THE ROMANTIC MOVEMENT IN
ENGLISH POETRY

THE
ROMANTIC MOVEMENT
IN
ENGLISH POETRY

BY

ARTHUR SYMONS

Phaeton Press
New York
1969

Originally Published 1909
Reprinted 1969

Library of Congress Catalog Card Number - 74-90371
Published by PHAETON PRESS, INC.

PREFACE

IN calling my book the 'Romantic Movement in English Poetry' I do not wish that title to be taken in too exclusive a sense. The word 'romantic,' I think, defines more clearly than any other what we find most characteristic in the renewal of poetry after its long banishment. The great poets of every age but the eighteenth have been romantic: what are Chaucer, Shakespeare, and Coleridge if not romantic? But in using the convenient word 'movement' I wish it to be understood that it is not meant in the usual historical sense, or with the definiteness with which we say, for example, the Tractarian or the Agrarian Movement. There a definite aim sets many minds working together, not in mere comradeship. No such thing ever happened in the creation of literature. It is each one of these poets whom I want to study, finding out, if I can, what he was in himself, what he made of himself in his work, and by what means, impulses, and instincts. The poet, the poem, — it is with these only that I am concerned.

And, again for convenience, I have set limits to my plan. The year 1800 is taken as a sort of centre; or shall I say a barrier, which shuts out every writer of verse who was born after that year, and lets through every one who survived from the eighteenth into the nineteenth century. My plan allows me no choice between good or bad writers in verse: I give each his due consideration, his due space, of a few lines or of many pages. And I have given each in chronological order, with the dates of his birth and death and of the first edition of his published volumes of verse. I have consulted no histories of literature, nor essays about it, except for the bare facts of a man's life or work; but I have tried to get at one thing only: the poet in his poetry, his poetry in the poet; it is the same thing.

CONTENTS

INTRODUCTION	3
JOHN HOME (1722–1808)	23
DR. ERASMUS DARWIN (1731–1802)	23
JAMES BEATTIE (1735–1803)	26
JOHN WOLCOT (1738–1819)	27
WILLIAM COMBE (1741–1823)	28
ANNA LÆTITIA BARBAULD (1743–1825)	30
HANNAH MORE (1745–1833)	30
WILLIAM HAYLEY (1745–1820)	32
CHARLES DIBDIN (1745–1814)	34
JOHN O'KEEFFE (1747–1833)	34
JOHN PHILPOT CURRAN (1750–1817)	36
WILLIAM GIFFORD (1756–1826)	37
WILLIAM BLAKE (1757–1827)	37
GEORGE CRABBE (1758–1832)	52
MRS. MARY ROBINSON (1758–1800)	61
JOANNA BAILLIE (1762–1851)	63
SIR SAMUEL EGERTON BRYDGES (1762–1837)	65
WILLIAM LISLE BOWLES (1762–1850)	65
GEORGE COLMAN THE YOUNGER (1762–1836)	67
SAMUEL ROGERS (1763–1855)	68
HENRY LUTTRELL (1765–1851)	73
CAROLINA, LADY NAIRNE (1766–1845)	73
ROBERT BLOOMFIELD (1766–1823)	74
JOHN HOOKHAM FRERE (1769–1846)	75
WILLIAM WORDSWORTH (1770–1850)	78
JAMES HOGG (1770–1835)	97
GEORGE CANNING (1770–1827)	106
HENRY BOYD (1770–1832)	107

CONTENTS

SIR WALTER SCOTT (1771–1832)	108
JAMES MONTGOMERY (1771–1854)	119
MRS. TIGHE (1772–1810)	121
HENRY FRANCIS CARY (1772–1844)	122
SAMUEL TAYLOR COLERIDGE (1772–1834)	123
ROBERT SOUTHEY (1774–1843)	148
ROBERT TANNAHILL (1774–1810)	161
CHARLES LAMB (1775–1834)	161
CHARLES LLOYD (1775–1839)	167
JOSEPH BLANCO WHITE (1775–1840)	169
THOMAS DERMODY (1775–1802)	170
DR. JOHN LEYDEN (1775–1811)	171
WALTER SAVAGE LANDOR (1775–1864)	172
JAMES AND HORATIO SMITH (1775–1839; 1779–1849)	189
THOMAS CAMPBELL (1775–1844)	191
THOMAS MOORE (1779–1852)	200
ROBERT EYRES LANDOR (1781–1869)	207
EDWARD, BARON THURLOW (1781–1829)	209
EBENEZER ELLIOTT (1781–1849)	209
WILLIAM NICHOLSON (1782–1849)	213
ANN AND JANE TAYLOR (1782–1866; 1783–1824)	213
REGINALD HEBER (1783–1826)	215
JAMES SHERIDAN KNOWLES (1784–1862)	216
BERNARD BARTON (1784–1849)	217
WILLIAM TENNANT (1784–1848)	217
JAMES HENRY LEIGH HUNT (1784–1859)	218
ALLAN CUNNINGHAM (1784–1842)	227
REV. CHARLES STRONG (1785–1864)	228
HENRY KIRKE WHITE (1785–1806)	228
THOMAS LOVE PEACOCK (1785–1866)	230
JOHN WILSON (1785–1841)	231
SIR AUBREY DE VERE (1786–1846)	232
CAROLINE ANNE BOWLES SOUTHEY (1786–1854)	233
GEORGE BEATTIE (1786–1823)	234

CONTENTS

MARY RUSSELL MITFORD (1787–1855)	234
BRYAN WALLER PROCTER: BARRY CORNWALL (1787–1874)	236
GEORGE GORDON, LORD BYRON (1788–1824)	239
RICHARD HARRIS BARHAM (1788–1845)	263
REV. HENRY HART MILMAN (1791–1868)	265
REV. CHARLES WOLFE (1791–1823)	266
PERCY BYSSHE SHELLEY (1792–1822)	268
REV. JOHN KEBLE (1792–1866)	286
DR. WILLIAM MAGINN (1793–1842)	286
JOHN CLARE (1793–1864)	288
FELICIA DOROTHEA HEMANS (1793–1835)	293
JOHN GIBSON LOCKHART (1794–1854)	295
THOMAS CARLYLE (1795–1881)	297
JOHN KEATS (1795–1821)	298
GEORGE DARLEY (1795–1846)	315
JEREMIAH JOSEPH CALLANAN (1795–1829)	318
SIR THOMAS NOON TALFOURD (1795–1854)	319
JOHN HAMILTON REYNOLDS (1796–1852)	320
DAVID HARTLEY COLERIDGE (1796–1849)	321
WILLIAM MOTHERWELL (1797–1835)	323
SAMUEL LOVER (1797–1868)	324
ROBERT POLLOK (1798–1827)	325
DAVID MACBETH MOIR (1798–1851)	325
WILLIAM THOM (1798–1848)	326
THOMAS HOOD (1799–1845)	328
THE MINORS	333
NOTE	340
INDEX	341

'Ages are all equal; but genius is always above the age.' — BLAKE.

THE ROMANTIC MOVEMENT IN ENGLISH POETRY

INTRODUCTION

I

COLERIDGE defined prose as 'words in good order,' poetry as 'the best words in the best order.' But there is no reason why prose should not be the best words in the best order. Rhythm alone, and rhythm of a regular and recurrent kind only, distinguishes poetry from prose. It was contended by an Oxford professor of poetry, Mr. W. J. Courthope, that the lines of Marlowe, —

> 'Was this the face that launched a thousand ships,
> And burned the topless towers of Ilium?'

are of a different substance from the substance of prose, and that it is certain that Marlowe 'could only have ventured on the sublime audacity that a face launched ships and burned towers by escaping from the limits of ordinary language, and conveying his metaphor through the harmonious and ecstatic movement of rhythm and metre.' To this it may be answered that any writer of elevated prose, Milton or Ruskin, could have said in prose precisely what Marlowe said in verse, and could have made fine prose of it: the imagination, the idea, a fine kind of form, would have been there; only one thing would have been lacking, the very finest kind of form, the form of verse. It would have been poetical substance, not poetry; the rhythm transforms it into poetry, and nothing but the rhythm.

When Wordsworth declares, in the Preface to the 'Lyrical Ballads,' that 'there neither is nor can be any essential difference between the language of prose and metrical composition,' he is perfectly right, and Coleridge is certainly wrong in saying, 'I write in metre because I am about to use a language different from that of prose.' Both forget that what must be assumed is poetical substance, and that, given poetical substance, the actual language of the prose and of the verse may very well be identical. When Coleridge says that he would have preferred 'Alice Fell' in prose, he is, very justly, criticising the substance of that 'metrical composition,' which is wholly unpoetical: there, and not in the language, is the distinction between its essential prose and poetry.

There is in prose, whenever it is good prose, but not necessarily inherent in it, a certain rhythm, much laxer than that of verse, not, indeed, bound by formal laws at all; but, in its essence, like the intonation which distinguishes one voice from another in the repetition of a single phrase. Prose, in its rudimentary stage, is merely recorded speech; but, as one may talk in prose all one's life without knowing it, so it may be that the conscious form of verse (speech, that is, reduced to rules, and regarded as partly of the nature of music) was of earlier origin. A certain stage of civilisation must have been reached before it could have occurred to any one that ordinary speech was worth being preserved. Verse is more easily remembered than prose, because of its recurrent beat, and whatever men thought worth remembering, either for its beauty (as a song or hymn) or for its utility (as a law), would naturally be put into verse. Verse may well have anticipated the existence of writing, but hardly prose. The writing-down of verse, to this day, is almost a materialization of it; but prose exists only as a written document.

The rhythm of verse, that rhythm which distinguishes it from prose, has never been traced with any certainty to its origin. It is not even certain whether its origin is consequent upon the origin of music, or whether the two are independent in their similar but by no means identical capacity. That a

INTRODUCTION

sense of regular cadence, though no sense of rhyme, is inherent in our nature, such as it now is, may be seen by the invariably regular rhythm of children's songs and of the half-inarticulate verse arrangements by which they accompany their games, and by the almost invariable inaccuracy of their rhymes. It is equally evident that the pleasure which we derive from the regular beat of verse is inherent in use, from the susceptibility of children to every form of regular rhythm, from the rocking of the cradle to the sound of a lullaby. Prose cuts itself sharply off from this great inheritance of susceptibility to regular rhythm, and thus, by what is looked upon as natural or instinctive in it, begins its existence a lawless and accidental thing.

In its origin, prose is in no sense an art, and it never has and never will become an art, strictly speaking, as verse is, or painting, or music. Gradually it has found out its capacities; it has discovered how what is useful in it can be trained to beauty; it has learned to set limits to what is unbounded in it, and to follow, at a distance, some of the laws of verse. Gradually it has developed laws of its own, which, however, by the nature of its existence, are less definite, less peculiar to it as a form, than those of verse. Everything that touches literature as literature affects prose, which has come to be the larger half of what we call literature.

It is the danger and privilege of prose that it has no limits. The very form of verse is a concentration; you can load every rift with more ore. Prose, with its careless lineage direct from speech, has a certain impromptu and casualness about it; it has allowed itself so much licence among trivialities that a too serious demeanour surprises; we are apt to be repelled by a too strait observance of law on the part of one not really a citizen. And there is one thing that prose cannot do; it cannot sing. A distinction there is between prose and lyrical verse, even in actual language, because here words are used by rhythm as notes in music, and at times with hardly more than that musical meaning. As Joubert has said, in a figure which is a precise definition: 'In the style of poetry every word reverberates like the sound of a well-tuned lyre, and leaves after it numberless undulations.' The words may be the same, no rarer; the construction may be the same, or, by preference, simpler; but, as the rhythm comes into it, there will come also something which, though it may be born of music, is not music. Call it atmosphere, call it magic; say, again with Joubert: 'Fine verses are those that exhale like sounds or perfumes'; we shall never explain, though we may do something to distinguish, that transformation by which prose is changed miraculously into poetry.

Again, it is Joubert who has said once and for all the significant thing: 'Nothing is poetry which does not transport: the lyre is in a certain sense a winged instrument.' Prose indeed may transport us, though not of the necessity with which poetry is bound to do so. But, in all the transport of prose, something holds us to the ground; for prose, though it may range more widely, has no wings. That is why substance is of so much greater importance in prose than in verse, and why a prose-writer, Balzac or Scott, can be a great writer, a great novelist, and yet not a great writer of prose; here, as elsewhere, prose makes conquest of new tracts of the earth, with leave to fix firm foundations there, by its very lack of skill in flight. The prose play, the novel, come into being as exceptions, are invented by men who cannot write plays in verse, who cannot write epics; and, the usurper once firmly settled, a new dynasty begins, which we come to call legitimate, as is the world's way with all dynasties.

Prose is the language of what we call real life, and it is only in prose that an illusion of external reality can be given. Compare, not only the surroundings, the sense of time, locality, but the whole process and existence of character, in a play of Shakespeare and in a novel of Balzac. I choose Balzac among novelists, because his mind is nearer to what is creative in the poet's mind than that of any novelist, and his method nearer to the method of the poet. Take King Lear and take Père Goriot. Goriot is a Lear at heart, and he suffers the same tortures and humiliations. But precisely where Lear grows up before the mind's eye into a vast cloud and shadowy monument of trouble, Goriot grows downward into the earth and takes root there, wrapping the dust about all his fibres. It is part of his novelty that he comes so close to us and is so recognisable. Lear may exchange his crown for the fool's bauble, knowing nothing of it; but Goriot knows well enough the value of every banknote that his daughters rob him of. In that definiteness, that new power of 'stationing' emotion in a firm and material way, lies one of the great opportunities of prose.

The novel and the prose play are the two great imaginative forms which prose has invented for itself. The essay corresponds in a sense to meditative poetry: has the lyric any analogue in prose? None, I think, in structural form, though there may be outbursts, in such elaborate prose as De Quincey's, which are perhaps only too lyrical, and seem to recognise a more fixed and releasing rhythm, that of verse. The prose of science, philosophy, and even history, has few fundamental duties to literature, or to prose as a fine art. Science, when it is not pure speculation, is concerned with mere facts, or theories of facts; and where a fact in itself is more important than the expression or illumination of that fact, there can be no literature. Philosophers have often been dreamers, poets turned inside out; and such may well bring concrete beauty into the domain of abstract thought. But for the most part philosophers have regarded prose much as ascetics have regarded the body; as a necessary part of matter, a necessary evil. To the historian prose becomes much more important, yet remains less important than it is to the novelist. The historian, after all, like the man of science, is concerned primarily with facts. He undertakes to tell us the truth about the past, and it is only when he competes with the novelist, and attempts psychology, that he is free to become a writer of actual literature. Much fine literature has been written under the name of criticism. But for the critic to aim at making literature is to take off something from the value of his criticism as criticism. It may produce a work of higher value. But it will cease to be, properly speaking, what we distinguish as criticism.

Only in the novel and in the prose play does prose become free to create, free to develop to the utmost limits of its vitality. Together with fiction I would include autobiography, perhaps of all forms of fiction the most convincing. In all these we see prose at work directly on life. 'The sense of cadence in prose,' says Rémy de Gourmont, 'has nothing in common with the sense of music; it is a sense wholly physiological. We set our sensations obscurely to rhythm, like prolonged cries of joy or sorrow. And thus everything can give finer shades, and adapt itself better to thought, in prose than in verse.' It is thus in prose that men confess themselves, with minute fidelity; Rousseau's 'Confessions' could have been written only in prose. All the best fiction, narrative or dramatic, is a form of confession, personal or vicarious; and, in a sense, it is all personal; for no novelist or dramatist ever rendered vitally a single sensation which he had not observed in himself or which he had not tested by himself. In verse even Villon cannot 'rhythme ses sensations' so minutely as Rousseau can in prose. The form forces him to give only the essence of his sensations, and to give them in a manner modified by that form. In prose we can almost think in words. Perhaps the highest merit of prose consists in this, that it allows us to think in words.

There is no form of art which is not an attempt to capture life, to create life over again. But art, in verse, being strictly and supremely an art, begins by transforming. Prose fiction transforms, it is true, it cannot help transforming; but by its nature it is able to follow line for line in a way that verse can never do. 'The artifices of rhythm,' said Poe, 'are an insuperable bar to the development of all points of thought or expression which have their basis in truth. . . . One writer of the prose tale, in short, may bring to his theme a vast variety of modes or inflexion of thought and expression — (the ratiocinative, for example, the sarcastic or humorous) which are not only antagonistical to the nature of the poem, but absolutely forbidden by one of its most peculiar and indispensable adjuncts: we allude, of course, to rhythm.' It is, in fact, that physiological quality which gives its chief power, its rarest subtlety, to prose. Prose listens at the doors of all the senses, and repeats their speech almost in their own tones. But poetry (it is again Baudelaire who says it) 'is akin to music through a prosody whose roots plunge deeper in the human soul than any classical theory has indicated.' Poetry begins where prose ends, and it is at its chief peril that it begins sooner. The one safeguard for the poet is to say to himself: What I can write in prose I will not allow myself to write in verse, out of mere honour towards my material. The further I can extend my prose, the further back do I set the limits of verse. The region of poetry will thus be always the beyond, the ultimate, and with the least possible chance of any confusion of territory.

II

Critics or historians of poetry are generally concerned with everything but what is essential in it. They deal with poetry as if it were a fashion, finding merit in its historical significance, as we find interest in an early Victorian bonnet, not because it is beautiful, but because people once thought it 'genteel.' But poetry is a reality, an essence, and is unchanged by any change in fashion; and it is the critic's business to find it where it is, to proclaim it for what it is, and to realise that no amount of historical significance or adaptability to a former fashion can make what is bad poetry in the present century good poetry in any century of the past.

There is a theory, at present much in vogue, by which the evolution of poetry is to be studied everywhere but in the individual poet. This theory has been summed up by M. Rémy de Gourmont in an essay on one of its chief practitioners, Ferdinand Brunetière: 'Literary history,' he says, 'is no longer to be a succession of portraits, of individual lives; the question is now of poetry or of history, not of poets or of historians; works are to be studied, without too much importance being given to their writers, and we are to be shown how these works give birth to one another by natural necessity; how from the species poetry are born the varieties sonnet and madrigal; how, under the influence of surroundings, the lyrical variety is transformed, without losing its essential characteristics, into eloquence, with many further metamorphoses.' The same point of view is expressed by Mr. Courthope when he tells us that 'it is unphilosophical to believe that a single poet can turn the art of poetry into any channel he will by his own genius: the greatest artists are those who best understood the conflict of tendencies in their own age, and who, though they rise above it into the region of universal truth, are moved by it to reflect in their work its particular form and character.' In other words, we are to believe that the cart drives the horse, that the taste of the time makes the genius of the poet. It is the poet who, by his genius, makes the taste of the time. All that 'conflicts of tendencies' and the like have to do with the poet is to help him now and again to a convenient form, to suggest to him the lute or the stage, to give him this or that malleable lump of material. He is supremely fortunate if, like Shakespeare, born with a genius for drama, he finds a stage already alive and awaiting him; comparatively unfortunate if, like Goethe, his dramatic genius, lacking a stage for its complete expression, can but create individual works, which, however great, lose their chance of

INTRODUCTION 11

wholly organic development. No great poet ever owed any essential part of his genius to his age; at the most he may have owed to his age the opportunity of an easy achievement.

Take, for instance, Chatterton. Chatterton's 'masculine persuasive force' is one of the most genuine things in our literature, and is in no degree affected by the mask which it pleased him to put on. Chatterton required no 'needs of the public taste' to guide him into a 'channel of great poetical expression.' He found for himself that 'channel of great poetical expression'; he found accounts in black-letter and turned them into living poetry, and it has been made a crime to him that he was an alchemist of the mind, and transmuted base metal into gold. It was his whim to invent a language for the expression of the better part of himself, a language which came as close as he could get it to come to that speech of the Middle Ages which he had divined in Gothic architecture and in the crabbed characters of old parchments. In Chatterton the whole modern romantic movement began, consciously and as a form of achieved art; and it is not necessary to remember that he died at an age when no other English poet had done work in any degree comparable with his, at least for those qualities of imagination typical of him, in order to give him his due place in English poetry. The existence of Chatterton, at the moment when he happened to exist, proves as conclusively as need be that the man of genius is not of his age, but above it.

The poet who typifies for us the eighteenth century, in which Chatterton was an exception, is Pope; and Pope was not a poet in the true sense, a born poet who had the misfortune to be modified by the influence of the age into which he was born, but a writer of extraordinary prose capacity and finish, who, if he had lived in another age and among genuine poets, would have had no more than a place apart, admired for the unique thing which he could do, but not mistaken for a poet of true lineage. Pope's poetic sensibility may be gauged by a single emendation which he made in the text of his edition of Shakespeare. Shakespeare had made Antony say to Cleopatra, 'O grave charm!' To Pope it seemed ridiculous that a light woman should possess gravity in charm. He proposed 'gay,' and nature seemed to be reasserted: 'O gay charm!' what more probable and sufficient?

The poetry of the eighteenth century has no fundamental relation with the rest of English poetry. The poets of every other age can be brought together under a single conception: they harmonise, for all their differences; but between the poets of every other age and the poets of the eighteenth century there is a gap, impossible to pass over. Here and there, as in the best work of Collins, we can distinguish some of the eternal signs of poetry. But, for the most part, the gap is so palpable that we find critics tacitly acknowledging it by their very efforts to bridge it over, and asking us, with Mr. Courthope, in speaking of Pope, to admit 'that it is on a false principle of criticism that Warton, and those who think with him, blame his poetry on account of the absence of qualities which they find in other poets.' If those qualities, which are to be found in other poets and not in Pope, are precisely the fundamental qualities which constitute poetry, why should these qualities be quietly laid aside for the occasion, and, the eighteenth century once over, taken up again as if nothing had happened?

The principles of poetry are eternal, and such divine accidents as Christopher Smart and Thomas Chatterton in an age in which the 'national taste' was turned persistently from those principles, are enough to show that no pressure of contemporary fashion can wholly hinder a poet from speaking out in his own and the only way. In the Preface to his 'Specimens of Later English Poets' Southey had the frankness to admit that 'the taste of the public may better be estimated from indifferent poets than from good ones; because the former write for their contemporaries, the latter for poster-

INTRODUCTION

ity.' And he asks, naïvely enough: 'Why is Pomfret the most popular of the English poets? The fact is certain, and the solution would be useful.' Who is aware to-day of the existence of a poem called 'The Choice' or of a poet called Pomfret? Pomfret held his own for a hundred years, and now is extinct. Enquiry as to why he was the most popular of the English poets is, however amusing for the social historian, beside the question for the student of poetry. What matters to him is not that 'The Choice' was once considered by the public to be an incomparable poem, but that it was and remains a tame and mediocre piece of verse, never really rising to poetry, and that precisely similar material could be and had been lifted into poetry by the genius of a genuine poet, such as Herrick.

Again, the influence of one poet on another has its interest, its importance even; but all that seriously matters is that part which was not influenced, the poet himself. The personal contact of Wordsworth and Coleridge, the Elizabethan reading of Keats, had their influence on the form and sometimes on the very impulse to existence of the poetry of each poet. But it was of the nature of a lucky or unlucky accident; it was at the most the equivalent of some natural excitement, a sunset or the face of a woman. Nor did the French Revolution create the poetry which gave it expression or moralised over it. King George the Third inspired the genius of Byron, but only better than the 'dark blue ocean,' because comic material was more valuable to Byron than heroic or sublime material. But that Shelley conceived himself to be atheist, philanthropist, or democrat; that Keats fell in love with Fanny Brawne and not with another woman; that Coleridge took opium and Wordsworth lived in the open air in Cumberland: these things go to the making of the man who is the poet; they touch or inspire him, in what is deepest or most sensitive in his nature; and though they will never explain to us how he came to have the power of creation, they will explain to us something more than his method.

To distinguish poetry, then, where it exists, to consider it in its essence, apart from the accidents of the age in which it came into being, to define its qualities in itself; that is the business of the true critic or student. And in order to do this he must cast aside all theories of evolution or the natural growth of genius, and remember that genius is always an exception, always something which would be a disease if it were not a divine gift. He must clear his mind of all limiting formulas, whether of *milieu*, *Weltschmerz*, or mode. He must disregard all schools or movements as other than convenient and interchangeable labels. He must seek, in short, only poetry, and he must seek poetry in the poet, and nowhere else.

III

The quality which distinguishes the poetry of the beginning of the nineteenth century, the poetry which we can roughly group together as the romantic movement, is the quality of its imagination, and this quality is seen chiefly as a kind of atmosphere, which adds strangeness to beauty. What is it in the atmosphere of an English landscape that seems at once to reveal and, in a sense, to explain that imaginative atmosphere which distinguishes the finest English poetry, and, in a special sense, the poetry of the nineteenth century, from almost all the fine poetry of the world? I was walking one afternoon along one of the slopes of Hampstead Heath, just above the Vale of Health, and I saw close beside me a line of naked autumn trees, every twig brown and separate: a definite, solid thing, beautiful in structure, sober and admirable in colour, just such branches as one would see in any clear country, where everything is distinctly visible, in Italy or in Spain. But, at some distance, on the higher edge of the heath, against the sky, there was another line of naked trees, and over their whole outline there was a soft, not quite transparent, veil of mist, like the down on fruit: you saw them and the general lines of their structure, but you saw them under a more exquisite

INTRODUCTION

aspect, like an image seen in a cloudy mirror. Nothing that was essential in their reality was lost, but they were no longer the naked, real thing; nature had transformed them, as art transforms nature. So imagination, in the English poets, transforms the bare outlines of poetical reality, clothing them with an atmosphere which is the actual atmosphere of England.

Is there in Homer, in Dante, in the poet of any bright, clear land, where men and things are seen detached against the sky, like statues or architecture, a passage like that passage in Keats, those two lines: —

> 'Charmed magic casements, opening on the foam
> Of perilous seas, in faery lands forlorn' ?

In those two lines we get the equivalent of that atmosphere which, in England, adds mystery to the beauty of natural things. The English sense of atmosphere, this imaginative transmutation of reality, is to be found in all English poetry from the beginning. But it is found incidentally, it is found subordinated to other characteristics; it is the rarest but not the most regarded part of great poetry. The best poetry of the nineteenth century is identical, in all essential respects, with the best poetry of every other but the eighteenth century; it is strictly in the tradition; but there is, in what we call the romantic movement, a certain economy which we do not always find in other periods, a sense of the limits of poetry, of exactly what we can and cannot do. No one has ever written more lucidly or more tenderly than Chaucer, more nobly or more musically than Spenser; but to Chaucer poetry was exclusively the telling of a story, and to Spenser it was partly picture-making and partly allegory. To the supreme Elizabethan it was life, every action of the will, the mind, and the soul; and there is not so much poetry to be found anywhere in the world, but it is more often than not in scattered splendours and fragments severally alive. The 'metaphysical' poets of the seventeenth century brought all the gifts of the Magi, and they brought pure gold, but some were clouded with incense and some too heavily perfumed with myrrh. Poetry at the beginning of the nineteenth century wastes surprisingly little of its substance, and one main reason of this is that it realises, as its main concern, what to most of the poets of the past had been, though their existence depended upon it, but lightly regarded, — that imaginative atmosphere which is the very breath of poetry, and adds strangeness to beauty.

Until the eighteenth century imagination, if not always a welcome guest, had never been refused admittance. The eighteenth century shut the door on imagination. Before that century was over Pan grew uneasy in the park, and impatient to return to the forest. Thomson and Cowper had pushed open the gate for him a little way, but by no means let him escape. A danger signal was heard but not heeded when Christopher Smart cried from his mad-house; the cry was not repeated till Chatterton really awoke. It was Dionysus that awoke in Burns, and has never been out of the blood of any authentic poet since. Burns is neither eighteenth nor nineteenth century, neither local nor temporary, but the very flame of man, speaking as a man has only spoken once or twice in the world. He taught no one anything that any one could learn, but this ploughman was Apollo to Admetus, incarnate song. After Burns, though no one could sing like him, no one has returned to the delusion that the poet need not be a singer. Romance rose out of the grave of Chatterton, and poetry, after Burns, was no longer in bondage to the prose and rational mind. Religion woke up when poetry did, and liberty seemed a fantastically delightful thing. Dilettantes like Leigh Hunt joined with pedants like Southey in helping to set poetry free. Even those who, like Byron, sided theoretically with the formulas of the past, brought in a new, personal manner of their own, sometimes upsetting more than they could rebuild. One after another, not learning of each other any more than Wordsworth learnt of Landor, or Shelley of Blake, a genera-

INTRODUCTION

tion of poets rose up, akin only in this, that they had returned instinctively to the eternal sources of poetry.

Mr. Watts-Dunton has used a phrase which has become famous, 'the Renaissance of Wonder,' for that 'great revived movement of the soul of man, after a long period of prosaic acceptance in all things, including literature and art,' which can be roughly indicated as the romantic movement. As a form of 'literary shorthand' it has its value, as had Matthew Arnold's phrase, 'the criticism of life.' But just as that partial phrase has become a shibboleth or an idol of the market-place, so is this summary or generalisation in danger of becoming one. It may be corrected by that definition of Zoroaster which Mr. Watts-Dunton himself has often quoted: 'Poetry is apparent pictures of unapparent realities.' Now the important thing is, not that there should be realities which are unapparent, but that the things which are unapparent, of which the poet gives apparent pictures, should be realities. To the great imaginative poet they are; and that, not his 'wonder' at them, is what matters. There is much, in the romantic attitude, of mere wonder; but what in Cyril Tourneur remains wonder, mere angry wonder, becomes in Shakespeare a divine certainty. Imagination, if there is any such thing, is sight, not wonder; a thing seen, not an opening of the eyes to see it. The great poets, the great visionaries, have always seen clearly; when they have seen furthest, as with Dante when he saw heaven and hell, they have seen without wonder.

What is really meant by all these phrases, and by the name of the romantic movement, is simply the reawakening of the imagination, a reawakening to a sense of beauty and strangeness in natural things, and in all the impulses of the mind and the senses. That reawakening was not always a conscious one. Thus Crabbe occupied himself in keeping out imagination as much as he could, yet could not keep out nature. It was at this time that nature, from being a background, came forward and seemed likely to dwarf the human figures in the landscape.

Objects, that had been seen detached, without atmosphere, were seen by Wordsworth in pure white light; which Keats caught in a prism of his own, and Shelley turned to moonlight. Then, lest nature should have undue worship, Byron set himself prominently in the foreground. Coleridge is fundamentally both naturalistic and romantic, but Shelley is not naturalistic at all, in any but a romantic sense. What all these poets, so different in inspiration and tendency, united in was in an aim at the emancipation of the world and of the mind and of the vehicle of poetry from the bondage of fact, opinion, formality, and tradition; and when fact, opinion, formality, and tradition go out, imagination comes in.

Wordsworth has been looked upon as the leader, as Coleridge was the more authentic lawgiver, of this emancipation. It is doubtful if Wordsworth was ever consciously under any special influence among his predecessors. Poetry came up in him naturally, and he was in intellectual revolt against whatever was not sincere in the substance and form of verse. He felt first and thought out afterwards, and his thoughts came to him slowly, often deviatingly, but by a kind of spiritual necessity. Thus the impulse came to him unconsciously to put off the misfitting fashionable clothes of the period's poetry, but it was with great deliberation that he put them off. He knew, by instinctive knowledge, what was essential in poetry, and that essential part of poetry was waiting in him to find fit expression. Coleridge, with his rarer literary genius, had been awakened by the gentle hint of Bowles, which was as if some one had touched him in a crowd, and he had turned and seen something wonderful passing. But while these men were finding out, each for himself, his own secret, Landor was rediscovering Greece not less privately, and Blake, 'his talents having been wholly devoted to the attainment of excellence in his profession' of engraver, was, long before any of the others and in deeper obscurity, inventing a new magic in English speech.

A general agreement as to first principles, when it is not a vital instinct, is apt to harden into formulas, and to hinder the free action of the mind. But in this revolt against the doctrinal and analysing principles of the eighteenth century, in this return to nature, to the natural part of man, it was as if a new Adam had returned to an old paradise. Almost nothing was attempted, except by a few experimental and not really genuine poets, that could not properly be done in verse; no one, after Erasmus Darwin, wrote a 'Botanic Garden.' And scarcely anything that could be done in verse was not attempted. The senses have never been served more purely than by Keats, the moral instinct more severely than by Wordsworth, intellectual beauty more ecstatically than by Shelley. While the lyric of Shakespeare's time was more universally perfect, a purer music, can we say that the age of Blake, Coleridge, and Shelley was inferior to that age in actual lyrical genius? The romantic narrative has never been done with more magic than by Keats, nor the reflective narrative more justified by achievement than by Wordsworth in 'The Leech Gatherer.' The ballad was re-created in a new and rarer form by Coleridge, who, with Hogg, brought a new witchcraft into poetry. The best sonnets of the period are among the best of English sonnets; and if any one has ever come recognisably near to the epic since 'Paradise Lost,' it is Landor in 'Gebir.' The drama is the form of poetry which was attempted least, and only once, in 'The Cenci,' with success. But 'The Cenci' is the greatest play since Shakespeare.

The romantic movement is an emancipation, and it cast off, not only the bandages of eighteenth-century limitation, but all bonds that had tightened about it in the mere acceptance of tradition. 'Beauty is truth, truth beauty,' is a saying not personal to Keats only. It was what Coleridge, who doubted everything else, never doubted; it characterises Wordsworth's poetry whenever it is poetry and not prose. That very revolt against 'poetic diction,' which seemed like a turning of one's back on the speech which poetry had chosen for itself, was really for the purpose of getting behind that speech. The battle in all ages has been between poetry and rhetoric, and there is unconquered rhetoric enough among all romantics. But no one seriously mistook rhetoric for poetry, as many poets in many ages have done. Nature was accepted, yet strangeness was sought rather than refused, that salt which gives savour to life; and there was an arduous and discreet cultivation of that 'continual slight novelty' without which poetry cannot go on in any satisfactory way. Imagination was realised as being, what only Blake quite clearly said, reality; and the beauty of imagination the natural element of that which it glorifies. Poetry was realised as a personal confession, or as an evocation, or as 'an instant made eternity.' It was realised that the end of poetry was to be poetry; and that no story-telling or virtue or learning, or any fine purpose, could make amends for the lack of that one necessity. Thus it may be affirmed that in studying this period we are able to study whatever is essential in English poetry; that is, whatever is essential in **poetry**.

THE ROMANTIC MOVEMENT IN
ENGLISH POETRY

JOHN HOME (1722-1808) [1]

JOHN HOME is known to every schoolboy by two lines in the play of 'Douglas': —

> 'My name is Norval: on the Grampian Hills
> My father feeds his flocks; a frugal swain.'

They occur in the second act, and are said in answer to the request: —

> Blush not, flower of modesty
> As well as valour, to declare thy birth.'

The lines are typical of a dramatist who, in his time, made theatrical successes in London and Edinburgh, and, by some strange delusion, led his contemporaries into an admiration which seems to us now unmerited and unintelligible. He shares with Joanna Baillie the doubtful honour of being compared with Shakespeare: she by Scott and he by Burns.

DR. ERASMUS DARWIN (1731-1802) [2]

IN one of his notes to 'The Feast of the Poets' Leigh Hunt says: 'The late Dr. Darwin, whose notion of poetical music, in common with that of Goldsmith and others, was of the school of Pope, though his taste was otherwise different, was perhaps the first who, by carrying it to its extreme pitch of sameness, and ringing it affectedly in one's ears, gave the public at large a suspicion that there was something wrong

---

[1] (1) *Douglas*, 1757. (2) *Agis, Douglas, The Siege of Aquileia*, 1760. (3) *Collected Works*, 3 vols. 1822.

[2] (1) *The Loves of the Plants*, 1789. (2) *The Economy of Vegetation*, 1792 (the two parts of *The Botanic Garden*). (3) *The Temple of Nature*, 1803. (4) *Poetical Works*, 1807.

in its nature.' No more deliberate endeavour of a prose mind to produce poetry of a formally accomplished kind has been seen than that of Dr. Darwin in his 'Botanic Garden,' who tells us that 'the general design of the following sheets is to enlist Imagination under the banner of Science.' In a prose 'interlude' to the second part of the poem, 'The Loves of the Plants' (in which he professes to contend with Ovid, and metamorphose 'by similar art' his trees and flowers, 'after having remained prisoners so long in their respective vegetable mansions,' back into men and women), he gives us his theory of poetry, which is so identical with his practice that we cannot doubt of his satisfaction with his own work as a poet. 'The Muses are young Ladies,' he tells us; 'we expect to see them dressed; though not like some modern beauties, with so much gauze and feather, that " the Lady herself is the least part of her."' But art is not to confine itself to nature: 'the further the artist recedes from nature, the greater novelty he is likely to produce.' The poet, it appears, 'writes principally to the eye'; and to prove his principle Darwin gives this instance: 'Mr. Pope has written a bad verse in the " Windsor Forest ": —

"And Kennet swift for silver eels *renowned*.'

The word renowned does not present the idea of a visible object to the mind, and is thence prosaic. But change the line thus: —

"And Kennet swift, where silver graylings *play*,"

and it becomes poetry, because the scenery is then brought before the eye.'

So easy, and so plain a matter of rule, did it seem to the scientific poet to convert prose into poetry. Turn from the sections in his 'argument,' as for instance 'Pumps explained — Charities of Miss Jones — Departure of the Nymphs like water spiders,' to the statements in verse, and it will be seen that he is always striving to trace the passage of light over

DR. ERASMUS DARWIN

an object, which is his only notion of the property of imagination illuminating science. Thus, treating of electricity, he bids his nymphs

> 'Beard the bright cylinder with golden wire,
> And circumfuse the gravitating fire';

while in a statue of Lotta (or Lot's wife) in the salt-mines of Cracow he observes how

> 'Cold dews condense upon her pearly breast,
> And the big tear rolls lucid down her vest.'

Elsewhere

> 'His cubic forms phosphoric Fluor prints,'

and some unpleasant personification is seen with

> 'The maudlin tear-drop glittering in her eyes.'

This steady mechanical glitter is I suppose what Hayley meant when he praised the 'radiant lays' of one whom he united with Cowper in praising. Of this praise he declared: —

> 'Time verifies it daily;
> Trust it, dear Darwin, on the word
> Of Cowper and of Hayley.'

But the 'Anti-Jacobin' was to come with its 'Loves of the Triangles,' text and notes inextricably moulded upon the text and notes of Darwin; and the reader of to-day is puzzled to know whether he is reading the original or the parody as he turns from

> 'Soft Sighs responsive whisper to the chords,
> And Indignations half unsheath their swords,'

to

> 'The obedient Pulley strong Mechanics ply,
> And wanton Optics roll the melting eye.'

JAMES BEATTIE (1735-1803) [1]

DOES any one ever open 'The Minstrel' of Beattie? In the preface to a little old undated copy, printed at Alnwick and decorated with quaint engravings, I find that in the opening lines of that poem it seemed to the editor that 'every point that imagination can conceive, constituting excellence in poetical composition, is there displayed in its fullest extent.' Beattie was more modest, and, in addressing what he called his 'Gothic lyre,' he declares: 'I only wish to please the simple mind.' His moralisings seem now a little out of date, yet it is still amusing to read: —

> 'Blest be the day I 'scaped the wrangling crew,
> From Pyrrho's maze, and Epicurus' stye,'

and to be reminded that these 'pointed lines' refer to Hume and his disciples, with whom the Gothic bard had had a famous controversy. Remembering that he was fond of music, and that he 'disliked his own favourite violoncello' after the death of his son, whom he used to accompany while he sang, we can still find a personal note in a stanza which is in every way characteristic of his style: —

> 'Is there a heart that music cannot melt?
> Alas! how is that rugged heart forlorn!
> Is there, who ne'er those mystic transports felt
> Of solitude and melancholy born?
> He needs not woo the Muse; he is her scorn.
> The sophist's rope of cobweb he shall twine;
> Mope o'er the schoolman's peevish page; or mourn
> And delve for life in Mammon's dirty mine;
> Sneak with the scoundrel fox, or grunt with glutton swine.'

Little village pictures, though of the cataloguing kind, have their fresh detail, where

> 'Crown'd with her pail the tripping milk-maid sings,'

[1] (1) *Original Poems and Translations*, 1761. (2) *The Judgement of Paris*, 1765. (3) *Verses on the Death of Churchill*, 1765. (4) *Poems on Several Subjects*, 1766. (5) *The Minstrel*, 1771. (6) *Poems on Several Occasions*, 1776. (7) *Poetical Works*, Aldine Edition, 1830.

and some of the descriptions of what seemed to him the best poetical materials in nature, —

> 'Rocks, torrents, gulfs, and shapes of giant size,
> And glittering cliffs on cliffs,'

or some 'vale romantic,' or some mountain from whose 'easy swell' might be seen

> 'Blue hills, and glittering waves, and skies in gold arrayed,'

still retain some faint glow of the enthusiasm that gave them their momentary existence. It is best not to go beyond the pages containing 'The Minstrel,' or we may come on epithets as innocently startling, in the eighteenth-century manner, as this, of 'the oblivious lap of soft Desire.'

JOHN WOLCOT (1738-1819)

THE vulgarity of the Englishman when he fights has never been seen so shamelessly in verse as in the voluminous rhymed verse of Peter Pindar. These rabid impromptus spare neither the living nor the dead, in their

> 'desultory way of writing,
> A hop and step and jump way of inditing,'

in which there is sometimes a coal-heaver's vigour of speech, as

> 'Once more forth volcanic Peter flames.'

He is himself his own best characteriser, and bids himself, though to no avail, —

> 'Envy not such as have in dirt surpassed ye;
> 'T is very, very easy to be nasty.'

Nor does he take the advice which he gives, when he says: —

> 'Build not, alas! your popularity
> On that beast's back ycleped Vulgarity.'

Such popularity as he got in his time was built on the back of just such a 'little old black beast.' 'The leading feature seems to be impudence,' he says of one of his own versicles, and declares rightly that another 'is verily exceeded by nothing in the annals of impertinence.' His jokes, which beslime most of the pages, are hardly ever funny, even when they are grossest; nor is there even fun in the attempts at serious sentiment which are strangely interlarded here and there. A bunch of 'New-Old Ballads,' done, we are told, 'as innocent deceptions,' seem not less out of place among the slatternly 'odes' which do not even imitate good models, but are content to be personal at the expense of every quality which could give them merit. Gifford has been blamed for outdoing Wolcot's defamatory and disreputable filth in an 'Ode to Peter Pindar,' which is not pleasant reading. But no punishment could be too humiliating for one whose doggerel is worse than anything left by the lowest brawlers of the Elizabethan age; for these were poets stooping to wield muckrakes, and this the stye's natural guardian.

WILLIAM COMBE (1741-1823)[1]

WILLIAM COMBE is still remembered as 'Dr. Syntax,' but it is because of Rowlandson's coloured etchings, for which the verses were written, rather than for any tolerable qualities

[1] (1) *The Diaboliad*, 1776. (2) *Additions to the Diaboliad*, 1777. (3) *The Diabolo-Lady; or, a Match in Hell*, 1777. (4) *Anti-Diabolo-Lady*, 1777. (5) *The First of April; or, The Triumph of Folly*, 1777. (6) *A Dialogue in the Shades*, 1777. (7) *Heroic Epistle to a Noble D——*, 1777. (8) *A Poetical Epistle to Sir Joshua Reynolds*, 1777. (9) *A Letter to her Grace the Duchess of Devonshire*, 1777. (10) *A Second Letter to the Duchess of Devonshire*, 1777. (11) *The Duchess of Devonshire's Cow, a Poem*, 1777. (12) *An Heroic Epistle to the 'Noble Author' of 'The Duchess of Devonshire's Cow,'* 1777. (13) *The Royal Register; or, Observations on the Principal Characters of the Church, State, Court, etc.*, 1777-84. (14) *Perfection; a Poetical Epistle*, 1778. (15) *The Diaboliad*, Part II, 1778. (16) *The Justification*, 1778. (17) *The Auction; a Town Eclogue*, 1778. (18) *An*

in the jogging couplets, tamely trying to be burlesque, with their broken and irrelevant narrative. The writer modestly enough explains that when the first print came to him he did not know what would be the subject of the second. Rowlandson's designs require no comment; the line and colour have the beauty of the finest burlesque, and they live a rollicking life of their own. Combe ambles after them with a halting gait, prosing and moralising. He supposed that he was imitating Butler in 'Hudibras.' Of the eighty-six publications which have been identified as his work, none were published under his name. His satires however, such as the 'Diaboliad' series, seem to have been undisguised in their application. In his dedication to the latter he said, needlessly, that he was a careless writer. 'I was not born,' he explains, 'to refine and polish my own compositions. The long habit of making rapid sketches of men and things has rendered me wholly incapable of filling up an outline with those effectual masses of light and shade, and that happy, harmonising mixture of colours, which distinguished the work of judicious application.' 'The Diaboliad' and its successors plaster crude daubs clumsily on unprepared canvases. Dashes, whole lines of asterisks, pretend to conceal meanings too definite to be written. What is written is never of any better quality than such a couplet as this: —

'With these supports, the modest Peer preferr'd
His claim, which Satan with attention hears.'

Interesting Letter to the Duchess of Devonshire, 1778. (19) *An Heroic Epistle to Sir James Wright*, 1778. (20) *An Heroic Epistle to an Unfortunate Monarch*, 1778. (21) *The Philosopher in Bristol*, 1778. (22) *The World as it goes*, 1779. (23) *The Fast Day; a Lambeth Eclogue*, 1780. (24) *The Traitor, a Poem*, 1781. (25) *The Royal Dream; or, the P—— in a Panic, an Eclogue*, 1791. (26) *Carmen Seculare*, 1796. (27) *Clifton, a Poem, in imitation of Spenser*, 1803. (28) *The Tour of Dr. Syntax in Search of the Picturesque*, 1812. (29) *Six Poems*, 1813. (30) *Poetical Sketches of Scarborough*, 1813. (31) *The English Dance of Death*, 2 vols. 1815–16. (32) *The Dance of Life*, 1816. (33) *The Second Tour of Dr. Syntax*, 1820. (34) *The Third Tour of Dr. Syntax in search of a wife*, 1821. (35) *Johnny Quae Genus; or, the Little Foundling*, 1822.

The aim of his 'Diabolo-Lady' he assures us was to 'damn Women to everlasting fame.' But his libels and his feeble evidences are happily forgotten.

ANNA LÆTITIA BARBAULD (1743–1825) [1]

ANNA LÆTITIA BARBAULD was a writer of great diligence, who had the good luck to concentrate her various talents into a single poem, which has been universally appreciated. The last lines, beginning 'Life! we've been long together,' are not less than an inspiration, a woman's, in which sadness, tenderness, and hope are mingled.

HANNAH MORE (1745–1833) [2]

HANNAH MORE was a copious writer of prose and verse. Her plays were acted by Garrick, her story of 'Cœlebs in Search of a Wife' has come down almost to our generation, and in her own time she was praised by Johnson and popular with the general and later in life with the pious public. I have a copy before me of the 'Sacred Dramas; chiefly intended for Young Persons,' and 'calculated,' we are told in the introductory memoir, 'to repress the luxuriance of juvenile imaginations,' a lamentable task which worse books and less intelligent women have undertaken. The little plays, 'the subjects taken from the Bible' with considerable skill and discretion, are still readable, on a dull afternoon, and though they are scarcely in the proper sense dramatic, it is

---

[1] (1) *Poems*, 1773. (2) *Poem, with Poetical Epistle to William Wilberforce*, 1792. (3) *Eighteen Hundred and Eleven*, 1811. (4) *Works*, 1825.

[2] (1) *The Inflexible Captive*, 1774. (2) *Sir Edred of the Bower, and the Bleeding Rock*, 1776. (3) *Percy*, 1777. (4) *The Fatal Falsehood*, 1779. (5) *Sacred Dramas*, 1782. (6) *Slavery*, 1788. (7) *The Feast of Freedom*, 1827. (8) *Collected Poems*, 1816 and 1829.

evident that the author has studied the methods of 'the excellent Racine,' and has realised 'the perfection of his dramatic art.' There are perhaps too many in view of

> 'The ostentatious virtues which still press
> For notice and for praise,'

as she says of them, in rebuke and without self-knowledge. But it seemed to her that the Muse, in her time, had drunk deep of some 'delicious ruin,' as she says with a curiously modern choice of epithet, and she prays

> 'for some balm
> Of sovereign power, to raise the drooping Muse
> To all the health of Virtue.'

The Muse, quieted by her balm, sinks into a state of very even health throughout these tiny plays, better fitted, as she is aware, for the nursery than for the stage. Her footnote, touching the question, shows foresight and is a permanent lesson. 'It would not be easy,' she says, 'nor perhaps proper, to introduce sacred tragedies on the English stage. The pious would think it profane, while the profane would think it dull.' It is for the supposed dulness that the name of Hannah More is mockingly, but unjustly, perpetuated. She gives one of her Bible kings this expressive line: —

> 'That world, whose gaze makes half the charm of greatness';

and we discover, in another play, a princess thanking her gods that they have made mercy a 'keen rapture exquisite,' before they imposed it on the virtuous as a duty. There can be no dulness where so alert a psychology is discernible between the sober lines, which are scarcely, all the same, as Johnson said of them, the production of 'the most powerful versificatrix in the English language.'

WILLIAM HAYLEY (1745–1820)[1]

HAYLEY is known to us now chiefly as a good but unsatisfactory friend to Blake, and for the amusing title of his 'Triumphs of Temper.' In his time he had a serious reputation, which he took with great solemnity. In the very personal preface to his 'Triumphs' he expresses the 'kind of duty incumbent on those who devote themselves to Poetry, to raise, if possible, the dignity of declining Art.' 'I wished indeed (but I fear most ineffectually),' he adds, 'for powers to unite some touches of the sportive wildness of Ariosto, and the more serious sublime painting of Dante, with some portions of the enchanting elegance, the refined imagination, and the moral grace of Pope; and to do this, if possible, without violating those rules of propriety which' did not exclude 'familiar Incident and allegorical picture from affording a strong relief to each other.' What Mr. Hayley could do in the direction of the 'serious sublime' of Dante may be seen in a translation of six lines of the 'Inferno.' Only the first need be quoted: 'Through me ye pass to Spleen's terrific dome.' But if we turn to his opinion of 'daring Dante,' we shall be surprised to understand his reason for wishing to share 'some touches,' of one who united ' The Seraph's Music and the Demon's yell.' The definition is unique of its kind. Ariosto's 'sportive wildness' may perhaps be meant to appear where the

[1] (1) *A Poetical Epistle on Marriage*, 1775. (2) *An Ode to Cheerfulness*, 1775. (3) *An Epistle to Dr. Long*, 1777. (4) *Epistle on Painting*, 1777. (5) *Poetical Epistle to Admiral Keppel*, 1779. (6) *An Elegy on the Ancient Greek Model*, 1779. (7) *Epistle on History*, 1780. (8) *Ode to Howard*, 1780. (9) *Epistle to a Friend*, 1780. (10) *The Triumphs of Temper*, 1781. (11) *Poetical Epistles on Epic Poetry*, 1782. (12) *Plays of Three Acts and in Verse*, 1784. (13) *Poetical Works*, 3 vols. 1785. (14) *The Happy Prescription*, 1785. (15) *The Two Connoisseurs*, 1785. (16) *Occasional Stanzas*, 1788. (17) *The Young Widow*, 1789. (18) *An Elegy on the Death of Sir K. Jones*, 1795. (19) *An Essay on Sculpture*, 1800. (20) *Triumphs of Music*, 1804. (21) *Ballads founded on Anecdotes of Animals*, 1805. (22) *Three Plays with a Preface*, 1811.

'cheerful banquet' underground at which very unpleasant persons sit down to 'rich liqueurs' is presented to the shocked heroine. Pope may be responsible for 'The spleenful outrage of the angry peer,' or perhaps when

'The light Serena to the window springs,
On curiosity's amusive wings.'

But where the attempt to 'raise, if possible, the dignity of a declining Art' is to be found in this mixture of 'familiar Incident and allegorical picture,' is beyond research.

Hayley tells us that he has given 'an air of novelty' to his 'Triumphs,' and he introduces his three plays in would-be comic verse with the hope that his 'liberal and enlightened readers will look with indulgence on a publication, which arose from his wish to introduce a striking, and he trusted, not a blameless variety into the amusements of English literature.' The novelty of Hayley's humour must, one imagines, have had something to do with some of Blake's best epigrams. Odes and Epistles, Essays in Verse, Sonnets, Songs, and occasional Verses, follow one another with dreary persistence, interspersed with notes longer than the poems, but better reading, and more nearly coming within the limits of that indulgence which he once claimed for 'those pleasing and innocent delusions in which a poetical Enthusiast may be safely indulged.'

Hayley was a poetical enthusiast, but remembering with Blake —

'the verses that Hayley sung
When my heart knocked against the roof of my tongue,'

we must conclude that it was not safe to indulge him in his innocent delusions. No one has the right to bore the world, or one great poet, with as little excuse as Hayley. He was a rich man, and, in the days of patrons, the prodigal patron of his own ineptitudes.

CHARLES DIBDIN (1745–1814) [1]

DIBDIN left an immense quantity of singable songs, not only ballads of the sea, but vigorous, often vulgar, not seldom amusing songs on all kinds of subjects, reminding one at times of George Morland's pictures. It is by 'Tom Bowling' that Dibdin is best known, and there is a good swing in it and some ingenious punning. It is a little self-conscious in its attempt to render a seaman's speech, and is only quite plausible from that point of view here and there. This way of song-writing, the building up, the final clench at the end, the actual rhythm, seem to anticipate some of the later characteristics of Mr. Albert Chevalier's cockney ballads. Dibdin had an illegitimate son, Thomas John (1771–1841), who was an actor and writer of comic plays and songs.

JOHN O'KEEFFE (1747–1833) [2]

JOHN O'KEEFFE was a copious and outrageous maker of comic plays, operas, and farces, of which it may well be said, in his own words in the refrain of one of his own songs, 'All is puff, rattle, squeak, and ding-dong.' He also wrote poems, which he left as a legacy to his daughter, and they are printed with all his own naïve comments on them. Of 'Bona the Rake; or, The Terrible Bony!' (Bona being Bonaparte) he says: 'This poem was with the exception of "War and Peace" (which he invariably called his Sublime Pedestal of Fame), decidedly the author's favourite of all his productions.' He began it, he says, as a song, and it comes finally to be eighty pages in this manner: —

[1] *Professional Life*, containing 600 songs, 4 vols. 1803.
[2] (1) *Dramatic Works*, 4 vols. 1798. (2) O'Keeffe's Legacy to his Daughter, being the *Poetical Works* of the late John O'Keeffe, Esq., the Dramatic Author, 1834.

'Great Constantine Christian-Imperial Premier,
Imperial Napoleon now eagles it there.'

But his most amusing and in every way best verse is to be found scattered all over the interminable pages of his plays. The prose is not less swift and toppling than the verse, as in this sentence from 'Tony Lumpkin in Town' : 'He gaped at the masks, roared most stertorously discordant with the music, overset the pyramids, pocketed the sweetmeats, broke the glasses, made love to an Arcadian dairy-maid, tripped up the heels of a harlequin, beat a hermit, who happened to be a captain of the guards, and gave a bishop a black eye.' Sometimes his verse, for a moment, turns serious, as in the song which begins: —

'Beauty in the street is sold,
And envy spatters fame with dirt,
And honour's now despised and old,
And genius sports a ragged shirt.'

And one of his metres anticipates a metre used afterwards by Darley and later still by Meredith, where it comes to perfection: —

'Fly, fly, refreshing gales, ah gently by me,
In passing softly whisper who is come;
No news of him I love, oh ne'er come nigh me —
Sing, sing, ye pretty birds, his welcome home.'

Refrains of preposterous oddity, not outdone till the time of Marzials' unforgettable

'Plop, plop,
The barges flop
Drip drop,'

are to be found in the 'amateur high musical' manner of

'Bounce!
Flounce!'

And better tunes too, as in

'Hey down,
Ho down,
Derry derry down,
All amongst the leaves so green-O.'

This boisterousness sinks at times to vulgarity, but of a wild, hearty sort, and is rarely without a real mastery of comic metre. O'Keeffe's most perfect extravagance, his rhythm at its best, is to be found in this splendid tune, which Leigh Hunt vainly tried to copy: —

> 'Amo, amas,
> I love a lass,
> As cedar tall and slender;
> Sweet cowslip's face
> Is her nominative case,
> And she's of the feminine gender.
> Horum quorum,
> Sunt divorum,
> Harum, scarum, Divo;
> Tag rag, merry derry, periwig and hatband,
> Hic, hoc, harum, genitivo.'

There, if you like, is nonsense; but how convincing to the ear!

JOHN PHILPOT CURRAN (1750–1817) [1]

CURRAN, a man of wit and a great speaker, of whom Byron said 'I have heard that man speak more poetry than I have ever seen written,' wrote one poem and one only which is worth remembering. It is in one of the good old Irish stanzas which Dr. Hyde has made familiar and beautiful to us, and it has a kind of laughter heard through a cry, an audacity in the face of death, which, in a 'Deserter's Meditation,' anticipates the great gallows-song of Burns. Here are the two stanzas: —

> 'If sadly thinking, with spirits sinking,
> Could more than drinking my cares compose,
> A cure for sorrow from sighs I'd borrow,
> And hope to-morrow would end my days.
> But as in wailing there's nought availing,
> And Death unfailing will strike the blow,
> Then for that reason, and for a season,
> Let us be merry before we go.

[1] *The Life of the Right Honourable John Philpot Curran.* By his son, William Henry Curran. 2 vols. 1822.

'To joy a stranger, a way-worn ranger,
In every danger my course I've run;
Now hope all ending, and Death befriending,
His last aid lending, my cares are done.
No more a rover, a hapless lover,
Those cares are over, and my glass runs low;
Then for that reason, and for a season,
Let us be merry before we go.'

If any one can read the refrain of this song without a stirring in the blood, there must be ice in him.

WILLIAM GIFFORD (1756-1826) [1]

IN the honest fragment of autobiography which prefaces his translation of Juvenal, Gifford tells us, perhaps needlessly, that he had no natural instinct for poetry. He comments on his 'gloom and savage unsociability' and on his waste of exertion on 'splenetic and vexatious tricks'; and 'The Baviad' and 'The Mæviad' are hardly more than so much waste, the waste of a prose-writer who takes up verse to chastise the writers of bad verse. Only from the actual evidence of the footnotes can we believe in the existence of 'Laura's tinkling trash' and the varied and unending ineptitudes of Della Crusca. The school existed, and Gifford killed it; yet such small game leaves but mangled carrion behind, and verse and notes are now equally unreadable.

WILLIAM BLAKE (1757-1827) [2]

I

BLAKE was twofold a poet, in words and in lines, and it has often been debated whether he was a greater poet in words

[1] (1) *Baviad*, 1794. (2) *Mæviad*, 1795. (3) *Epistle to Peter Pindar*, 1800. (4) *Juvenal*, 1820. (5) *Persius*, 1821.
[2] (1) *Poetical Sketches*, privately printed, 1783. (2) *Songs of Innocence*, 1789. (3) *The Book of Thel*, 1789. (4) *The Marriage of Heaven*

38 ROMANTIC MOVEMENT IN ENGLISH POETRY

or in lines. If greatness includes, as I think it must, a technique able not only to suggest, but to embody, then the writer of the 'Songs of Innocence' and the 'Songs of Experience' is unquestionably greater than the designer of all those magnificent suggestions which may be more justly compared with the scattered splendours of the Prophetic Books. In the writings of the Prophetic Books there are fine passages, but no achieved fineness of result: inspiration comes and goes, unguided; while in the best of the lyrics we have an inspiration which is held firmly under control. In the best of the lyrics there is an art of verse which neither Coleridge nor Shelley has ever surpassed; can it quite be said of even the very best of the designs, that they have not been surpassed, in the actual art of design, by Leonardo and Michael Angelo?

It is only in his earliest work, in the volume of 'Poetical Sketches,' printed in 1783 but never published, that any origins can be found for the poetry of Blake, and even there they are for the most part uncertain and of little significance. We are told in the 'advertisement' at the beginning of the book that 'the following Sketches were the production of

and Hell, probably 1790. (5) *Visions of the Daughters of Albion*, 1793. (6) *For Children; The Gates of Paradise*, 1793. (7) *America*, 1793. (8) *Europe*, 1794. (9) *Songs of Experience*, 1794. (10) *The First Book of Urizen*, 1794. (11) *The Song of Los*, 1795. (12) *The Book of Los*, 1795. (13) *The Book of Ahania*, 1795. (14) *Milton*, 1804. (15) *Jerusalem*, 1804. (16) *The Ghost of Abel*, 1822. All these, except the first, are engraved by Blake, with his own illustrations on the pages. The first collected edition of the *Poems*, without the Prophetic Books, but containing the poems in the Rossetti manuscript, first printed in Gilchrist's *Life of Blake*, 1863, was edited for the Aldine Series by Mr. W. M. Rossetti in 1874. *The Works of William Blake, Poetic, Symbolic, and Critical*, edited by E. J. Ellis and W. B. Yeats, followed in 1893, in three volumes, containing facsimiles of most of the Prophetic Books and the first printed conjectural text of *Vala*. Other editions of the poems have followed, but the only authoritative text is that of Mr. John Sampson, Oxford, 1904. This edition, however, does not contain the Prophetic Books; *Jerusalem* and *Milton* were printed under the editorship of A. G. B. Russell and R. D. Maclagan in 1904 and 1907, and the complete text of the Prophetic Books was given by Mr. Edwin Ellis in his *Poetical Works of William Blake*, 2 vols. 1906.

untutored youth, commenced in his twelfth, and occasionally resumed by the author till his twentieth year'; that is to say, between the years 1768 and 1777. The earliest were written while Goldsmith and Gray were still living, the latest (if we may believe these dates) after Chatterton's death but before his poems had been published. 'Ossian' had appeared in 1760, Percy's 'Reliques' in 1765. The 'Reliques' probably had their influence on Blake, Ossian certainly, an influence which returns much later, curiously mingled with the influence of Milton, in the form taken by the Prophetic Books. It has been suggested that some of Blake's mystical names, and his 'fiend in a cloud,' came from Ossian; and Ossian is very evidently in the metrical prose of such pieces as 'Samson' and even in some of the imagery ('their helmed youth and aged warriors in dust together lie, and Desolation spreads his wings over the land of Palestine'). But the influence of Chatterton seems not less evident, an influence which could hardly have found its way to Blake before the year 1777. In the fifth chapter of the fantastic 'Island in the Moon' (probably written about 1784) there is a long discussion on Chatterton, while in the seventh chapter he is again discussed, in company with Homer, Shakespeare, and Milton. As late as 1826 Blake wrote on the margin of Wordsworth's preface to the 'Lyrical Ballads': 'I believe both Macpherson and Chatterton that what they say is ancient is so'; and, on another page: 'I own myself an admirer of Ossian equally with any poet whatever: of Rowley and Chatterton also.' Whether it be influence or affinity, it is hard to say, but if the 'Mad Song' of Blake has the hint of any predecessor in our literature, it is to be found in the abrupt energy and stormy masculine splendour of the High Priest's Song in 'Aella,' 'Ye who hie yn mokie ayre'; and if, between the time of the Elizabethans and the time of 'My silks and fine array' there had been any other song of similar technique and similar imaginative temper, it was certainly the Minstrel's Song in 'Aella': 'O! synge untoe mie roundelaie.'

Of the direct and very evident influence of the Elizabethans we are told by Malkin, with his quaint preciseness: 'Shakespeare's "Venus and Adonis," "Tarquin and Lucrece," and his Sonnets, . . . poems, now little read, were favourite studies of Mr. Blake's early days. So were Johnson's Underwoods and his Miscellanies.' 'My silks and fine array' goes past Johnson, and reaches Fletcher if not Shakespeare himself. And the blank verse of 'King Edward the Third' goes straight to Shakespeare for its cadence and for something in its manner of speech. And there is other blank verse which, among much not even metrically correct, anticipates something of the richness of Keats.

Some rags of his time did indeed cling about him, but only by the edges; there is even a reflected ghost of the pseudo-Gothic of Walpole in 'Fair Elenor,' who comes straight from the 'Castle of Otranto'; as 'Gwin King of Norway' takes after the Scandinavian fashion of the day, and may have been inspired by 'The Fatal Sisters' or 'The Triumphs of Owen' of Gray. 'Blindman's Bluff,' too, is a piece of eighteenth-century burlesque realism. But it is in the ode 'To the Muses' that Blake for once accepts, and in so doing clarifies the smooth convention of the eighteenth-century classicism, and, as he reproaches it in its own speech, illuminates it suddenly with the light it had rejected:—

> 'How have you left the ancient love
> That bards of old enjoyed in you!
> The languid strings do scarcely move,
> The sound is forced, the notes are few!'

In those lines the eighteenth century dies to music; and from this time forward we find, in the rest of Blake's work, only a proof of his own assertion: that 'the ages are all equal; but genius is above the age.'

To define the poetry of Blake one must find new definitions for poetry; but, these definitions once found, he will seem to be the only poet who is a poet in essence; the only poet who could, in his own words, 'enter into Noah's rainbow, and make a friend and companion of one of these images of wonder, which always entreat him to leave mortal things.' In this verse there is, if it is to be found in any verse, the 'lyrical cry'; and yet, what voice is it that cries in this disembodied ecstasy? The voice of desire is not in it, nor the voice of passion, nor the cry of the heart, nor the cry of the sinner to God, nor of the lover of nature to nature. It neither seeks nor aspires nor laments nor questions. It is like the voice of wisdom in a child, who has not yet forgotten the world out of which the soul came. It is as spontaneous as the note of a bird; it is an affirmation of life; in its song, which seems mere music, it is the mind which sings; it is lyric thought. What is it that transfixes one in any couplet such as this: —

> 'If the sun and moon should doubt
> They'd immediately go out'?

It is no more than a nursery statement, there is not even an image in it, and yet it sings to the brain, it cuts into the very flesh of the mind, as if there was a great weight behind it. Is it that it is an arrow, and that it comes from so far, and with an impetus gathered from its speed out of the sky?

The lyric poet, every lyric poet but Blake, sings of love; but Blake sings of forgiveness: —

> 'Mutual forgiveness of each vice,
> Such are the gates of Paradise.'

Poets sing of beauty, but Blake says: —

> 'Soft deceit and idleness,
> These are Beauty's sweetest dress.'

They sing of the brotherhood of men, but Blake points to the 'divine image': —

> 'Cruelty has a human heart,
> And Jealousy a human face;
> Terror the human form divine,
> And Secrecy the human dress.'

Their minds are touched by the sense of tears in human things, but to Blake 'a tear is an intellectual thing.' They sing of 'a woman like a dewdrop,' but Blake of 'the lineaments of gratified desire.' They shout hymns to God over a field of battle or in the arrogance of material empire; but Blake addresses the epilogue of his 'Gates of Paradise' 'to the Accuser who is the God of this world' : —

> 'Truly, my Satan, thou art but a dunce,
> And dost not know the garment from the man;
> Every harlot was a virgin once,
> Nor canst thou ever change Kate into Nan.
> Though thou art worshipped by the names divine
> Of Jesus and Jehovah, thou art still
> The son of morn in weary night's decline,
> The lost traveller's dream under the hill.'

Other poets find ecstasy in nature, but Blake only in imagination. He addresses the Prophetic Book of 'The Ghost of Abel' 'to Lord Byron in the Wilderness,' and asks: 'What doest thou here, Elijah? Can a poet doubt of the visions of Jehovah? Nature has no outline, but Imagination has. Nature has no Time, but Imagination has. Nature has no supernatural, and dissolves. Imagination is eternity.' The poetry of Blake is a poetry of the mind, abstract in substance, concrete in form; its passion is the passion of the imagination, its emotion is the emotion of thought, its beauty is the beauty of idea. When it is simplest, its simplicity is that of some 'infant joy' too young to have a name, or of some 'infant sorrow' brought aged out of eternity into the 'dangerous world,' and there

> 'Helpless, naked, piping loud,
> Like a fiend hid in a cloud.'

There are no men and women in the world of Blake's poetry, only primal instincts and the energies of the imagination.

His work begins in the Garden of Eden, or of the childhood of the world, and there is something in it of the naïveté of beasts: the lines gambol awkwardly, like young lambs. His utterance of the state of innocence has in it something of the grotesqueness of babies, and enchants the grown man, as they do. Humour exists unconscious of itself, in a kind of awed and open-eyed solemnity. He stammers into a speech of angels, as if just awakening out of Paradise. It is the primal instincts that speak first, before riper years have added wisdom to intuition. It is the supreme quality of this wisdom that it has never let go of intuition. It is as if intuition itself ripened. And so Blake goes through life with perfect mastery of the terms of existence, as they present themselves to him; 'perfectly happy, wanting nothing,' as he said, when he was old and poor; and able in each stage of life to express in art the corresponding stage of his own development. He is the only poet who has written the songs of childhood, of youth, of mature years, and of old age; and he died singing.

II

Blake is the only poet who sees all temporal things under the form of eternity. To him reality is merely a symbol, and he catches at its terms, hastily and faultily, as he catches at the lines of the drawing-master, to represent, as in a faint image, the clear and shining outlines of what he sees with the imagination; through the eye, not with it, as he says. Where other poets use reality as a spring-board into space, he uses it as a foothold on his return from flight. Even Wordsworth seemed to him a kind of atheist, who mistook the changing signs of 'vegetable nature' for the unchanging realities of the imagination. 'Natural objects,' he wrote in a copy of Wordsworth, 'always did and now do weaken, deaden, and obliterate imagination in me. Wordsworth must know that what he writes valuable is not to be found in nature.' And so his poetry is the most abstract of all poetry, although in a sense the most concrete. It is everywhere an affirmation, the register of vision; never observation. To him Observation was one of the daughters of memory, and he had no use for her among his Muses, which were all eternal, and the children of the imagination. 'Imagination,' he said, 'has nothing to do with memory.' For the most part he is just conscious that what he sees as 'an old man grey' is no more than 'a frowning thistle':

> 'For double the vision my eyes do see,
> And a double vision is always with me.
> With my inward eyes, 't is an old man grey,
> With my outward, a thistle across my way.'

In being so far conscious, he is only recognising the symbol, not admitting the reality.

In his earlier work, the symbol still interests him, he accepts it without dispute; with indeed a kind of transfiguring love. Thus he writes of the lamb and the tiger, of the joy and sorrow of infants, of the fly and the lily, as no poet of mere observation has ever written of them, going deeper into their essence than Wordsworth ever went into the heart of daffodils, or Shelley into the nerves of the sensitive plant. He takes only the simplest flowers or weeds, and the most innocent or most destroying of animals, and he uses them as illustrations of the divine attributes. From the same flower and beast he can read contrary lessons without change of meaning, by the mere transposition of qualities; as in the poem which now reads: —

> 'The modest rose puts forth a thorn,
> The humble sheep a threatening horn;
> While the lily white shall in love delight,
> Nor a thorn, nor a threat, stain her beauty bright.'

Mr. Sampson tells us in his notes: 'Beginning by writing —

> '"The rose puts envious . . ."

he felt that "envious" did not express his full meaning, and deleted the last three words, writing above them "lustful rose," and finishing the line with the words "puts forth a thorn." He then went on —

> '"The coward sheep a threatening horn;
> While the lily white shall in love delight,
> And the lion increase freedom and peace;"

at which point he drew a line under the poem to show that it was finished. On a subsequent reading he deleted the last line, substituting for it —

'"The Priest loves war, and the soldier peace,"

but here, perceiving that his rhyme had disappeared, he cancelled this line also, and gave the poem an entirely different turn by changing the word "lustful" to "modest," and "coward" to "humble," and completing the quatrain (as in the engraved version) by a fourth line simply explanatory of the first three! This is not merely obeying the idle impulse of a rhyme, but rather a bringing of the mind's impulses into that land where "contraries mutually exist."'

And when I say that he reads lessons, let it not be supposed that Blake was ever consciously didactic. Conduct does not concern him; not doing, but being. He held that education was the setting of a veil between light and the soul. 'There is no good in education,' he said. 'I hold it to be wrong. It is the great sin. It is eating of the tree of the knowledge of good and evil. This was the fault of Plato. He knew nothing but the virtues and vices, and good and evil. There is nothing in all that. Everything is good in God's eyes.' And, as he says with his excellent courage: 'When I tell the truth it is not for the sake of convincing those who do not know it, but for the sake of defending those who do'; and again, with still more excellent and harder courage: 'When I am endeavouring to think rightly, I must not regard my own any more than other people's weaknesses'; so, in his poetry, there is no moral tendency, nothing that might not be poison as well as antidote; nothing indeed but the absolute affirmation of that energy which is eternal delight. He worshipped energy as the well-head or parent fire of life; and to him there was no evil, only a weakness, a negation of energy, the ignominy of wings that droop and are contented in the dust.

And so, like Nietzsche, but with a deeper innocence, he finds himself 'beyond good and evil,' in a region where the soul is naked and its own master. Most of his art is the unclothing of the soul, and when at last it is naked and alone, in that 'thrilling' region where the souls of other men have at times penetrated, only to shudder back with terror from the brink of eternal loneliness, then only is this soul exultant with the supreme happiness.

III

In his earlier work Blake is satisfied with natural symbols, with nature as symbol; in his later work, in the final message of the Prophetic Books, he is no longer satisfied with what then seems to him the relative truth of the symbols of reality. Dropping the tools with which he has worked so well, he grasps with naked hands after an absolute truth of statement, which is like his attempt in his designs to render the outlines of vision literally, without translation into the forms of human sight. He invents names harsh as triangles, Enitharmon, Theotormon, Rintrah, for spiritual states and essences, and he employs them as Wagner employed his leading motives, as a kind of shorthand for the memory. His meaning is no longer apparent in the ordinary meaning of the words he uses; we have to read him with a key, and the key is not always in our hands; he forgets that he is talking to men on the earth in some language which he has learnt in heavenly places. He sees symbol within symbol, and as he tries to make one clear to us he does but translate it into another, perhaps no easier, or more confusing. And, it must be remembered when even interpreters like Mr. Ellis and Mr. Yeats falter, and confess 'There is apparently some confusion among the symbols,' that after all we have only a portion of Blake's later work, and that probably a far larger portion was destroyed when the Peckham 'angel,' Mr. Tatham (co-partner in foolish wickedness with Warburton's cook) sat down to burn the books which he did not understand. Blake's great system of wheels within wheels remains no better than a ruin, and can but at the best be pieced together tentatively by those who are able to trace the connection of some of its parts. It is no longer even possible to know how much consistency Blake was able to give to his symbols, and how far he failed to make them visible in terms of mortal understanding. As we have them, they evade us on every side, not because they are meaningless, but because the secret of their meaning is so closely kept. To Blake actual contemporary names meant even more than they meant to Walt Whitman. 'All truths wait in all things,' said Walt Whitman, and Blake has his own quite significant but perplexing meaning when he writes: —

'The corner of Broad Street weeps; Poland Street languishes
To Great Queen Street and Lincoln's Inn: all is distress, and woe.'

He is concerned now only with his message, with the 'minutely particular' statement of it; and as he has ceased to accept any mortal medium, or to allow himself to be penetrated by the sunlight of earthly beauty, he has lost the means of making that message visible to us. It is a miscalculation of means, a contempt for possibilities: not, as people were once hasty enough to assume, the irresponsible rapture of madness. There is not even in these crabbed chronicles the wild beauty of the madman's scattering brain; there is a concealed sanity, a precise kind of truth, which, as Blake said of all truth, 'can never be so told as to be understood, and not be believed.'

Blake's form, or apparent formlessness, in the Prophetic Books, was no natural accident, or unconsidered utterance of inspiration. Addressing the public on the first plate of 'Jerusalem' he says: 'When this verse was first dictated to me, I considered a monotonous cadence like that used by Milton and Shakespeare and all writers of English blank Verse, derived from the bondage of rhyming, to be a necessary and indispensable part of verse. But I soon found that in the mouth of a true orator such monotony was not only awkward, but as much a bondage as rhyme itself. I have therefore produced a variety in every line, both of cadences and number of syllables. Every word and every letter is studied and put into its fit place; the terrific numbers are reserved for the terrific parts, the mild and gentle for the mild and gentle parts, and the prosaic for inferior parts; all are necessary to each other.' This desire for variety at the expense of unity is illustrated in one of Blake's marginal notes to Reynolds' 'Discourses.' 'Such harmony of colouring' (as that of Titian in the Bacchus and Ariadne) 'is destructive of Art. One species of equal hue over all is the cursed thing called harmony. It is the smile of a fool.' This is a carrying to its extreme limit of the principle that 'there is no such thing as softness in art, and that everything in art is definite and minute . . . because vision is determinate and perfect'; and that 'colouring does not depend on where the colours are put, but on where the lights and darks are put, and all depends on form and outline, on where that is put.' The whole aim of the Prophetic Books is to arrive at a style as 'determinate and perfect' as vision, unmodified by any of the deceiving beauties of nature or of the distracting ornaments of conventional form. What is further interesting in his statement is that he aimed, in the Prophetic Books, at producing the effect, not of poetry but of oratory, and it is as oratory, the oratory of the prophets, that the reader is doubtless meant to take them.

Throughout the Prophetic Books Blake has to be translated out of the unfamiliar language into which he has tried to translate spiritual realities, literally, as he apprehended them. Just as, in the designs which his hand drew as best it could, according to its limited and partly false knowledge, from the visions which his imagination saw with perfect clearness, he was often unable to translate that vision into its real equivalent in design, so in his attempts to put these other mental visions into words he was hampered by an equally false method, and often by reminiscences of what passed for 'picturesque' writing in the work of his contemporaries. He was, after all, of his time, though he was above it; and just as he knew Michelangelo only through bad reproductions, and could never get his own design wholly free, malleable, and virgin to his 'shaping spirit of imagination,' so, in spite of all his marvellous lyrical discoveries, made when his mind was less burdened by the weight of a controlling message, he found himself, when he attempted to make an intelligible system out of the 'improvisations of the spirit,' and to express that system with literal accuracy, the half-helpless captive of formal words, conventional rhythms, a language not drawn direct from its source. Thus we find, in the Prophetic Books, neither achieved poems nor an achieved philosophy. The philosophy has reached us only in splendid fragments (the glimmering of stars out of separate corners of a dark sky), and we shall never know to what extent these fragments were once part of a whole. Had they been ever really fused, this would have been the only system of philosophy made entirely out of the raw material of poetry. As it has come to us unachieved, the world has still to wait for a philosophy untouched by the materialism of the prose intelligence.

IV

'There are three powers in man of conversing with Paradise,' said Blake, and he defined them as the three sons of Noah who survived the flood, and who are Poetry, Painting, and Music. Through all three powers, and to the last moments of his life on earth, Blake conversed with Paradise. We are told that he used to sing his own songs to his own music, and that, when he was dying, 'he composed and uttered songs to his Maker,' and 'burst out into singing of the things he saw in heaven.' And with almost the last strength of his hands he had made a sketch of his wife, before he 'made the rafters ring,' as a bystander records, with the improvisation of his last breath.

Throughout life, his desire had been, as he said, 'To converse with my friends in eternity, see visions, dream dreams, and prophesy and speak parables unobserved.' He says again: —

> 'I rest not from my great task
> To open the eternal worlds, to open the immortal eyes
> Of Man inwards into the worlds of thought, into eternity,
> Ever expanding in the bosom of God, the human imagination.'

And writing to the uncomprehending Hayley (who had called him 'gentle, visionary Blake'), he says again: 'I am really drunk with intellectual vision whenever I take a pencil or graver into my hand.' To the newspapers of his time, on the one or two occasions when they mentioned his name, he was 'an unfortunate lunatic'; even to Lamb, who looked upon him as 'one of the most extraordinary persons of the age,' he was a man 'flown, whither I know not — to Hades or a mad house.' To the first editor of his collected poems there seemed to be 'something in his mind not exactly sane'; and the critics of to-day still discuss his sanity as a man and as a poet.

It is true that Blake was abnormal; but what was abnormal in him was his sanity. To one who believed that 'The ruins of Time build mansions in eternity,' that 'imagination is eternity,' and that 'our deceased friends are more really with us than when they were apparent to our mortal part,' there could be none of that confusion at the edge of mystery which makes a man mad because he is unconscious of the gulf. No one was ever more conscious than Blake was of the limits of that region which we call reality and of that other region which we call imagination. It pleased him to reject the one and to dwell in the other, and his choice was not the choice of most men, but of some of those who have been the greatest saints and the greatest artists. And, like the most authentic among them, he walked firmly among those realities to which he cared to give no more than a side-glance from time to time; he lived his own life quietly and rationally, doing always exactly what he wanted to do, and with so fine a sense of the subtlety of mere worldly manners, that when, at his one moment of worldly success, in 1793, he refused the post of drawing-master to the royal family, he gave up all his other pupils at the same time, lest the refusal should seem ungracious on the part of one who had been the friend of revolutionaries. He saw visions, but not as the spiritualists and the magicians have seen them. These desire to quicken mortal sight, until the soul limits itself again, takes body, and returns to reality; but Blake, the inner mystic, desired only to quicken that imagination which he knew to be more real than the reality of nature. Why should he call up shadows when he could talk 'in the spirit with spiritual realities'? 'Then I asked,' he says, in the 'Marriage of Heaven and Hell,' 'does a firm persuasion that a thing is so make it so? He replied: "All poets believe that it does."'

Of the definite reality of Blake's visions there can be no question; no question that, as he once wrote, 'nothing can withstand the fury of my course among the stars of God, and in the abysses of the accuser.' But imagination is not one, but manifold: and the metaphor, professing to be no more than metaphor, of the poet, may be vision as essential as the thing actually seen by the visionary. The difference between imagination in Blake and in, say, Shakespeare, is that the one (himself a painter) has a visual imagination and sees an image or metaphor as a literal reality, while the other, seeing it not less vividly but in a more purely mental way, adds a 'like' or an 'as,' and the image or metaphor comes to you with its apology or attenuation, and takes you less by surprise. But to Blake it was the universe that was a metaphor.

GEORGE CRABBE (1758–1832) [1]

COLERIDGE, who usually said the right thing about poetry, said of Crabbe: 'In Crabbe there is an absolute defect of the high imagination; he gives me little or no pleasure: yet, no doubt, he has much power of a certain kind.' It is this power of a certain kind, not, obviously at least, of an essentially poetic kind, that we have to disentangle and define, if we can, in the work of the poet who, more than any other, carried on into the nineteenth the traditions of the eighteenth century.

In several of his prefaces, Crabbe was at the pains to explain and even to justify what he had done in his poetry. With his admirable frankness he confesses: 'With me the way I take is not a matter of choice, but of necessity': or, as he puts it elsewhere: 'What I thought I could best describe, that I attempted.' 'I have,' says a manuscript fragment printed by his son, 'chiefly, if not exclusively, taken my subjects and characters from that order of society where the least display of vanity is generally to be found, which is placed between the humble and the great. It is in this class of mankind that more originality of character, more variety of fortune, will be met with.' In a letter to his friend in old age, Mrs. Leadbeater, he says: 'I will tell you readily about my creatures, whom I endeavoured to paint as nearly as I could and dared. . . . There is not one of whom I had not in my mind the original; but I was obliged, in some cases, to take them from their real situations, in one or two instances to change even the sex, and, in many, the circumstances. . . . Indeed, I do not know that I could paint merely from my own fancy; and there is no cause why we should.'

In the preface to the 'Tales' of 1812, Crabbe makes his most

[1] (1) *Inebriety* (anonymous), 1774. (2) *The Candidate*, 1780. (3) *The Library*, 1781. (4) *The Village*, 1783. (5) *The Newspaper*, 1785. (6) *The Parish Register*, 1807. (7) *The Borough*, 1810. (8) *Tales in Verse*, 1812. (9) *Tales of the Hall*, 1819. (10) *Poetical Works*, 8 vols. 1834.

serious attempt to meet the criticisms of those who doubted whether his original and powerful work was, in the strict sense, poetry. 'It has been already acknowledged,' he says, 'that these compositions have no pretensions to be estimated with the more lofty and heroic poems; but I feel great reluctance in admitting that they have not a fair and legitimate claim to the poetic character.' He is one of those, he says, 'who address their productions to the plain sense and sober judgment of their readers, rather than to their fancy and imagination'; and he affirms that many genuine poems 'are adapted and addressed to the common-sense of the reader, and prevail by the strong language of truth and nature.' 'Who will complain,' he asks in a passage intended for this preface, 'that a definition of poetry, which excludes a great part of the writings of Pope, will shut out him'? For, he says, both in Pope and Dryden, there is, 'no small portion of this actuality of relation, this nudity of description, and poetry without an atmosphere.'

Actuality of relation, nudity of description, and poetry without an atmosphere: was there ever so just a description, so severe a condemnation, of a great part of the poetry of Crabbe? It is rarely needful to judge any writer except out of his own mouth: be sure that, if once he begins to justify himself against objections, he will confess by the way more fatal deficiencies than those he was already charged with. In a note added by Wordsworth in later life to the early poem of 'Lucy Gray,' he says pointedly: 'The way in which the incident was treated and the spiritualising of the character might furnish hints for contrasting the imaginative influences which I have endeavoured to throw over common life with Crabbe's matter of fact style of treating subjects of the same kind.' It was here that Crabbe had the critics of the day on his side, and it was because this 'strong language of truth and nature' was set to the fixed eighteenth-century cadences, and was untinged by any 'light that never was, on sea or land,' that he was accepted, while Wordsworth was only laughed at. Crabbe did, indeed, do something which was out of fashion then: he took nature fearlessly at first hand, and set down what he saw as he saw it; and so he was a liberating influence. But he was no revolutionary; his sympathies, in matters of literature, were always with the past through which he had lived.

The life of Crabbe takes us back into the heart of the eighteenth century. When, at the age of twenty-four, standing by 'a shallow, muddy piece of water, as desolate and gloomy as his own mind, called the Leech-pond,' he determines 'to go to London and venture all,' Chatterton had but just committed suicide, and his only acquaintances in London warn him of a fate that may well come to be his, they think. He starves in poor lodgings, tries the booksellers in vain 'with a view to publication,' and looks out, in the way of the period, for a patron. He finds one, just not too late, in Burke, and the way is made smooth for him. Lord Thurlow asks him to breakfast, and puts an envelope into his hand as he is leaving; it contains one hundred pounds. A living is found for him in the Church, and he goes back to his native town as a curate, having met Sir Joshua Reynolds, and been growled at by Dr. Johnson, who bids him 'Never fear putting the strongest and best things you can think of into the mouth of your speaker, whatever may be his condition.'

His first poem, we must remember, was published at Ipswich in 1775; and between 'The Newspaper' of 1785, in which the better start of 'The Village' is abandoned for a mere imitation of Pope, and the next poem which he published, 'The Parish Register,' his first really poetical work, there was an interval of twenty-two years. By that year, 1807, a new century had come with new ideals, men were fighting for the existence of their old models, Wordsworth had brought in a new humanity, Coleridge a new magic, Scott a new romance. How much had Wordsworth learnt from the close grappling with reality in 'The Village' of 1783, which appeared five years before the 'Lyrical Ballads'? And is it fanciful to think that Crabbe, in turn, during those years of silence, had learnt something from the 'Lyrical Ballads'? 'There were few modern works,' says his son, 'which he opened so frequently' as 'the earlier and shorter poems of what is called the Lake School.' He did not learn what he could not quite unlearn from his eighteenth-century training, for in the fifth line of his poem of 1807 he still says 'Nymphs and Swains' when he means the young men and women of his parish. But I can imagine the work of Wordsworth coming to him as work which after all did, in its different way, something which he was trying to do, equally without a model, and in another form of the 'strong language of truth and nature.'

What we know of the life of Crabbe, as it is told in the excellent memoir by his elder son, can be seen, from the first, building up the poet, with all his strength and limitations. He was born on the East Coast, at Aldborough, where his father, 'a man of imperious temper and violent passions,' was Salt-master, or collector of the salt-duties. The house in which he was born was long since washed away by the sea; it was a dark house with small windows, glazed with diamond panes. Aldborough was then a small town of two unpaved streets, in which hardly any one but fishermen and pilots lived. The spring-tides battered down the houses, from time to time. Inland, the land was sandy and full of weeds, the trees few and stunted; marshy land lay between the river and the beach. The whole desolation of the coast, and of the discoloured sea, has gone into the verse of Crabbe, to which it has indeed given its harsh and gloomy colouring. At eighteen he began to write verse and to study botany, on which he wrote a book, which, on the advice of a friend, he burned; to find out later on that he had made some discoveries which were left for others to name and classify. His son tells us that he never saw him doing nothing; 'out of doors he had always some object in view, a flower, or a pebble, or his note-book, in his hand;

and in the house, if he was not writing, he was reading.' He would compose his verse while he was searching for plants, insects, or minerals; and he would take out his note-book and write down what he had composed. Near the end of his life, when he was staying with Scott at Edinburgh, he had a lamp and writing materials placed by his bedside every night; and he told Lady Scott that he would have lost 'many a good hit' if he had not set down at once things that occurred to him in his dreams. He wrote best in autumn, and found an extraordinary stimulus in a sudden fall of snow. He did not care for music, or painting, or architecture, or what is usually held to be the beauty of natural scenes or things. But once, when he was living sixty miles inland, at Stathern, he was seized with so sharp a desire for the sea that he mounted his horse, rode the sixty miles to the coast, bathed, and rode back again. In botany, he cared chiefly for grasses, and had few showy flowers, but many rare weeds, in his garden; in minerals, he studied mostly the earths and sands; and, in entomology, small insects. He thought little of any ordered beauty, from what his son 'must call his want of taste'; but he loved any form of exact science, and 'could at all times find luxury in the most dry and forbidding calculations.'

Crabbe was the botanist and geologist of the rockier strata of men and of the weeds and grasses of nature. He botanises among the village hedgerows, finding 'specimens' of abnormal growth, or picks with his hammer at the village streets, turning up quartz or flint with an odd relish. He is always the investigator, the collector, and was indeed really a man of science, to whom science was so vital that it became almost, only never quite, a thing of the imagination, or the equivalent of that 'shaping spirit.' His stories are built up, with method and patience, detail added to detail, in a strenuous effort to be truthful in regard to 'the manners moving in his way.' He wonders

'That books which promise much of life to give,
Should show so little how we truly live,'

and resolves for his part to let in 'truth, terror, and the day.' At times he is a masculine Jane Austen, observing the trivialities of provincial life with unshrinking, sometimes with gravely humorous eyes. But, in his attempt to find

'What shapes the Proteus-passions take
And what strange waste of life and joy they make,'

he is drawn most powerfully to those mean tragedies in which Hogarth had found the matter of his designs, to prisons, workhouses, to

'The lame, the blind, and, far the happier they!
The moping idiot, and the madman gay,' —

lines in which his curious feeling about distraction of mind, as a relief from the too heavy burdens of reality, comes in significantly. The nearest road for him from truth to something which is a form of imagination lies in a feeling for solitude in people and things; the interaction of two solitudes. His finest effects are got from the picture of Peter Grimes, enduring his slow misery, alone in his boat : —

'At the same time the same dull views to see,
The bounding marsh-bank and the blighted tree;
The water only, when the tides were high,
When low, the mud half-covered and half-dry :'

of Abel Keene pining away wherever he can find 'a sad and silent place,' by the seashore, the riverside, or among the rushes in the fen; of the condemned felon in his cell, counting his meals, because each brings him by one meal nearer to the last hour,

'And dreams the very thirst which then will be.'

It may be noticed in passing, as an instance of Crabbe's satisfied conventionality of attitude, that, though he pities the highwayman for his fate, he never doubts the justice of the law which has condemned him to death for taking a purse. What remained, to the end, conventional in his way of rendering very downright fact may be seen equally in the powerful poem of 'Ellen Orford,' when Ellen's husband hangs himself, and we are told, —

> 'His son suspended saw him, long bereft
> Of life, nor prospect of revival left.'

That false kind of writing, with its worse echo of a bad style, alternates everywhere with a naturalness which can go so near, and so agreeably near, to the actual cadence of ordinary conversation as this: —

> 'But he had chosen — we had seen how shy
> The girl was getting, my good man and I.'

And the bare, pedestrian style can lift, too, now and again, into such a line as: —

> 'So like a ghost that left a grave for love';

or, in the more thoroughly warmed cadences of the poems in shorter lines, into such a hurry and heaping up of repeated sounds as this: —

> 'Their watchmen stare, and stand aghast,
> As on we hurry through the dark;
> The watch-light blinks as we go past,
> The watch-dog shrinks and fears to bark:
> The watch-tower's bell sounds shrill; and, hark!
> The free wind blows.'

There are moments in the poem from which I take these lines, the early poem of 'Sir Eustace Grey,' in which certain effects of two writers so dissimilar as Poe and Browning seem actually to be forestalled. There are lines in 'Johannes Agricola in Meditation' (originally one of two 'Madhouse Cells') which have a curious resemblance with one stanza in particular (the ninth stanza after the 'Patient' has started on his uninterrupted narration to the 'Visitor' and the 'Physician') of this scene in a madhouse. I am reminded of Poe in the cool terror of some of the vaguer and more striking tortures inflicted by the 'two fiends of darkness.' Throughout, there is imagination, never quite rising to the freedom of the poetic imagination, always held in by the long logical leash of prose invention; but genuine, that 'power of a certain kind,' which Coleridge speaks of. To see the whole difference between these two kinds of imaginative power, we need only contrast a passage representing the affliction of 'Ellen Orford' after her desertion with a single couplet from Wordsworth. Ellen says: —

> 'My dreams were dismal — wheresoe'er I strayed,
> I seemed ashamed, alarmed, despised, betrayed,
> Always in grief, in guilt, disgraced, forlorn,
> Mourning that one so weak, so vile, was born;
> The earth a desert, tumult in the sea,
> The birds affrighted fled from tree to tree,
> Obscured the setting sun, and everything like me.'

The mother, in Wordsworth, talking wildly to her baby, says: —

> 'The breeze I see is in the tree!
> It comes to cool my babe and me.'

In those two ways of representing a similar distraction, the strong feeling and methodical force of the one, and the sudden, incalculable vision of the other, we see precisely where prose stops short and the whole gulf before poetry begins.

The writer whom Crabbe perhaps most resembles is Mathurin Regnier, but in Regnier there is a violent personal quality which is lacking in Crabbe, who, unlike the sixteenth-century satirist, kept a wise distance between the low tragedy of his verse and the middle-class comforts of his life. Regnier was 'tout aux tavernes et aux filles,' and in 'Le Souper Ridicule' and 'Le Mauvais Giste' he has painted both with a realism which has something of Villon's sharp personal outcry in it. His 'Macette' is a type in whom Crabbe would have delighted, but nothing in Crabbe is so critical of human nature. The point of view of both is not dissimilar.

> 'Voyez que c'est du monde, et des choses humaines:
> Toujours à nouveaux maux naissent nouvelles peines,'

Regnier tells us, drawing on his own experience, however, for the nearest illustration, 'estant né pour souffrir.' It was life, unlucky personal adventure, more than philosophy or observation, that made Regnier a poet; and, even when he sets out, more deliberately than Crabbe, to be the satirist, he is never able to control his wayward energies into that disinterested calm which makes of Crabbe perhaps the one really objective poet.

Byron, in a line that has become proverbial, defined Crabbe (whom he called 'the first of living poets') as being,

'Though nature's sternest painter, yet her best.'

And Wordsworth, after the death of Crabbe, writing to his son in praise of his father's works, says: 'They will last, from their combined merits as Poetry and Truth, full as long as anything that has been expressed in verse since they first made their appearance.' It was for those 'combined merits,' as we have seen, that Crabbe looked to be welcomed and remembered. And the poetry, it seemed to him, was to be the natural product of the truth. In a note to Letter XVI of 'The Borough,' Crabbe says: 'Benbow may be thought too low and despicable to be admitted here; but he is a Borough-character, and however disgusting in some respects a picture may be, it will please some, and be tolerated by many, if it can boast that one merit of being a faithful likeness.'

The point of view is the point of view of Zola. How strange a delusion, that truth, without beauty, can have any place in art; and how strange an ignorance of beauty, that looks upon the fairest daughter of life as if she were Pygmalion's marble, condemned to remain forever on her pedestal, a stony despair to all mortal lovers. What strenuous qualities Crabbe would have added to poetry, if there had been in him the poetry to add them to! He has a psychology which is not only hard, firm, persistent, and, in a good sense, pitiless, but subtle as well. He would have made one of the greatest of our novelists, anticipating Hardy and recalling Defoe. There is not a line in his verse, not the finest, that would have suited ill with a simple and flexible prose, capable of such dark splendours as those two lines of 'Peter Grimes' in which the delirious man, haunted by the sight of the father whose life he has threatened but not taken, says: —

> 'He cried for mercy, which I kindly gave,
> But he has no compassion in his grave.'

What a novelist was lost in the burning of those three novels which were written in the winters in Suffolk, during one or two of those twenty-two years of silence! The third novel, says Crabbe's son in his biography, 'opened with a description of a wretched room, similar to some that are presented in his poetry,' and he remembers that, 'on my mother's telling him frankly that she thought the effect very inferior to that of the corresponding pieces in verse, he paused in his reading, and, after some reflection, said, " Your remark is just."' Whereupon the three manuscripts were burnt.

Perhaps, however, Mrs. Crabbe was right; and this poet with the genius of prose could never have written in prose so well as he wrote in verse. Nature is as capricious in the assortment of tendency and capacity as in the assortment of body and mind. As certainly as we find inner beauty robed in mean flesh, timid souls faltering under fierce beards, and the lees of all corruption under an aspect of lilied candour, so certainly do we find men of genius condemned to labour all their lives at a task which is not their task, and in which they must seem to be no more than half themselves.

MRS. MARY ROBINSON (1758-1800) [1]

THE Perdita of the Prince of Wales, Mary Robinson, began writing verses in the King's Bench prison at the age of seventeen; she went on the stage, where she was famous, and,

[1] *The Poetical Works of the late Mrs. Mary Robinson*, 3 vols. 1806.

after many conquests and adventures, returned to the writing of verse, and called herself by the name of the English Sappho. It is under that signature that she wrote an ode to Coleridge, in which she says archly: —

>'Spirit divine! with *thee* I'll trace
>Imagination's boundless space!'

She had just before sent him another ode, on his latest baby, 'born Sept. 14, 1800, at Keswick, in Cumberland': Derwent, that would be. Not the least ardent or accomplished of her poems was a sonnet sequence: 'Sappho and Phaon, in a series of legitimate sonnets,' where she characterises her 'whose lyre throbbed only to the touch of love' as 'the brightest planet of the eternal sphere.' The subject lends her eloquence, and she bursts out: —

>'Ye, who in alleys green and leafy bowers,
>Sport, the rude children of fantastic births;
>Where frolic nymphs, and shaggy tribes of mirth,
>In clamorous revels waste the midnight hours.'

She is not always so good, and her attempt at drama, in 'The Sicilian,' is distinctly amusing. 'He lives! he lives! It is my Alferenzi!' shouts one character, and another, taking the opposite view, believes that Alferenzi is dead.

>'I fear he was: most sure I am he died!
>His cheek was pale, and petrified, and cold!
>But I entreat you let us change the matter,
>For 't is a wounding subject.'

Odes overflow the pages, 'Lines to him who will understand them,' perhaps one of those

>'whose soul like mine,
>Beams with poetic rays divine,'

or Della Crusca perhaps, 'enlightened Patron of the sacred Lyre.' All these overflow with feminine italics and capitals and dashes and notes of exclamation. At times, quieting down, she can characterise those who 'seek fame by different roads' in eight stanzas done after this manner: —

'Ladies gambling night and morning;
Fools the work of genius scorning;
Ancient dames for girls mistaken,
Youthful damsels quite forsaken.'

And in another poem in the same metre she becomes a little bewilderingly personal; for, —

'Where conscious Rectitude retires;
Instructive Wisdom; calm Desires;
Prolific Science — lab'ring Art;
And Genius, with expanded heart' —

there, on her own authority, Mrs. Mary Robinson also is.

JOANNA BAILLIE (1762-1851) [1]

CRABB ROBINSON tells us in his diary that Wordsworth said to him of Joanna Baillie: 'If I had to present any one to a foreigner as a model of an English gentlewoman it would be Joanna Baillie.' It was this good lady who proposed to herself the aim, in a 'Series of plays, in which it is attempted to delineate the stronger passions of the mind, each passion being the subject of a tragedy and a comedy,' to 'add a few pieces to the stock of what may be called our national or permanently acting plays.' She begins with a plan perfectly matured, and reproaches those dramatists who have 'made use of the passions to mark their several characters, and animate their scenes, rather than to open to our view the nature and portraitures of those great disturbers of the human breast, with whom we are all, more or less, called upon to contend.' She had already written some scattered lyrics, some of them, especially those in the Scottish dialect, not without the lyrical touch, and it does not seem to have occurred to her to ask her-

---

[1] (1) *Fugitive Verses*, 1790. (2) *Plays on the Passions*, 3 vols., 1798, 1802, 1812. (3) *Miscellaneous Plays*, 1804. (4) *Metrical Legends of Exalted Characters*, 1821. (5) *Poetic Miscellanies*, 1823. (6) *The Martyr* 1826. (7) *Miscellaneous Plays*, 1836.

self whether such an aim at close truth to nature, and the exclusion of imagination, as she approved of in the writing of moral drama, might not have been better attained in prose than in verse. In one of the tragic plays she does, indeed, with some apology, use prose, and to the advantage of the somewhat melodramatic material, surprisingly direct, and with a certain human feeling in it, which comes to us in the verse, as if disguised under a thin clothing. This fixed, formal study of the passions leads naturally to something too deliberate for drama; passion being too often treated as if it were a form of logic, or followed recognisable rules of human nature. It was a brave adventure, and had many lessons to teach the more fantastic, Germanising dramatists of her time. 'Modern Poetry,' she laments in a preface, 'within these last thirty years, has become so imaginative, impassioned, and sentimental, that more homely subjects, in simple diction, are held in comparatively small estimation.' Throughout we feel and respect the woman's diligent application to a task or mission: the creation of a serious drama, the elevation of the theatre. And what is most surprising, and all that remains interesting to us now, when the plays themselves have dropped quietly out of existence, is to see the practical sense of the conditions of the stage which comes out in preface and foot-notes, really anticipating discoveries which are only now being put into practice. She protests against the footlights, on the analogy of the art of the painter, who, when he 'wishes to give intelligence and expression to a face, does not make his lights hit upon the under part of his chin, the nostrils, and the under curve of the eyebrows.' And, she adds, 'daylight comes from heaven, not from the earth; even within doors our whitened ceilings are made to throw down reflected light upon us, while our pavements and carpets are of a darker colour.' And she imagines, in those days of boxes on the stage, almost the 'mystic gulf' of Wagner: 'The front-piece at the top; the boundary of the stage from the orchestra at the bottom; and the pilasters at each side, would then represent the frame of a great moving picture, entirely separated and distinct from the rest of the theatre.'

SIR SAMUEL EGERTON BRYDGES (1762-1837) [1]

SIR EGERTON BRYDGES, who must be respected for the editions printed at his Lee Priory Press, in an 'Invocation to Poetry,' which he wrote at the age of twenty, but, twenty years afterwards, still put at the beginning of his poems, represents himself as calling that 'wild maid' to go with him into the woods ('and let not coy excuse thy steps retard') and then falling asleep in her company, and dreaming of 'fame immortal.' The episode seems characteristic; Sir Egerton Brydges always fell asleep when he found himself in the company of Poetry.

WILLIAM LISLE BOWLES (1762-1850) [2]

WILLIAM LISLE BOWLES was born in 1762 and died in extreme old age, a canon of Salisbury, in 1850. His first volume, a collection of twenty sonnets, 'written amidst various interesting scenes, during a tour under youthful dejection,' was pub-

[1] (1) *Sonnets and Other Poems*, 1785. (2) *Select Poems*, 1814. (3) *Occasional Poems*, 1814. (4) *Bertram*, 1814. (5) *Dunlace Castle*, 1814. (6) *Fragment of a Poem*, 1814. (7) *To the Friends and Admirers of Robert Bloomfield*, 1816. (8) *Verses addressed to Lady Brydges* (?). (9) *To a Lady*, 1817. (10) *Odo Count of Lingen*, 1824. (11) *A Poem on Birth*, 1831. (12) *Elegiac Lines*, 1832. (13) *Lake of Geneva*, 1832. (14) *Human Fate*, 1846. (15) *Darkness, An Ode*, 1870.

[2] (1) *Fourteen Sonnets*, written chiefly on Picturesque Spots during a journey, 1789. (2) *Verses to John Howard*, 1789. (3) *Coombe Ellen*, 1798. (4) *St. Michael's Mount*, 1798. (5) *The Battle of the Nile*, 1799. (6) *The Sorrows of Switzerland*, 1801. (7) *The Picture*, 1803. (8) *The Spirit of Discovery*, 1804. (9) *Bowden Hill*, 1806. (10) *The Missionary of the Andes*, 1815. (11) *The Grave of the Last Saxon*, 1822. (12) *Ellen Gray*, 1823. (13) *Days Departed*, 1828. (14) *St. John in Patmos*, 1833. (15) *Scenes and Splendours of Days Departed*, 1837. (16) *The Village Hymnbook*, 1837. (17) *Poetical Works*, 1855.

lished in 1789, and a copy of it, coming into the hands of Coleridge, at the age of seventeen, did much to decide the early course of Coleridge's poetry, for he had not then seen any of the work of Cowper, and, as he tells us in the 'Biographia Literaria,' 'of the then living poets Bowles and Cowper were, to the best of my knowledge, the first who combined natural thoughts with natural diction: the first who reconciled the heart with the head.' Bowles was afterwards to enter into a controversy with Byron, on the side of nature against the formal art of Pope, and in contention, as he says, that 'passions of nature, not morals, or manners of life, constitute the eternal basis of what is sublime or beautiful in poetry.' It was this tendency, quite out of fashion at the time, that had its effect upon Coleridge, and though the work itself was uninspired, it was unforced. In one of his prefaces Bowles says, 'There is a great difference between *natural* and *fabricated* feelings, even in poetry,' and there is something which at that time would seem exceptionally natural and direct in sonnets which, as he puts it with his usual awkward straightforwardness, 'exhibit occasional reflections which naturally arose in his mind, chiefly during various excursions undertaken to relieve, at the time, depression of spirits,' due, he tells us, 'to the sudden death of a deserving young woman.' Bowles tells us that he inherited a love of landscape from his father, and from his mother a susceptibility to music, and especially to the sound of bells, of which he says: —

> 'The mournful magic of their mingling chime
> First waked my wondering childhood into tears.'

Coleridge's moralising landscapes are distinctly foreshadowed in those of Bowles, and something not altogether of his best manner, something of the over-sweetness of its simplicity, can be seen in lines like these: —

> 'Her voice was soft, which yet a charm could lend
> Like that which spoke of a departed friend,
> And a meek sadness sat upon her smile.'

Bowles himself, who repaid Coleridge's early devotion with a charming gratitude, guessed that if in future years any one cared to ask 'who was W. L. Bowles?' it might be for Coleridge's sake, and it is true that we turn to these gentle amiabilities of verse chiefly because they showed Coleridge that contemporary poetry was not obliged to be 'glittering, cold, and transitory,' after the manner of Darwin's 'Botanic Garden,' and that it was possible to look at natural things with the eyes and to express the natural feelings of the heart. 'Genius of the sacred fountain of tears,' Lamb wrote to Coleridge in 1796, with unusual pomp, 'it was he who led you through all this valley of weeping.'

GEORGE COLMAN THE YOUNGER (1762-1836) [1]

GEORGE COLMAN the Younger was, in his time, a prolific writer of farce; he attempted, in a futile way, to write seriously in blank verse; and to this day his name has not disappeared entirely from the records of acted stage plays. He also attempted humorous verse, and wrote a vulgar kind of it copiously. In his 'Poetical Vagaries,' a quarto heaped up with humourless garbage, after announcing: —

'Yet, here, will I apostrophize thee, Time!
If not in reason, why in Crambo Rhime,'

he is reasonable enough to admit to the reader: —

'But, should I grow prolix, alas!
Thou never would'st kill Time by reading Me.'

The main part of the volume consists in a coarse and inept parody of 'The Lady of the Lake,' which is called 'The Lady of the Wreck or Castle Blarneygig' and introduced in this man-

[1] (1) *Songs from Two to One*, 1784. (2) *My Night-Gown and Slippers*, 1797. (3) *Broad Grins*, 1802. (4) *Poetical Vagaries*, 1812. (5) *Vagaries Vindicated*, 1813. (6) *Eccentricities for Edinburgh*, 1816. (7) *The Humorous Works of George Colman*, no date. 7 plays, 4 vols., Paris, 1827.

ner: 'The author of this Work has attempted, in this instance, to become a Maker of the *Modern-Antique;* a Vender of a new Coinage, being rimed with the ancient *oerugo;* a Constructor of the *dear pretty Sublime,* and *sweet little Grand.*' 'How is such a Writer to be class'd?' he ends by asking. But he has written himself down already as a factor of 'Broad Grins,' and needs no further classing.

SAMUEL ROGERS (1763–1855) [1]

SAMUEL ROGERS was not a poet, but he was an unaffected and pleasantly old-fashioned writer of verse; and as he was rich, and kind-hearted, and sharp-tongued, he lived to be a very old man without losing a kind of unofficial leadership of the poetry of his period, though for long, as Byron said, 'retired upon half-pay.' It was Byron who gave him the most thorough praise he got, putting him next to Scott, and thus only just below the apex of his 'triangular Gradus ad Parnassum,' in which Moore and Campbell came third, and Southey, Wordsworth, and Coleridge just above the indistinguishable 'many.' And when Byron set him there ('more as the last of the best school') he professed to have 'ranked the names upon my triangle more upon what I believe popular opinion than any decided opinion of my own.' This was merely a way of trying to add weight to what was really his own decided opinion; for he returns to Rogers again and again, in his letters and controversial writings, ranking him with Goldsmith and Campbell as 'the most successful' of the disciples of Pope, and with Crabbe as the only poet of the day who was not 'in the wrong,' 'upon a wrong revolutionary poetical system.' 'And thou, melodious Rogers!' he had in-

[1] (1) *An Ode to Superstition,* 1786. (2) *The Pleasures of Memory,* 1792. (3) *Epistle to a Friend,* 1798. (4) *Columbus,* privately printed, 1812. (5) *Jacqueline,* 1814. (6) *Human Life,* 1819. (7) *Italy,* 1822. (8) *Italy,* second part, 1828.

voked him, in the 'English Bards and Scotch Reviewers,' bidding him 'restore Apollo to his vacant throne.' Fifty years afterwards Rogers is still a notable person to Elizabeth Barrett, who, 'not a devout admirer of "The Pleasures of Memory," does admire this perpetual youth and energy' of the poet of eighty-one whose bank has been robbed of £40,000, and who 'says witty things on his own griefs.' And, in 1850, we find Ruskin still valuing him as a poet and inspirer, and writing to him from Venice: 'Whenever I found myself getting utterly hard and indifferent, I used to read over a little bit of the " Venice " in your " Italy," and it put me always into the right tone of thought again.' The old man to whom he was writing had seen Haydn play at a concert in a tie-wig, with a sword by his side, and had met more than one person who remembered Mr. Alexander Pope.

Rogers was born in 1763, before any of those who may be properly called his contemporaries among the poets of the nineteenth century, except Blake and Crabbe, and he died in 1855, after all of them but Landor and Leigh Hunt. He was famous in 1793 as the writer of 'The Pleasures of Memory,' the most popular poem which had appeared since Cowper's 'Task,' seven years earlier; more popular indeed than that poem had ever been. Nearly twenty years afterwards, the 'Edinburgh Review,' in not too amiable an article, could say of it that it was 'to be found in all libraries and in most parlour windows.' Rogers seemed, to the critics of that time, by his 'correctness of thought, delicacy of sentiment, variety of imagery, and harmony of versification,' to be the legitimate 'child of Goldsmith.' Burns was still alive, and he, with Blake and Crabbe, had already published the poems which were the real heralds of the new poetry; but neither Burns nor Crabbe was universally known, and Blake was wholly unknown. Rogers seemed to his contemporaries more 'classical,' more in the tradition, than Cowper; his ease and finish made Hayley and the Della Cruscans impossible. He was accepted instantly, as Byron was to accept him later, at least in theory, as the chief adherent to 'the Christianity of English Poetry, the poetry of Pope.'

We can read worse things now, but we cannot read 'The Pleasures of Memory.' It is not poetry, and there is nothing in its smooth commonplaces to make up for its not being poetry, as, to some extent, there certainly is in the later, never quite so popular, 'Italy.' But, before 'Italy,' there had been 'An Epistle to a Friend,' which begins to be more personal and thus more interesting; 'The Voyage of Columbus,' which suggested to Byron 'the idea of writing a poem in fragments,' 'The Giaour,' dedicated to Rogers; and 'Jacqueline,' which Byron found 'all grace, and softness, and poetry,' and which was actually published under the same covers with 'Lara.' We can read none of these now, but we can read the 'Italy,' almost as if it were prose, but with no distaste at its being in verse.

'The Pleasures of Memory' fitted the fashion of its day, a fashion which was even then passing; but it could not outlast that fashion, as the work of many poets has done, because it had no energy of life or imagination within it. It was sincere, and we can respect it for its sincerity; but it was the work of one who had trained himself up to be a poet as he trained himself up to appreciate and collect beautiful things, and to acquire worldly wisdom by 'always listening to the conversation of older persons.' His nephew tells us that 'he thought every man ought to have a pursuit, such as the writing of a book, which gave an interest to life such as was not known without it.' His poetry was simply the most serious interest in life of a dilettante who would have lacked only an interest in life without it. 'On all subjects of taste,' said Byron, 'his delicacy of expression is as pure as his poetry.'

And so it is in the 'Italy' that he came nearest to writing anything of value, for that pleasant road-book to Italy is done with a real personal gusto, and in a blank verse which, as

Lamb said, 'gallops like a traveller, as it should do,' and is a form which we can read to-day more easily than those couplets out of which Rogers confesses that he got with so much difficulty. Wordsworth found in it 'rather too strong a leaning to the pithy and concise'; but Rogers does not aim appreciably higher than prose, and is wise in not doing so. 'Happy should I be,' he says, 'if by an intermixture of verse and prose, of prose illustrating the verse and verse embellishing the prose, I could furnish my countrymen on their travels with a pocket-companion.' Was not an aim so humble more than attained when Ruskin, in his 'Præterita,' confessed that it was the birthday gift, at the age of thirteen, of Rogers' 'Italy'. that 'determined the main tenor of his life'?

To go to Italy was for Rogers to make a pilgrimage to his Holy Land. In his epilogue he says: —

'Nature denied him much,
But gave him at his birth what most he values;
A passionate love for music, sculpture, painting,
For poetry, the language of the gods,
For all things here, or grand or beautiful.'

It is the idolater of art who writes to a friend from Venice: 'Oh, if you knew what it was to look upon a lake which Virgil has mentioned, and Catullus has sailed upon, to see a house in which Petrarch has lived, and to stand upon Titian's grave as I have done, you would instantly pack up and join me.' His poem is the warm direct record of this enthusiasm; only, the verse is less warm than the prose, the sentiment cools a little in its passage into verse, the sharp details of the journal are softened, generalised, lose much of their really poetical substance. When Byron went on the grand tour, much less impressed really than Rogers by what he saw, he transfigured all these things in some atmosphere of his own, and 'Childe Harold' is a bad guide-book, and not always an honest or intelligent comment of the observer, but at least a very startling and personal poem. Rogers will put into his notes or prose interludes such a vigorous utterance as this: 'When a despot lays his hand on a free city, how soon must he make the discovery of the rustic, who bought Punch of the puppet-show man, and complained that he would not speak'! Turning to the verse, you find vaguer epithets or a fainter discourse, as in the inexpressive lines which call forth that beautiful and significant note (which Rogers says he wrote ten times over before he was satisfied with it) on the Dominican at Padua, who, looking on his companions at the refectory table and then at the Last Supper fading off the painted wall, was 'sometimes inclined to think that we, and not they, are the shadows.' Had he but realised it, it is as a prose-writer that Rogers might have lived.

Rogers was a man of letters, and holds a position in the history of letters in England, almost apart from the actual quality of his work. This 'grim old dilettante, full of sardonic sense,' as Carlyle called him, was the typical man of taste of his time: 'his god was harmony,' Mrs. Norton said of him. His house was as carefully studied as his poems, and as elaborately decorated; the Giorgione 'Knight in Armour,' now in the National Gallery, was one of his pictures. Byron paid Rogers many extravagant compliments, but he was defining him very justly when in 'Beppo,' he classed him with Scott and Moore as 'Men of the world, who know the world like men.' He was not a great talker, but he had and deserved a reputation for neat, not always amiable, wit. 'They tell me I say ill-natured things,' he said to Sir Henry Taylor. 'I have a very weak voice; if I did not say ill-natured things no one would hear what I said.' He was a benefactor to Wordsworth, to Campbell, to Sheridan, to Moore; a peacemaker among poets; a friend to men of genius and children. It was written of him by one of his guests: 'I suppose there is hardly any hero or man of genius of our time, from Nelson or Crabbe downwards, who has not dined at Rogers' table.' He loved beauty, and honoured genius, perhaps beyond any man of his time.

HENRY LUTTRELL (1765-1851) [1]

HENRY LUTTRELL was described by Lady Blessington as a talker who makes one think, and by Byron as the most epigrammatical conversationalist whom he had ever met. No one, said Rogers (of whom he had said wickedly, speaking of his 'Italy,' that it would have dished but for the plates), could stick in a brilliant thing with greater readiness. His 'Advice to Julia' and, in a less degree, 'Crockford House' are typical of the intelligent and observant man about town. The Julia letters are written fluently, and respond to the motto from Rousseau: 'J'ai vu les mœurs de mon tems, et j'ai publié cette lettre.' Luttrell's brilliant society verses have their smaller place between Gay and Praed, perpetuating some of his finest qualities as a wit and talker.

CAROLINA, LADY NAIRNE (1766-1845) [2]

LADY NAIRNE was one of the many 'restorers' of old Scottish songs. She began by writing 'words suited for refined circles,' which were to replace the original words in a collection of national airs, called 'The Scottish Minstrel,' published in six volumes, from 1821 to 1824. Her admiration of Burns showed itself in the desire to publish a 'purified' edition of his songs. But she found that 'some of his greatest efforts of genius,' having 'a tendency to inflame the passions,' 'would n't do,' would n't be purified, that is; and the edition was happily abandoned. How far her desire to introduce 'words suited for refined circles' contributed to the artistic bettering of the songs which she restored may remain questionable. But there is no question of the merit of her own

---

[1] (1) *Lines on Ampthill Park*, 1819. (2) *Advice to Julia*, a letter in Rhyme, 1820. (3) *A Letter to Julia*, 1822. (4) *Crockford House*, 1827.
[2] (1) *Lays from Strathearn*, 1846. (2) *Life and Songs*, 1869.

songs, whose authorship she concealed during the main part of her life. Her sense of form was generally sure, she had a firm grasp on the ballad-metre, and a personal originality, in which ready humour and womanly feeling were mingled. The Jacobite songs are rarely without a light gallop of their own; there is a delightful sly chuckle in 'The Laird of Cockpen'; and 'Caller Herrin',' the best of all her songs, is a sad and gay fisherwomen's song with a changing rhythm always in tune. The most famous of her poems, 'The Land o' the Leal,' is the expression of a sentiment verging upon sentimentality; but something, perhaps in the slow, monotonous cadence of the verse, has helped to keep it alive, like an old tune in the memory.

ROBERT BLOOMFIELD (1766–1823) [1]

Robert Bloomfield was born at Honington, a village near Bury St. Edmunds, on December 3, 1766; he was the son of a tailor, and though for a short time a 'farmer's boy,' was too sickly for the work, and was sent to work at tailoring in a London garret. 'The Farmer's Boy,' written in another garret after his marriage, was published in 1800, and nearly thirty thousand copies of it were sold in three years. Bloomfield was lionised, patronised, and then left to himself, when, says Mr. Bullen in the Dictionary of National Biography, 'having now become hypochondriacal and half blind, he retired to Shefford, where he died in great poverty on 19 August, 1823, leaving a widow and four children. Had he lived longer he would probably have gone mad.'

When Lamb said that Bloomfield had 'a poor mind' he has sometimes been taken to mean no more than a rather cruel

[1] (1) *The Farmer's Boy*, 1800. (2) *Rural Tales, Ballads and Songs*, 1802. (3) *Good Tidings; or News from the Farm*, 1804. (4) *Wild Flowers*, 1806. (5) *The Banks of the Wye*, 1811. (6) *May-Day with the Muses*, 1822. (7) *Hazlewood Hall;* a Village Drama, 1823. (8) *Works*, 1824.

pun. But the epithet is strictly just. At his best he goes no further than a stiff and good-humoured realism; his point of view is anecdotal; the language is on the village level or is strained to a formal fitness; never is there an original epithet, a touch of illumination. In his homely ballads he uses his material in the strict manner of prose, getting nothing from his form; his stories never go beyond triviality; his songs have the yokel's simper. Addressing his 'old oak table,' he says that on it

> 'I poured the torrent of my feelings forth,
> Conscious of truth in Nature's humble track,
> And wrote "The Farmer's Boy" upon thy back.'

But the detail of 'The Farmer's Boy,' which is copious, is diluted or disguised by a vague acquired manner, which tries to give a traditional turn to what can only interest us if it is set down frankly, as Clare set it down. How preferable is Clare's

> 'Hodge whistling at the fallow plough'

to Bloomfield's gibe: —

> 'His heels deep sinking every step he goes,
> Till dirt adhesive loads his clouted shoes.'

The writer of those lines was trying to write elegantly.

JOHN HOOKHAM FRERE (1769–1846) [1]

JOHN HOOKHAM FRERE was a politician and scholar, who, in the intervals of a fastidious and unambitious career, found time to do certain poems and translations of an unique kind,

[1] (1) *Prospectus and Specimen of an intended National Work*, by William and Robert Whistlecraft, of Stowmarket in Suffolk, Harness and Collar Makers, 2 vols., 1817, 1818. (2) *The Monks and the Giants* (same as above), 1821. (3) *Fables for Five-Year Olds*, 1830. (4) *The Frogs*, 1839. (5) *Aristophanes*, a Metrical Version of the *Acharnians*, the *Knights*, and the *Birds*, 1840. (6) *Theognis Restitutus*, 1842. (7) *Psalms*, 1848. (8) *Works*, 3 vols., 1874.

which he required persuasion even to publish. He wrote, with Canning in 1797-98 the better part of the 'Anti-Jacobin'; then, still anonymously, in 1817 the 'Prospectus and Specimen of an intended National Work, by William and Robert Whistlecraft, of Stow-Market, in Suffolk, harness and collar-makers, intended to comprise the most interesting particulars relating to King Arthur and his Round Table,' afterwards called 'The Monks and the Giants'; and, as late as 1831, practically for private circulation, the first part of his translation of Aristophanes, done ten years earlier. A translation and commentary on 'Theognis' was published in 1845 to 'show the Germans that an Englishman can do something, though not exactly in their own way.'

As lately as forty years ago, an American, Mr. Charles Eliot Norton, found in 'The Monks and the Giants' 'one of the most playful, humorous, and original poems in English, a perfect success in its kind, and that kind one of the rarest and most difficult.' And he reports to us Coleridge's preference for the superior metrical skill of the poem as compared with Byron's imitation in 'Beppo.' Perfect technique there is, and a wellbred quality of pleasantry which is perhaps the most distinguished kind of nonsense-making that we have had. But can it be read to-day with anything like the interest with which we can read 'Beppo'? To compare it with 'Don Juan' would be out of the question: the great poem, owing the origin of its form to him, which Frere tried to suppress, on moral grounds, before publication. Frere tells us that his intention was to introduce a new kind of burlesque into English, using the stanza of 'Morgante Maggiore,' which had lain dormant in England since the Elizabethan age, and had never been used then for more than plain narrative purposes. It was to be such burlesque as we get in Sancho Panza: 'the burlesque treatment of lofty and serious subjects by a thoroughly common but not necessarily low-minded man — a Suffolk harness-maker.' Southey rightly defined the result as 'too good in itself and too inoffensive to become popular; for it attacked nothing and nobody.' People tried to find a meaning in it, and resented so well-bred and generalised a joke. It has indeed none of the qualities that live, and has become an instructive fossil. It did what new and perfect technique can sometimes do: it set a fashion in poetry. It gave Byron exactly the weapon and plaything he was in want of. 'Whistlecraft,' he wrote in 1818, 'was my immediate model'; from Whistlecraft he turned back to Berni, and from Berni to 'the parent of all jocose Italian poetry,' Pulci. But when he took the form from Frere he took it ready-made; he had only to fill it with his own energy and exuberance.

Frere was one of the scholars of letters who create nothing for themselves, but discover many things for others. Having discovered a form for Byron, and invented, with Canning, a scholarly and brilliant manner of parody in the 'Anti-Jacobin,' he attempted little more except translation, an art for which he was peculiarly fitted, and, as it was his nature to do, the translation of perhaps the most difficult of all poets to render, Aristophanes. It was his opinion that 'the talent and attainments requisite are not of the highest order, and if we add to these a natural feeling of taste, and a disposition to execute the task, with the degree of perfection of which it is capable, it should seem, that little else would be requisite.' It is with these modest words that he anticipates a series of translations, interspersed with notes, commentaries, and copious stage-directions, of 'the half-divine humourist,' as Mr. Swinburne has called him, 'in whose incomparable genius the highest qualities of Rabelais were fused and harmonised with the supremest gifts of Shelley.' Only Mr. Swinburne himself, in the translation of the chorus of Birds to which these words were appended, has so far shown us the possibility of going beyond Frere's sinuous versatility and fine speed and vivid fooling. I cannot but think that it is from his rhymes that Barham and Gilbert learnt some of their technique of nonsense-rhyming. Few translators have had so just a conception of the laws of that delicate and sensitive art, which he has defined in these words: 'The language of translation ought, we think, to be a pure, impalpable, and invisible element, the medium of thought and feeling, and nothing more; it ought never to attract attention to itself; hence all phrases that are remarkable in themselves, either as old or new, are as far as possible to be avoided.' Speech and rhythm are alike brought to an extraordinary flexibility, the blank verse really doing, with its artful crowdings and elisions, precisely that familiar service which Leigh Hunt and others were then fumbling after. The hand on it is firm enough to loosen it to its full length; it never strays from the leash.

WILLIAM WORDSWORTH (1770–1850) [1]

SINCERITY was at the root of all Wordsworth's merits and defects; it gave him his unapproachable fidelity to nature, and also his intolerable fidelity to his own whims. Like Emerson, whom he so often resembled, he respected all intuitions, but, unlike Emerson, did not always distinguish between a whim

[1] (1) *An Evening Walk*, 1793. (2) *Descriptive Sketches*, 1793. (3) *Lyrical Ballads, with a few other Poems*, 1798. (4) *Lyrical Poems, with other Poems*, 2 vols., by W. Wordsworth, 1800. (5) *Lyrical Ballads, with Pastoral and other Poems*, 2 vols., 1802. (6) *The Excursion*, being a portion of *The Recluse, a Poem*, 1814. (7) *Poems*, 2 vols., 1815. (8) *The White Doe of Rylstone; or The Fate of the Nortons*, 1815. (9) *Thanksgiving Ode*, 1816. (10) *Peter Bell*, a tale in verse, 1819. (11) *The Waggoner*, 1819. (12) *The River Duddon*, a Series of Sonnets: *Vaudracour and Julia: and other Poems*, 1820. (13) *The Miscellaneous Poems of William Wordsworth*, 4 vols., 1820. (14) *Ecclesiastical Sketches*, 1822. (15) *Poetical Works*, 5 vols., 1827. (16) *Yarrow Revisited*, 1835. (17) *Poetical Works* 6 vols., 1836–37. (18) *The Sonnets of William Wordsworth*, 1838. (19) *Poems chiefly of Early and Late Years*; including *The Borderers, a Tragedy*, 1842. (20) *Ode, performed in the Senate House, Cambridge*, 1847. (21) *The Prelude, or Growth of a Poet's Mind*; an Autobiographical Poem, 1850. (22) *The Recluse* (posthumous), 1888. (23) *Complete Poetical Works*, 1888.

and an intuition. His life was spent in a continual meditation, and his attitude towards external things was that of a reflective child, continually pondering over the surprise of his first impressions. I once heard Mr. Aubrey de Vere, who had been a friend of Wordsworth for many years, say that the frequent triviality of Wordsworth's reflections was due to the fact that he had begun life without any of the received opinions which save most men from so much of the trouble of thinking; but had found out for himself everything that he came to believe or to be conscious of. Thus what seems to most men an obvious truism not worth repeating, because they have never consciously thought it, but unconsciously taken it on trust, was to Wordsworth a discovery of his own, which he had had the happiness of taking into his mind as freshly as if he had been the first man and no one had thought about life before; or, as I have said, with the delighted wonder of the child. Realising early what value there might be to him in so direct an inheritance from nature, from his own mind at its first grapple with nature, he somewhat deliberately shut himself in with himself, rejecting all external criticism; and for this he had to pay the price which we must deduct from his ultimate gains. Wordsworth's power of thought was never on the level of his power of feeling, and he was wise, at least in his knowledge of himself, when he said : —

> 'One impulse from a vernal wood
> May teach you more of man,
> Of moral evil and of good,
> Than all the sages can.'

He felt instinctively, and his feeling was nature's. But thought, coming to him thus immediately as it did, and representing the thinking part of himself with unparalleled fidelity, spoke out of an intellect by no means so responsive to the finer promptings of that supreme intellectual energy of which we are a part. It is thus often when he is most solemnly satisfied with himself that he is really showing us his weakness most ingenuously: he would listen to no external criticism, and there was no inherent critical faculty to stand at his mind's elbow and remind him when he was prophesying in the divine language and when he was babbling like the village idiot.

Wordsworth desired to lead a continuously poetic life, and it seemed to him easy, inevitable, in one whose life was a continual meditation. It seemed to him that, if he wrote down in verse anything which came into his mind, however trivial, it would become poetry by the mere contact. His titles explain the conviction. Thus the beautiful poem beginning, 'It is the first mild day of March,' is headed, 'To my Sister. Written at a small distance from my house, and sent by my little boy.' In its bare outline it is really a note written down under the impulse of a particular moment, and it says: 'Now that we have finished breakfast, let us go for a walk; put on a walking dress, and do not bring a book; it is a beautiful day, and we should enjoy it.' Some kindly inspiration helping, the rhymed letter becomes a poem: it is an evocation of spring, an invocation to joy. Later on in the day Wordsworth will fancy that something else in his mind calls for expression, and he will sit down and write it in verse. There it will be; like the other, it will say exactly what he wanted to say, and he will put it in its place among his poems with the same confidence. But this time no kindly inspiration will have come to his aid; and the thing will have nothing of poetry but the rhymes.

What Wordsworth's poetic life lacked was energy, and he refused to recognise that no amount of energy will suffice for a continual production. The mind of Coleridge worked with extraordinary energy, seemed to be always at high thinking power, but Coleridge has left us less finished work than almost any great writer, so rare was it with him to be able faultlessly to unite, in his own words, 'a more than usual state of emotion with more than usual order.' Wordsworth was unconscious even of the necessity, or at least of the part played by skill and patience in waiting on opportunity as it comes, and seizing it as it goes. When one has said that he wrote instinctively, without which there could be no poetry, one must add that he wrote mechanically, and that he wrote always. Continual writing is really a bad form of dissipation; it drains away the very marrow of the brain. Nature is not to be treated as a handmaid of all work, and requires some coaxing before she will become one's mistress. There is a kind of unconscious personal vanity in the assumption that whatever interests or concerns me, however slightly, must be of interest to all the world. Only what is of intense interest to me, or concerns me vitally, will be of interest to all the world; and Wordsworth often wrote about matters which had not had time to sink into him, or the likelihood of taking root in any but the upper surface of his mind.

But there was another kind of forgetfulness which has had almost the most fatal consequences of any. Wordsworth never rightly apprehended what is essential in the difference between prose and poetry. Holding rightly that poetry can be a kind of religion, he admitted what Gautier has called 'the heresy of instruction.' He forgot that religion has its sacred ritual, in which no gesture is insignificant, and in which what is preached from the pulpit is by no means of higher importance than what is sung or prayed before the altar. He laboured to make his verse worthy, but he was not always conscious that a noble intention does not of itself make great art. In 'The Prelude' he tells the story of his own mind, of his growth, not so much as a man, but as a poet; and he has left us a document of value, together with incidental fragments of fine poetry. But it is not a poem, because what Wordsworth tried to do was a thing which should have been done in prose. It is a talking about life, not a creation of life; it is a criticism of the imagination, not imagination at work on its own indefinable ends.

And yet, just here, out of this unconsciousness which leaves him so often at the mercy of all intrusions, clogged by fact, tied to scruple, a child in the mischief-working hands of his own childishness, we come upon precisely the quality which gives him his least questionable greatness. To Wordsworth nothing is what we call 'poetry,' that is, a fanciful thing, apart from reality; he is not sure whether even the imagination is so much as a transfiguring, or only an unveiling, of natural things. Often he gives you the thing and his impressions of the thing, and then, with a childlike persistence of sincerity, his own doubt as to the precise truth of the thing. Whether I am right or wrong, he says to us gravely, I indeed scarcely know; but certainly I saw or heard this, or fancied that I saw or heard it; thus what I am telling you is, to me at least, a reality. It is thus that, as Matthew Arnold has said finely, 'it might seem that nature not only gave him the matter for his poem, but wrote his poem for him.' He has none of the poet's pride in his own invention, only a confidence in the voices that he has heard speaking when others were aware of nothing but silence. Thus it is that in the interpretation of natural things he can be absolutely pellucid, like pure light, which renders to us every object in its own colours. He does not 'make poetry' out of these things; he sets them down just as they came to him. It is the fault of 'Laodamia,' and of some pieces like it, that there Wordsworth breaks through his own wise rule, and sets himself to compose, not taking things as they come. 'Laodamia' is an attempt to be classic, to have those classic qualities of calmness and balance and natural dignity which, in a poem like 'The Leech-Gatherer,' had come of themselves, through mere truth to nature, to the humbleness of fact and the grandeur of impassioned thought illuminating it. Here, on the contrary, Wordsworth would be Greek as the Greeks were, or rather as they seem to us, at our distance from them, to be; and it is only in single lines that he succeeds, all the rest of the poem showing an effort to be something not himself. Thus this profoundly natural poet becomes for once, as Matthew Arnold has noted, 'artificial,' in a poem which has been classed among his masterpieces.

In the sonnets, on the other hand, we find much of Wordsworth's finest work, alike in substance and in form. 'The sonnet's scanty plot of ground' suited him so well because it forced him to be at once concise and dignified, and yet allowed him to say straight out the particular message or emotion which was possessing him. He felt that a form so circumscribed demanded not only something said in every line, but something said with a certain richness; that when so few words could be used, those words must be chosen with unusual care, and with an attention to their sound as well as to their meaning. The proportion, it is true, of his bad sonnets to his good sonnets is so great, that, even in Matthew Arnold's scrupulous selection, at least six out of the sixty would have been better omitted. Taking them at their best, you will find that nowhere in his work has he put so much of his finest self into so narrow a compass. Nowhere are there so many splendid single lines, lines of such weight, such imaginative ardour. And these lines have nothing to lose by their context, as almost all the fine lines which we find in the blank verse poems have to lose.

Wordsworth's blank verse is so imperfect a form, so heavy, limp, drawling, unguided, that even in poems like 'Tintern Abbey' we have to unravel the splendours, and, if we can, forget the rest. In 'The Prelude' and 'The Excursion' poetry comes and goes at its own will, and even then, for the most part,

'Its exterior semblance doth belie
Its soul's immensity.'

What goes on is a kind of measured talk, which, if one is in the mood for it, becomes as pleasant as the gentle continuance of a good, thoughtful, easy-paced, prosy friend. Every now and then an ecstasy wakes out of it, and one hears singing, as if the voices of all the birds in the forest cried in a human chorus.

Wordsworth has told us in his famous prefaces exactly what was his own conception of poetry, and we need do no more than judge him by his own laws. 'Poetry,' he says, 'is the breath and finer spirit of all knowledge; it is the impassioned expression which is in the countenance of all science.' 'The poet thinks and feels in the spirit of human passions.' The poet is 'a man pleased with his own passions and volitions, and who rejoices more than other men in the spirit of life that is in him.' 'I have said,' he reiterates, 'that poetry is the spontaneous overflow of powerful feelings; it takes its origin from emotion recollected in tranquillity; the emotion is contemplated till, by a species of reaction, the tranquillity gradually disappears, and an emotion kindred to that which was before the subject of contemplation is gradually produced, and does itself actually exist in the mind.' The poet, then, deals with 'truth, carried alive into the heart by passion.' 'I have at all times,' he tells us, 'endeavoured to look steadily at my subject,' and, as for the subject, 'I have wished to keep the reader in the company of flesh and blood, persuaded that by so doing I shall interest him.' 'Personifications of abstract ideas rarely occur in these volumes, and are utterly rejected as an ordinary device to elevate the style and raise it above prose.' 'Poetic diction,' which is always insincere, inasmuch as it is not 'the real language of men in *any situation*,' is to be given up, and, 'it may safely be affirmed that there neither is, nor can be, any essential difference between the language of prose and metrical composition.' The language which alone is suitable for verse, and which requires no change in its transference from the lips of men to the printed page, is defined, not very happily, in the original preface of 1798, as 'the language of conversation in the middle and lower classes of society,' and, in the revised preface of 1800, with perfect exactitude, as 'a selection of the real language of men in a state of vivid sensation.'

When these true, but to us almost self-evident things were said, Wordsworth was daring, for the first time, to say what others, when they did it, had done without knowing; and he was supposed to be trying to revolutionise the whole art of poetry. In reality, he was bringing poetry back to its senses, which it had temporarily lost under the influence of that lucid madness which Pope imposed upon it. The style of Pope was still looked upon as the type of poetical style, though Blake and Burns had shown that the utmost rapture of personal passion and of imaginative vision could be expressed, even in the eighteenth century, in a style which was the direct utterance of Nature in her two deepest moods. Pope is the most finished artist in prose who ever wrote in verse. It is impossible to read him without continuous admiration for his cleverness, or to forget, while reading him, that poetry cannot be clever. While Herrick or Crashaw, with two instinctively singing lines, lets us overhear that he is a poet, Pope brilliantly convinces us of everything that he chooses, except of that one fact. The only moments when he trespasses into beauty are the moments when he mocks its affectations; so that

'Die of a rose in aromatic pain'

remains his homage, unintentional under its irony, to that 'principle of beauty in all things' which he had never seen.

But it was not only against the directly anti-poetical principles of Pope that Wordsworth protested, but against much that was most opposed to it, against the hyperbolical exaggerations of the so-called 'metaphysical poets' of the seventeenth century, and against the half-hearted and sometimes ill-directed attempts of those who, in a first movement of reaction against Pope, were trying to bring poetry back to nature, against Thomson, Cowper, and Crabbe. He saw that Thomson, trying to see the world with his own eyes, had only to some degree won back the forgotten 'art of seeing,' and that, even when he saw straight, he could not get rid of that 'vicious style' which prevented him from putting down what he had seen, just as he saw it. Cowper's style is mean, rather than vicious; 'some critics,' says Wordsworth, after quoting some lines from a poem of Cowper, then and afterwards popular, 'would call the language prosaic; the fact is, it would be bad prose, so bad that it is scarcely worse in metre.' With Crabbe, who may have taught Wordsworth something, we have only to contrast, as the note to 'Lucy Gray' asks us to do, 'the imaginative influences which [Wordsworth] endeavoured to throw over common life with Crabbe's matter-of-fact style of handling subjects of the kind.' For, seeming, as Wordsworth did to the critics of his time, to bring poetry so close to prose, to make of it something prosaic, he is really, if we will take him at his word, and will also judge him by his best, the advocate of a more than usually lofty view of poetry.

In saying that there is no essential difference between the language of prose and of verse, Wordsworth is pointing straight to what constitutes the essential difference between prose and poetry: metre. An old delusion reappeared the other day, when a learned writer on æsthetics quoted from Marlowe: —

'Was this the face that launched a thousand ships,
And burned the topless towers of Ilium?'

and assured us that 'it is certain that he could only have ventured on the sublime audacity of saying that a face launched ships and burned towers by escaping from the limits of ordinary language, and conveying his metaphor through the harmonious and ecstatic movements of rhythm and metre.' Now, on the contrary, any writer of elevated prose, Milton or Ruskin, could have said in prose precisely what Marlowe said, and made fine prose of it; the imagination, the idea, a fine kind of form, would have been there; only one thing would have been lacking, the very finest kind of form, the form of verse. It would have been poetical substance, not poetry; the rhythm transforms it into poetry, and nothing but the rhythm.

When Wordsworth says 'that the language of a large portion of every good poem, even of the most elevated character, must necessarily, except with reference to the metre, in no respect differ from that of good prose,' he is admitting, on behalf of metre, all that any reasonable defender of 'art for art's sake' ever claimed on its behalf. But he is not always, or not clearly, aware of the full meaning of his own argument, and not always consistent with it. He is apt to fall back on the conventional nicety of the worst writers whom he condemns, and can speak of

'The fowl domestic and the household dog,'

or can call a gun 'the deadly tube,' or can say of the organ,

'While the tubed engine feels the inspiring blast.'

He is frequently provincial in thought, and thus trivial in expression, as when he says with conviction:—

'Alas! that such perverted zeal
Should spread on Britain's favoured ground.'

He can be trivial for so many reasons, one of which is a false theory of simplicity, not less than a lack of humour.

'My little Edward, say why so;
My little Edward, tell me why,'

is the language of a child, not of a grown man; and when Wordsworth uses it in his own person, even when he is supposed to be speaking to a child, he is not using 'the real language of men,' but the actual language of children. The reason why a fine poem like 'The Beggars' falls so immeasurably below a poem like 'The Leech-Gatherer' is because it has in it something of this infantile quality of speech. I have said that Wordsworth had a quality of mind which was akin to the child's fresh and wondering apprehension of things. But he was not content with using this faculty like a man; it dragged him into the depths of a second childhood hardly to be distinguished from literal imbecility. In a famous poem, 'Simon Lee,' he writes:—

> 'My gentle reader, I perceive
> How patiently you've waited;
> And now I fear that you expect
> Some tale will be related.'

There are more lines of the kind, and they occur, as you see, in what is considered one of Wordsworth's successes. If one quoted from one of the failures!

It was from Burns, partly, that Wordsworth learnt to be absolutely straightforward in saying what he had to say, and it is from Burns that he sometimes even takes his metres, as in the two fine poems written in his memory.

> 'Well might I mourn that He was gone
> Whose light I hailed when first it shone,
> When, breaking forth as nature's own,
> It showed my youth
> How Verse may build a princely throne
> On humble truth.'

That has the very quality of Burns, in its admission of a debt which is more obvious than any other, except that general quickening of poetic sensibility, of what was sometimes sluggish in his intellect, which he owed to Coleridge, and that quickening of the gift of seeing with emotion, which he owed to his sister Dorothy. But, at his best and worst, hardly any poet seems so much himself, so untouched by the influence of other poets. When he speaks he is really speaking, and when speech passes into song, as in some of those happy lyrics which preserve a gravity in delight, the words seem to sing themselves unconsciously, to the tune of their own being. In what seems to me his greatest, as it is certainly his most characteristic poem, 'The Leech-Gatherer,' he has gathered up all his qualities, dignity, homeliness, meditation over man and nature, respectful pity for old age and poverty, detailed observation of natural things, together with an imaginative atmosphere which melts, harmonises, the forms of cloud and rock and pool and the voices of wind and man into a single composition. Such concentration, with him, is rare; but it is much less rare than is commonly supposed to find an almost perfect expression of a single mood or a single aspect of nature, as it has come to him in his search after everything that nature has to say to us or to show us.

In Haydon's portrait, the portrait by which Wordsworth is generally known, the eyes and the forehead seem to be listening, and the whole head droops over, as if brooding upon some memory of sound or sight. It is typical of a poet who, at his best, had a Quaker wisdom, and waited on the silent voices 'in a wise passiveness,' with that 'happy stillness of the mind' in which truth may be received unsought. For, as he says, summing up into a kind of precept what nearly all of his work represents to us indirectly: —

> 'The eye — it cannot choose but see;
> We cannot bid the ear be still;
> Our bodies feel, where'er they be,
> Against, or with our will.
>
> 'Nor less I deem that there are Powers
> Which of themselves our minds impress;
> That we can feed this mind of ours
> In a wise passiveness.
>
> 'Think you, 'mid all this mighty sum
> Of things for ever speaking,
> That nothing of itself will come
> But we must still be seeking?'

And, in 'The Prelude,' defining what he most hopes for as a poet, it is

> 'A privilege whereby a work of his
> Proceeding from a source of untaught things,
> Creative and enduring, may become
> A force like one of Nature's.'

To see, more clearly than any one had seen before, seeing things as they are, not composed into pictures, but in splendid natural motion or in all the ardour of repose; and then to see deeply into them, to feel them,

> 'not as in the hour
> Of thoughtless youth, but hearing oftentimes
> The still, sad music of humanity':

that is his aim, his ambition. In the note to a very early poem he tells us of some natural aspect that struck him in boyhood: 'It was in the way between Hawkshead and Ambleside, and gave me extreme pleasure. The moment,' he adds, 'was important in my poetical history, for I date from it my consciousness of the infinite variety of natural appearances which had been unnoticed by the poets of any age or country, so far as I was acquainted with them; and I made a resolution to supply, in some degree, the deficiency.' It was only gradually that the human figures came into the landscape, and at first as no more than a completion to the picture. He sees the Cumberland shepherd like one 'in his own domain,' among the rocks, and outlined against the sky: —

> 'Thus was man
> Ennobled outwardly before my sight,
> And thus my heart was early introduced
> To an unconscious love and reverence
> Of human nature':

still visual, you see, part of the honour and majesty of the eyes; and still secondary to nature: —

> 'a passion, she,
> A rapture often, and immediate love
> Ever at hand; he, only a delight
> Occasional, an accidental grace,
> His hour being not yet come.'

The hour came with a consciousness, henceforward deeply, but not passionately, felt, with a moved, grave, pitying and respectful, but not passionate, sympathy with passion, of

> 'Man suffering among awful Powers and Forms.'

When Wordsworth resolved to

> 'make verse
> Deal boldly with substantial things,'

WILLIAM WORDSWORTH

he turned, somewhat apprehensively, to what he feared and valued most in humanity, the elementary passions, and to those in whom they are seen most simply, the peasants of his countryside. It was

> 'the gentle agency
> Of natural objects'

that had led him gradually to feel for passions not his own, and to think

> 'On man, the heart of man, and human life.'

And so these 'dwellers in the valley' come to us with some of the immobility of natural objects, set there among their rocks and stones like a part of them, scarcely more sentient, or scarcely less interpenetrated with the unconscious lesson of nature. They are stationary, a growth of the soil, and when they speak, with the emphatic slowness of the peasant, we are almost surprised that beings so rudimentary can become articulate.

> 'Words are but under-agents in their souls;
> When they are grasping with their greatest strength
> They do not breathe among them.'

There is something sluggish, only half awake, in the way 'Michael' is told: —

> ''T is a common tale,
> An ordinary sorrow of man's life';

and it is seen as if with the eyes of the old man, and told as if always with his own speech. Turn to those poems in which Wordsworth is most human, and at the same time most himself as a poet, 'The Leech-Gatherer,' 'Michael,' 'Animal Tranquillity and Decay,' 'The Old Cumberland Beggar,' and you will see that they are all motionless, or moving imperceptibly, like the old beggar: —

> 'He is so still
> In look and motion, that the cottage curs,
> Ere he have passed the door, will turn away,
> Weary of barking at him.'

And Wordsworth conveys this part of natural truth to us as no other poet has ever done, no other poet having had in him so much of the reflective peasant. He seems to stop on the other side of conscious life, and I think we may apply to his general attitude towards the human comedy what he says in 'The Prelude' of his attitude towards a play on the stage: —

> 'For though I was most passionately moved
> And yielded to all changes of the scene
> With an obsequious promptness, yet the storm
> Passed not beyond the suburbs of the mind.'

In one of his poems Wordsworth rebukes Byron because he

> 'dares to take
> Life's rule from passion craved for passion's sake';

and, in an utterance reported in Mr. Myers' Life, takes credit to himself for his moderation, in words which can hardly be read without a smile: 'Had I been a writer of love-poetry, it would have been natural to me to write it with a degree of warmth which could hardly have been approved by my principles, and which might have been undesirable for the reader.' Not unnaturally, Wordsworth was anxious for it to be supposed that he had not attained tranquillity without a struggle, and we hear much, from himself and others, of his restlessness, which sent him wandering about the mountains alone, of his nervous exhaustion after writing, of his violence of feeling, the feeling for his sister, for instance, which seems to have been the one strong and penetrating affection of his life. Were not these stirrings, after all, no more than breaths of passing wind ruffling the surface of a deep and calm lake? I think almost the most significant story told of Wordsworth is the one reported by Mr. Aubrey de Vere about the death of his children. 'Referring once,' he tells us, 'to two young children of his who had died about *forty years* previously, he described the details of their illnesses with an exactness and an impetuosity of troubled excitement, such as might have been expected if the bereavement had taken place but a few weeks before. The lapse of time seemed to have left the sorrow submerged indeed, but still in all its first freshness. Yet I afterwards heard that at the time of the illness, at least in the case of one of the two children, it was impossible to rouse his attention to the danger. He chanced to be then under the immediate spell of one of those fits of poetic inspiration which descended on him like a cloud. Till the cloud had drifted, he could see nothing beyond.' The thing itself, that is to say, meant little to him: he could not realise it; what possessed him was the 'emotion recollected in tranquillity,' the thing as it found its way, imaginatively, into his own mind.

And it was this large, calm, impersonal power, this form of imagination, which, as he says,—

> 'Is but another name for absolute power
> And clearest insight, amplitude of mind,
> And Reason in her most exalted mood,'

which made him able to

> 'Sit without emotion, hope, or aim,
> In the loved presence of his cottage fire,'

and yet to look widely, dispassionately, into what in man is most akin to nature, seeing the passions almost at their origin, where they are still a scarcely conscious part of nature. Speaking of his feeling for nature, he tells us that,

> 'As if awakened, summoned, roused, constrained,
> I looked for universal things, perused
> The common countenance of earth and sky.'

And so, in his reading of 'the great book of the world,' of what we call the human interest of it, he looked equally, and with the same sense of a constraining finger pointing along the lines, for universal things.

> 'Him who looks
> In steadiness, who hath among least things
> An under-sense of greatest; sees the parts
> As parts, but with a feeling of the whole,'

is his definition of what he has aimed at doing: it defines exactly what he has done. The links of things as their roots begin to form in the soil, their close intertexture underground: that is what he shows us, completing his interpretation of nature. We must go to other poets for any vivid consciousness or representation of all that waves in the wind when sap and fibre become aware of themselves above ground.

All Wordsworth's work is a search after

> 'The bond of union between life and joy.'

The word joy occurs in his work more frequently than perhaps any other emotional word. Sometimes, as in his own famous and awkward line, it is

> 'Of joy in widest commonalty spread'

that he tells us; sometimes of the joy embodied in natural things, as they are taken in gratefully by the senses; sometimes of disembodied joy, an emotion of the intellect:—

> 'And I have felt
> A presence that disturbs me with the joy
> Of elevated thought; a sense sublime
> Of something far more deeply interfused,
> Whose dwelling is the light of setting suns,
> And the round ocean and the living air,
> And the blue sky, and in the mind of man.'

Ecstasy, with him, is

> 'The depth, and not the tumult, of the soul';

and his highest joy comes to him in a sacramental silence. Even at this height, any excess of joy seems to him so natural, that he can speak of it quite simply, without any of the unfaith of rhetoric.

To Wordsworth there was an actual divine inhabitant of woods and rocks, a divinity implicit there, whom we had only to open our eyes to see, visible in every leaf and cranny. What with other men is a fancy, or at the most a difficult act of faith, is with him the mere statement of a fact. While other men search among the images of the mind for that poetry which they would impute to nature, Wordsworth finds it there, really in things, and awaiting only a quiet, loving glance. He conceives of things as loving back in return for man's love, grieving at his departure, never themselves again as they had been when he loved them. 'We die, my friend,' says the Wanderer, looking round on the cottage which had once been Margaret's;

> 'Nor we alone, but that which each man loved
> And prized in his particular nook of earth
> Dies with him, or is changed.'

Even the spring in the garden seems conscious of a grief in things.

> 'Beside yon spring I stood,
> And eyed its waters till we seemed to feel
> One sadness, they and I. For them a bond
> Of brotherhood is broken: time has been
> When, every day, the touch of human hand
> Dislodged the natural sleep that binds them up
> In mortal stillness; and they ministered
> To human comfort.'

What a responsiveness of the soul to the eye, 'the most despotic of our senses,' the sense of sight, as he calls it, truly! It is his chief reason for discontentment with cities, that in them the eye is starved, to the disabling or stunting of the growth of the heart: —

> 'Among the close and overcrowded haunts
> Of cities, where the human heart is sick,
> And the eye feeds it not, and cannot feed.'

The eye is realised by him as the chief influence for good in the world, an actual moral impulse, in its creation and radiation of delight. Sight, to him, is feeling; not, as it is with Keats, a voluptuous luxury, but with some of the astringent quality of mountain air. When he says that the valley 'swarms with sensation,' it is because, as he tells us of one living among the Lakes, 'he must have experienced, while looking on the unruffled waters, that the imagination by their aid is carried into recesses of feeling otherwise impenetrable.' It is into these recesses of feeling that the mere physical delight of the eye carries him, and, the visible world so definitely apprehended, the feeling latent in it so vividly absorbed, he takes the further step, and begins to make and unmake the world about him.

> 'I had a world about me — 't was my own,
> I made it, for it only lived to me.'

The Beatific Vision has come to him in this tangible, embodied form, through a kind of religion of the eye which seems to attain its final rapture, unlike most forms of mysticism, with open eyes. The tranquillity, which he reached in that consciousness of

> 'A motion and a spirit, that impels
> All thinking things, all objects of all thought,
> And rolls through all things,'

is his own form of perfect spiritual happiness, or attainment. That 'impassioned contemplation' of nature, which he prized above all things, was his way of closing the senses to all things external to his own contemplation. It came to him through sight, but through sight humanised into feeling, and illuminated by joy and peace. He saw nature purely, with no uneasy or unworthy emotions, which nature might need to purify. Nature may, indeed, do much to purify the soul of these emotions, but until these are at rest it cannot enter fully, it cannot possess the soul with itself. The ultimate joy, as Wordsworth knew, that comes to the soul from the beauty of the world, must enter as light enters a crystal, finding its own home there and its own flawless mirror.

Yet, as there is an ecstasy in which joy itself loses so much of separateness as to know that it is joy, so there is one further step which we may take in the companionship of nature; and this step Wordsworth took. In the note to that ode into which he has put his secret doctrine, the 'Intimations of Immortality from Recollections of Early Childhood,' he says, speaking of his early years: 'I was often unable to think of external things as having external existence, and I communed with all that I saw as something not apart from, but inherent in, my own immaterial nature. Many times while going to school have I grasped at a wall or tree to recall myself from this abyss of idealism to the reality.' To Wordsworth, external things existed so visibly, just because they had no existence apart from the one eternal and infinite being; it was for the principle of infinity in them that he loved them, and it was this principle of infinity which he seemed to recognise by a simple act of memory. It seemed to him, quite literally, that the child really remembers 'that imperial palace whence we came'; less and less clearly as human life sets all its veils between the soul and that relapsing light. But, later on, when we seem to have forgotten, when the world is most real to us, it is by an actual recognition that we are reminded, now and again, as one of those inexplicable flashes carries some familiar, and certainly never seen, vision through the eyes to the soul, of that other, previous fragment of eternity which the soul has known before it accepted the comfortable bondage and limit of time. And so, finally, the soul, carried by nature through nature, transported by visible beauty into the presence of the source of invisible beauty, sees, in one annihilating flash of memory, its own separate identity vanish away, to resume the infinite existence which that identity had but interrupted.

JAMES HOGG (1770-1835) [1]

JAMES HOGG, better known as the Ettrick Shepherd, began to work for his living at the age of seven, by herding cows on the hills of Selkirk; his wages for the half year being a ewe

---

[1] (1) *Donald McDonald*, patriotic song, 1800. (2) *Scottish Pastorals*, 1801. (3) *The Mountain Bard*, 1807. (4) *The Forest Minstrel*, 1810.

lamb and a pair of shoes. At twenty he could not write all the letters of the alphabet; at twenty-six, after reading many books, he began to make up verses in his head, which he wrote down slowly, 'four or six lines at a sitting,' on sheets of paper which he had stitched together and carried in his pocket, sitting on the hillside with his unruly sheep about him. In the following year, 1797, he first heard of Burns, who had just died; a half-daft man came to him on the hill, and repeated 'Tam o' Shanter,' which he got by heart. The half-daft man told him that it had been made by a ploughman called Robert Burns, and that he was the sweetest poet who ever lived, and that he was dead now, and his place would never be filled. Hogg thought deeply of the matter, and resolved to be a poet, and to fill Burns' place in the world.

His first songs were printed in 1801. He believed that by this time he had become 'a grand poet,' and being in Edinburgh to sell his sheep, and having to wait till market-day, he wrote out some of his poems from memory, 'and gave them all to a person to print,' at his own expense. They sold, but he was more anxious, just then, to be a farmer than a poet. In this he failed, but having been discovered by Scott, who came out to his mother's cottage to take down the old ballads from her lips, he was able to bring out his 'Mountain Bard,' in which, as in Scott's 'Minstrelsy of the Scottish Border,' there were old ballads and imitations of old ballads. He made money, tried farming again, and lost all his money. After that, 'having appeared as a poet, and a speculative farmer besides,' no one would even take him as a shepherd, and he decided to give himself wholly to the more profitable business of writing. He went to Edinburgh, started and wrote a newspaper called 'The Spy,' which had a brief existence; and, in the spring of 1813, brought out 'The Queen's Wake,' which con-

(5) *The Queen's Wake*, 1813.   (6) *The Pilgrims of the Sun*, 1815.
(7) *Mador of the Moor*, 1816.   (8) *The Poetic Mirror*, 1816.   (9) *Queen Hynde*, 1826.   (10) *Works*, 2 vols., 1865.

tains the best work he was ever to do, and which immediately gave him a recognised position as a poet. He found a friend in John Wilson, who has given him a dubious celebrity as the Ettrick Shepherd of his once popular 'Noctes Ambrosianæ.' From first to last he took himself with all a peasant's dogged and stolid and unshakable vanity. He seems to have had many good sober qualities, but no charm to make up for what Wordsworth considered his 'coarse manners.' His face, as one sees it in engravings, is full of hard power, but without flexibility. The poetry is hidden away, no doubt, somewhere behind that high, narrow forehead; but the mouth is unattractively obstinate and the eyes are cold.

The poetry of Hogg is wholly destitute of passion; nothing human moves him, except the unearthly drollery of things. He reverences religion, with a sober conviction; preaches morality, the obvious duties, with an experienced sense of their necessity to a man who wishes to get on in the world. And he touches frankly on love, taking it from various points of view, as a quite natural instinct and as a feeling capable of elaborate refinements. But neither he nor any of the persons of his songs and ballads can touch one with a single personal thrill. When, in his fantastic 'Russiadde,' Russell is lying in the arms of Venus, in the depths of the sea, all Hogg can find to say of his feelings is: —

> 'True love he ne'er before had felt,
> Love, pure as purest cryst'lization,
> The sweetest, fondest admiration';

and Russell turns away from Venus to watch 'the little fishes wandering by.' Hogg is warmed to an efficacious enthusiasm only by something inhuman. He can write ringingly to the sound of 'battles long ago,' sometimes, as in 'Lock the door, Lariston,' in almost his best manner; but there are no tears for him in the thought that some 'sweet war-man is dead.' Even in what is meant to move you by its horror, as in 'The Lord of Balloch,' nothing human returns to one, only the splendid and unearthly image of the eagle sailing on a cloud, and screaming from the height, —

> 'For he saw the blood below his feet,
> And he saw it red, and he knew it sweet.'

His men and women love, hate, suffer, and go through all the acts of life, like strangers who copy the manners of those they see about them, but without ever quite understanding the language of their fellows. It is as if his heart too had been captured and turned cold by the fairies.

In his feeling for nature there is the same strangeness of attitude. Though, as he says, 'I consider myself exquisite at descriptions of nature, and mountain scenery in particular,' and though he valued some of such descriptions in 'Mador of the Moor,' above everything else that he had written, he is rarely able to do much with nature, taken simply, and observed without transposition. Now and then he sets down a new, fresh detail, just as he has seen it; such as : —

> 'Or dark trout spreads his waxing O.'

And in the poem called 'Storm of Thunder among Mountains' there is genuine observation of natural moods, only put into what he thought the 'grand manner.' But he is never quite himself unless he is looking down on the earth, from a witch's broomstick, as in 'The Witch of Fife,' from 'far up the welkin,' as in 'The Russiadde,' from higher worlds, as in 'The Pilgrims of the Sun.'

> 'Russ never saw a scene so fair
> As Scotland from the ambient air,'

we are told, and in the introduction to 'Mador' the poet longs that 'some spirit at the midnight noon' would bear him aloft into middle space, so that he might see all Scotland at once. It is certain that his descriptions from this point of view are much better than those done on a mere earthly level. One sees that inhuman trait coming out again, in his relations with nature, just as in his relations with men and women.

And I do not think it is fanciful to set down to a somewhat similar reason that genius for parody which makes 'The Poet's Mirror.' the most subtly poetical of all parodies of poetry. The parody of Scott ('Wat o' the Cleuch') is like a more amusing, a more abounding, piece of Scott himself, into which some tricksy imp has brought a little companionable mischief; the parodies of Wordsworth ('James Rigg,' for example) and of Coleridge ('Isabelle') are thought out from inside the skin of Wordsworth and Coleridge, with a serene and devilish sympathy; sympathy, to his inhuman nature, being an uncanny thing, and evil-disposed. In his original writing he is often out of key; here, never, so faultlessly he lets himself be guided, like the medium who has invoked spirits. The imitative faculty, once set in motion, acts almost unconsciously; it is the failure of so much of his original work that it is half imitative, without being wholly so.

Hogg is nearest humanity when he abandons himself to his humour; yet, at its best, his humour is almost more unearthly than his more obviously romantic qualities. In songs like that enchanting one whose refrain is: —

> 'O love, love, love!
> Love is like a dizziness!
> It winna let a puir body
> Gang about his business';

there is a kind of quizzical sly Scotch fooling with grave things and gay things, jumbled together by a shrewd common-sense. 'The Village of Balmaquhapple' is like the very best Irish work in that kind, more headlong in its gallop than most Scotch songs. And there are others of his songs in which it is the undercurrent of humour which brings into them what they have of human nature. In the too lengthy ballad called 'The Powris of Moseke' the humour, becoming fantastic, runs blindfold into imagination, and turns its somersaults half in and half out of a fairies' ring on the grass. 'The Gude Greye Katte,' which was meant for a parody on himself, and 'The

Witch of Fife,' which it parodies (and, as he fancied, excels) are danced wholly within the ring, and have but another, and not less genuine, nor less rare, magic of their own than 'Kilmeny,' in which for once he has achieved pure beauty.

It is by 'Kilmeny' that Hogg first became famous, and it is by 'Kilmeny' that his fame is still kept alive, among those who know his work at all. It is the story, so frequent in all Celtic folk-lore, and believed in to-day by every Irish peasant, of a maiden stolen by the fairies, and brought back to the earth after seven years, no longer human with desire. 'Besides the old tradition,' says Hogg, 'on which this ballad is founded, there are some modern incidents of a similar nature, which cannot well be accounted for, yet are as well attested as any occurrence that has taken place in the present age.' There had been witches in Hogg's family, notably one old woman, a contemporary of Michael Scott, known as Lucky Hogg. And never, he says, 'in the most superstitious ages, was the existence of witches, or the influence of their diabolical power, more firmly believed in, than by the inhabitants of the mountains of Ettrick Forest at the present day.' But, he laments, 'the fairies have now totally disappeared; and it is a pity they should; for they seem to have been the most delightful little spirits that ever haunted the Scottish dells.' Hogg brought back the fairies to Scotland, and by a magic of which he was rather the slave than the master. He tells us that he 'quaked by night and mused by day' on the Ettrick hills: —

> 'And sore I feared in bush or brake might be
> Things of unearthly make';

yet he was only too ready to talk of 'superstition,' and to reason away the fears that were rather in his blood than in his brain. The fairies were to him almost as merely poetical material as they might have been to Southey; but they were material for that thin flame of genius which was in him. 'Kilmeny' is an inspiration, and it escaped from him, by some never-repeated accident, almost flawless. He could not have told you how that poem is at once music and vision, and why the best words came for once almost always into the best places. It was not because of any literal, peasant belief in these 'superstitious' things; but, as certainly as with Coleridge, from a poet's 'willing suspension of belief.'

Only, the magic is there; unconsciously, I say, because, with all his trying, he could never repeat it. Perhaps no poet has ever evoked fairyland so simply; the very weaknesses or trivialities, here and there, aiding in the effect. The melody of the poem is the most lulling melody that I know in verse, full of a sweet, sleepy monotony. No philosophy is wrapped up in the flowers and beasts of it; there is no undercurrent of meaning to be teased out of its pictures. There is only what Hogg, speaking of something else, calls 'wild unearthly nakedness.'

Inspiration came to Hogg rarely; the desire to write verse almost continually. There was in him that one small, bright flame of genius; and for the rest, he was the professional literary man, only without the requisites of his profession. He tells us how, having finally, in 1810, failed in all his attempts at farming, 'I took my plaid about my shoulders, and marched away to Edinburgh, determined, since no better could be, to push my fortune as a literary man.' From that time till his death, twenty-five years later, he lived by writing, making the most he could of the fact that he had begun by being a shepherd in the mountains. He wrote many poems and many stories, with only here and there a good poem, and, in whole long cantos, not a good line; and with one admirable story, 'The Private Memoirs and Confessions of a Justified Sinner.' 'It being a story replete with horrors, after I had written it,' says Hogg, 'I durst not venture to put my name to it'; and it has often been asserted that part of the writing was Lockhart's. It is very nearly a masterpiece of its kind, a kind somewhere between Bunyan and a spiritual Defoe. It might have suggested Poe's 'William Wilson,' and it has a horror which even Poe has hardly exceeded. But it is as a piece of psychology that it is most remarkable: the lean, dry record of a wrinkled soul, which projects its own devil upon the outer air, and dies the suicide of its enemy, itself.

Here, for once (was this really some helping influence of Lockhart?), Hogg is grimly self-possessed, master of his material. He tells us proudly that he never re-wrote. Not to revise means, to him, 'to hold fast my integrity'; he will try to write better next time, but what he has written he has written. The consequence of this proud incapacity is that all but his very best work is both spun out to weakness and marred by absurdities of language. The Scotch dialect was at once a help and a disguise to him. Sometimes the difference is only apparent, but for the most part he is better able to mould words to his thought out of the homely dialect whose shades of meaning were so much clearer to him than those of English. In English he uses words that express his meaning, but whose poverty or formality as words he does not realise. He does not hear the absurdity of writing, —

> 'No torrent, no rock, her velocity staid,'

or, —

> 'And hauberk, armlet, cuirass, rung
> Promiscuous on the green.'

In Scotch his ear tells him when a word rings true, and he can write stanza after stanza with this fine and masterly swing: —

> 'And the bauld windis blew, and the fire flauchtis flew
> And the sea ran to the skie;
> And the thunder it growlit, and the sea-dogs howlit,
> As we gaed scouryng bye.'

Hogg knew that a song, at least a Scotch song, was 'made for singing, an' no for reading,' as his mother told Scott, when Scott had spoilt the old ballads by printing them; his first poems, made before he could write them down, were 'songs and ballads made up for the lasses to sing in chorus.' When he was fourteen he had saved five shillings of his wages, and bought an old fiddle. You hear the fiddle jigging away through his verse for singing, with its recaptured refrains: —

> 'There wals ane auld caryl wonit in you howe,
> Lemedon! lemedon! ayden lillelu!
> His face was the geire, and his hayre was the woo,
> Sing Ho! Ro! Gillan of Allanhu!'

But it was his mistake, the mistake partly of ignorance, partly of that 'inherent vanity' to which he confesses with so evident a satisfaction, to have the 'fixed opinion, that if a person could succeed in the genuine ballad style, his muse was adequate for any other.'

When Hogg was not at his best, and he was rarely at his best, considering the amount of work which he produced, he was almost totally worthless. Much of 'The Queen's Wake,' nearly all of 'Mador of the Moor,' 'The Pilgrims of the Sun,' and 'Queen Hynde,' is not even interestingly bad, but consistently feeble. He imitated not only Scott and Byron, but Professor Wilson, whose 'fanciful and visionary scenes' he was 'so greatly taken with'; and to imitate Wilson was to dilute an already thrice-diluted source. The main part of this work, on the weakest portions of which he was ready to 'stake his credit,' is not even readable, and it has no personal quality, nothing to make up for its imitative feebleness. He thought he had produced 'the best epic poem that had been produced in Scotland,' and reformed the Spenserian stanza 'to its proper harmony.' When he said to Robert Montgomery, who had asked his opinion on his poems, 'I daresay, Robert, they're gey gude, but I never a' my life could thole college poetry — it's sae desperate stupid,' he did not realise that he himself had only been making 'college poetry' whenever he stepped outside that tiny local ring in which the fairies danced in homespun, or when he spoke in a language that he had not used to his cows, 'when the kye comes hame.'

GEORGE CANNING (1770-1827)[1]

AMONG the political satires of the age, crude, townish, and temporary, we need not linger over 'The Criticisms of the Rolliad,' which appeared in 1784-85, and were followed by 'Probationary Odes for the Laureateship'; they were the work of many contributors, now mostly forgotten, and they are now amusing only to those who are acquainted with Mason and Warton, and Lord Monboddo, who invented the human ourang-outang before Peacock, and cantankerous scholars like Sir John Hawkins, and Mrs. George Anne Bellamy, the impecunious actress. The prose parodies are the best, and anticipate the prose of the 'Anti-Jacobin,' while the verse of the probationary odes must have suggested part of the plan of the 'Rejected Addresses.' But it is in the 'Anti-Jacobin' (1799-1800) that we have the finest satire. It was written mainly by Canning, Frere, and George Ellis, and Canning was the finest wit among them.

The satire was directed against the stultification of ideas, the absurdities of literature and politics, and, unlike most satires, it has survived its occasion. The 'Poetry of the Anti-Jacobin' has been imitated ever since, by political and social and literary satirists, but it has never been excelled in its own way; and the salt in it has not yet lost its savour. It set a fashion, and one can trace Barham and Calverley in it, and later men. The needy knife-grinder's answer to the friend of humanity is one of the remembered lines of English poetry, and the inscription on Mrs. Brownrigg is one of the classics of parody. And, throughout, there are lyric high-spirits, and the dancers brandish real swords.

[1] *Poems*, 1823.

HENRY BOYD (1770–1832)[1]

HENRY BOYD (probably born about 1770; he died in 1832) is generally said to be the first translator of Dante into English verse. His 'Inferno' was published in 1785, and Hayley, in the voluminous notes to his 'Essay on Epic Poetry,' had already, in 1782, published a translation in terza rima of the first three cantos. 'I believe,' he says, 'no entire Canto of Dante has hitherto appeared in our language. . . . He has endeavoured to give the English reader an idea of Dante's peculiar manner, by adopting his triple rhyme; and he does not recollect that this mode of versification has ever appeared before in our language.' He adds, with his usual imperturbable impertinence, that he had been solicited to execute an entire translation of Dante: 'but the extreme inequality of this Poet would render such a work a very laborious undertaking.' From the specimens, we may be grateful that Hayley carried his translation no further. It is just possible, however, that Blake may have got his first lessons in Dante and Italian from these parallel columns in the two languages, at the later period when Hayley notes in one of his letters: 'Read Klopstock aloud to Blake.' For Hayley's version though not a poet's of a poet, is almost word for word (so that *fastidiosi verme* figures as 'fastidious worms'), and would have been useful as a lesson.

It was not only in his translation of Dante that Hayley anticipated Boyd, but in an analysis and partial rendering of the 'Araucana' of the Spanish poet Ercilla. Boyd's translation was finished, though apparently not printed, in 1805. Hayley, in the notes to this third epistle, gives a hundred pages to Ercilla, whom he finds more palatable than Dante. Like Dante, he finds him 'unequal, but, with all his defects, one of the

[1] (1) *Dante's 'Inferno,'* 1785. (2) *Poems, Chiefly Dramatic and Lyric*, 1793. (3) *Dante's 'Divina Commedia,'* 3 vols., 1802. (4) *Monti's 'Penance of Hugo, a Vision,'* 1805. (5) *The Woodman's Tale*, 1805. (6) *The Triumphs of Petrarch*, 1807.

most extraordinary and engaging characters in the poetical world.' 'This exalted character,' he says, 'is almost unknown in our country'; although his style, 'notwithstanding the restraint of rhyme, has frequently all the ease, the spirit, and the volubility of Homer.'

The metre used by Boyd in his Dante and Monti is a six-line stanza, formed of two couplets divided by two single lines; for Ariosto he used the Spenserian stanza, and for Petrarch, to his disadvantage, the heroic couplet. The Dante is not without merit; Boyd is always aware that he is translating a poet. Left alone, he wrote but mediocre verse, a temperance allegory called 'The Woodman's Tale,' a drama on David and Bathsheba, and some odes and epitaphs.

SIR WALTER SCOTT (1771–1832) [1]

SCOTT was twenty-six, the age of Keats at his death, before he wrote any original verse. He then wrote two poems to two ladies: one out of a bitter personal feeling, the other as a passing courtesy; neither out of any instinct for poetry. At twenty-four he had translated the fashionable 'Lenore' of Bürger; afterwards he translated Goethe's youthful play, 'Goetz von Berlichingen.' In 1802 he brought out the first two volumes of the 'Minstrelsy of the Scottish Border,' in which the resurrection of the old ballad literature, begun in 1765 by Percy's 'Reliques,' was carried on, and brought nearer to the interest of ordinary readers, who, in Scott's admirable introductions and notes, could find almost a suggestion of what

---

[1] (1) *The Eve of St. John*, 1800. (2) *Lay of the Last Minstrel*, 1805. (3) *Ballads and Lyrical Pieces*, 1806. (4) *Marmion*, 1808. (5) *The Lady of the Lake*, 1810. (6) *The Vision of Don Roderick*, 1811. (7) *Glenfinlas and other Ballads*, 1812. (8) *Rokeby*, 1813. (9) *The Bridal of Triermain*, 1813. (10) *The Lord of the Isles*, 1815. (11) *The Field of Waterloo*, 1815. (12) *Harold the Dauntless*, 1817. (13) *Miscellaneous Poems*, 1820. (14) *Halidon Hall*, 1822.

was to come in the Waverley Novels. The 'Lay of the Last Minstrel' was begun in 1802, and published, when Scott was thirty-four, in 1805. It was begun at the suggestion of the Duchess of Buccleugh, and continued to please her. Lockhart tells us: 'Sir John Stoddart's casual recitation of Coleridge's unfinished " Christabel " had fixed the music of that noble fragment in his memory; and it occurred to him that, by throwing the story of Gilpin Horner into somewhat similar cadence, he might produce such an echo of the later metrical romances as would seem to connect his conclusion of the primitive "Sir Tristrem" with the imitation of the popular ballad in the " Grey Brother" and the "Eve of St. John."' Its success was immediate, and for seven years Scott was the most popular poet in England. When the first two cantos of 'Childe Harold's Pilgrimage' appeared in 1812, there was a more popular poet in England, and Scott gave up writing verse, and, in the summer of 1814, took up and finished a story which he had begun in 1805, simultaneously with the publication of the 'Lay of the Last Minstrel,' — the story of 'Waverley.' The novelist died eleven years later, in 1825; but the poet committed suicide, with 'Harold the Dauntless,' in 1817.

Until he was thirty-one Scott was unconscious that he had any vocation except to be a 'half-lawyer, half-sportsman.' At forty-three he discovered, sooner than all the world, that he had mistaken his vocation; and with that discovery came the other one, that he had a vocation, which he promptly accepted, and in which, with his genius for success, he succeeded, as instantaneously, and more permanently. He was always able to carry the world with him, as he carried with him his little world of friends, servants, dogs, and horses. And how deeply rooted in the work itself was this persuasive and overcoming power is proved by the fact that 'Waverley' was published anonymously, and that the other novels were only known, for many years, as by the author of 'Waverley.' None of the prestige of the poet was handed over to the novelist. Scott attacked the public twice over, quite independently, and conquered it both times easily.

Success with the public of one's own day is, of course, no fixed test of a man's work; and, while it is indeed surprising that the same man could be, first the most popular poet and then the most popular novelist of his generation, almost of his century, there is no cause for surprise that the public should have judged, in the one case, justly, and in the other unjustly. The voice of the people, the voice of the gods of the gallery, howls for or against qualities which are never qualities of literature; and the admirers of Scott have invariably spoken of his verse in praise that would be justified if the qualities for which they praise it were qualities supplementary to the essentially poetic qualities: they form no substitute. First Scott, and then Byron, partly in imitation of Scott, appealed to the public of their day with poems which sold as only novels have sold before or since, and partly because they were so like novels. They were, what every publisher still wants, 'stories with plenty of action'; and the public either forgave their being in verse, or for some reason was readier than usual, just then, to welcome verse. It was Scott himself who was to give the novel a popularity which it had never had, even with Fielding and Richardson; and thus the novel had not yet flooded all other forms of literature for the average reader. Young ladies still cultivated ideals between their embroidery frames and their gilt harps. An intellectual democracy had not yet set up its own standards, and affected to submit art to its own tastes. This poetry, so like the most interesting, the most exciting prose, came at once on the wave of a fashion: the fashion of German ballads and 'tales of wonder' and of the more genuine early ballads of England and Scotland; and also with a new, spontaneous energy all its own. And it was largely Scott himself who had helped to make the fashion by which he profited.

The metrical romance, as it was written by Scott, was avowedly derived from the metrical romances of the Middle Ages,

SIR WALTER SCOTT

one of which Scott had edited and even concluded in the original metre: the 'Sir Tristrem' which he attributed to Thomas of Ercildoune. This 'Sir Tristrem' is but one among many fragmentary versions of a lost original, giving the greatest of all legends of chivalry, the legend of Tristan and Iseult. The most complete and the finest version which we have is the poem in octosyllabic couplets written in German by Gottfried of Strassburg at the beginning of 1200. In this poem we see what a metrical romance can be, and it is no injustice to Scott if we put it for a moment beside his attempts to continue that heroic lineage.

A friend of mine, an Irish poet, was telling me the other day that he had found himself, not long ago, in a small town in the West of Ireland, Athenry, a little lonely place, with its ruined castle; and having to wait there, because he had taken the wrong train, he took out of his pocket a prose version of Gottfried's poem, and sat reading it for some hours. And suddenly a pang went through him, with an acute sense of personal loss, as he said to himself: 'I shall never know the man who wrote that; I have never known any man who was such a gentleman.' The poem, with all its lengthy adventures, its lengthy comments, is full of the passion of beauty; the love of Tristan and Iseult is a grave thing, coming to them in one cup with death. 'Love,' says the poet, 'she who turneth the honey to gall, sweet to sour, and dew to flame, had laid her burden on Tristan and Iseult, and as they looked on each other their colour changed from white to red and from red to white, even as it pleased Love to paint them. Each knew the mind of the other, yet was their speech of other things.' And, at their last parting, Iseult can say: 'We two have loved and sorrowed in such true-fellowship unto this time, we should not find it over-hard to keep the same faith even to death. . . . Whatever land thou seekest, have a care for thyself — *my* life; for if I be robbed of that, then am I, *thy* life, undone. And myself, *thy* life, will I for thy sake, not for mine, guard with all care.

For thy body and thy life, that know I well, they rest on me.
Now bethink thee well of me, thy body, Iseult.' This, remember, is in a metrical romance, written in the metre of the
'Lady of the Lake.' Now turn to that poem, and read there:—

> 'Nor while on Ellen's faltering tongue
> Her filial welcomes crowded hung,
> Marked she, that fear (affection's proof)
> Still held a graceful youth aloof;
> No! not till Douglas named his name,
> Although that youth was Malcolm Graeme.'

Much has been claimed for Scott's poetry because of its appeal to unpoetical persons, who, in the nature of things, would be likely to take an interest in its subject-matter; and it has been thought remarkable that poetry composed, like much of 'Marmion,' in the saddle, by one 'through whose head a regiment of horse has been exercising since he was five years old,' should have seemed genuine to sportsmen and to soldiers. A striking anecdote told by Lockhart allows us to consider the matter very clearly. ' In the course of the day, when the " Lady of the Lake " first reached Sir Adam Ferguson, he was posted with his company on a point of ground exposed to the enemy's artillery, somewhere no doubt on the lines of Torres Vedras. The men were ordered to lie prostrate on the ground; while they kept that attitude, the captain, kneeling at the head, read aloud the description of the battle in Canto VI, and the listening soldiers only interrupted him by a joyous huzza when the French shot struck the bank close above them.' 'It is not often,' says Mr. Hutton in his 'Life of Scott,' 'that martial poetry has been put to such a test.' A test of what? Certainly not a test of poetry. An audience less likely to be critical, a situation less likely to induce criticism, can hardly be imagined. The soldiers would look for martial sentiments expressed with clear and matter-of-fact fervour. They would want no more and they would find no more; certainly no such intrusion of poetry as would have rendered the speech of

SIR WALTER SCOTT

Henry V before the battle of Agincourt but partially intelligible to them, though there Shakespeare is writing for once almost down to his audience. Scott's appeal is the appeal of prose, the thing and the feeling each for its own sake, with only that 'pleasurable excitement,' which Coleridge saw in the mere fact of metre, to give the illusion that one is listening to poetry.

Let me give an instance from another art. If, on his return to England, you had taken one of Sir Adam Ferguson's soldiers into a picture gallery, and there had been a Botticelli in one corner, and a Titian in another, and between two Bellini altar-pieces there had been a modern daub representing a battle, in which fire and smoke were clearly discernible, and charging horses rolled over on their riders, and sabres were being flourished in a way very like the trooper's way, is there much doubt which picture would go straight home to the soldier? There, it might be said, is a battle-piece, and the soldier goes up to it, examines it, admires it, swears that nothing more natural was ever painted. Is that a 'test' of the picture? Are we to say: this picture has been proved to be sincere, natural, approvable by one who has been through the incident which it records, and therefore (in spite of its total lack of every fine quality in painting) a good picture? No one, I think, would take the soldier's word for that: why should we take his word on a battle-piece which is not painted, but written?

A great many of the merits which people have accustomed themselves to see in Scott come from this kind of miscalculation. Thus, for instance, we may admit, with Mr. Palgrave, that Scott 'attained eminent success' in 'sustained vigour, clearness, and interest in narration.' 'If we reckon up the poets of the world,' continues Mr. Palgrave, 'we may be surprised to find how very few (dramatists not included) have accomplished this, and may be hence led to estimate Scott's rank in his art more justly.' But is not this rather a begging of the question? Scott wrote in metre, of which Hogg said acutely, that it had 'spirit and animation, and a sort of battle rapidity quite peculiar, but seldom any true melody,' and in some of his metrical narratives he attained 'sustained vigour, clearness, and interest in narration.' But is there anything except the metre to distinguish these stories in verse from what, as Scott himself afterwards showed, might have been much better if they had been told in prose? Until this has been granted, no merit in narration will mean anything at all, in a consideration of poetry as poetry; any more than the noughts which you may add to the left of your figure 1, in the belief that you are adding million to million.

The fact is, that skill in story-telling never made any man a poet, any more than skill in constructing a drama. Shakespeare is not, in the primary sense, a poet because he is a great dramatist; he is a poet as much in the sonnets as in the plays, but he is a poet who chose to be also a playwright, and in measuring his greatness we measure all that he did as a playwright along with all that he did as a poet; his especial greatness being seen by his complete fusion of the two in one. And it is the same thing in regard to story-telling. Look for a moment at our greatest narrative poet, Chaucer. Chaucer tells his stories much better, much more pointedly, concisely, with much more of the qualities of the best prose narrative, than Scott, who seems to tell his stories rather for boys than for men, with what he very justly called 'a hurried frankness of composition, which pleases soldiers, sailors, and young people of bold and active dispositions.' Chaucer is one of the most masculine of story-tellers, and if you read, not even one of the 'Canterbury Tales,' but a book of 'Troilus and Cressida,' you will find in it something of the quality which we applaud in Balzac: an enormous interest in life, and an absorption in all its details, because those details go to make up the most absorbing thing in the world. But in Chaucer all this is so much prose quality added to a consummate gift for poetry. Chaucer is first of all a poet; it is almost an accident, the accident of his period, that he wrote tales in verse. In the Elizabethan age he would have been a great dramatist, and he has all the qualities that go to the making of a great lyrical poet. His whole vision of life is the vision of the poet; his language and versification have the magic of poetry; he has wisdom, tenderness, a high gravity, tinged with illuminating humour; no one in our language has said more touching and beautiful things, straight out of his heart, about birds and flowers and grass; he has ecstasy. In addition to all this he can tell stories: that was the new life that he brought into the poetry of his time, rescuing us from 'the moral Gower' and much tediousness.

Now look at Scott: I do not say, ask Scott to be another Chaucer; but consider for a moment how much his admirers have to add to that all-important merit of 'sustained vigour, clearness, and interest in narration.' Well, it has been claimed, first and most emphatically, I think, by Sir Francis Doyle, that his poetry is 'Homeric.' Sir Francis Doyle says, in one of his lectures on Scott, given when Professor of Poetry at Oxford: 'Now, after the immortal ballads of Homer, there are no ballad poems so full of the spirit of Homer as those of Scott.' Homer, indeed, wrote of war and warriors, and so did Scott; Homer gives you vivid action, in swiftly moving verse, and so does Scott. But I can see little further resemblance, and I can see an infinite number of differences. No one, I suppose, would compare the pit-a-pat of Scott's octosyllabics with 'the deep-mouthed music' of the Homeric hexameter. But Sir Francis Doyle sees in the opening of the 'Lay of the Last Minstrel,' and not in this alone, 'the simple and energetic style of Homer.' Let me, then, take one single sentence from that battle in Canto VI of the 'Lady of the Lake,' and set against it a single sentence from one of the battle-pieces in the Iliad, in the prose translation of Mr. Lang. Here is Scott's verse: —

> 'Forth from the pass, in tumult driven,
> Like chaff before the wind of heaven,
> The archery appear;

> For life! for life! their flight they ply,
> And shriek, and shout, and battle-cry,
> And plaids and bonnets waving high,
> And broadswords flashing to the sky,
> Are maddening in the rear.'

And here is Homer in English prose: 'And as the gusts speed on, when shrill winds blow, on a day when dust lies thickest on the roads, even so their battle clashed together, and all were fain of heart to slay each other in the press with the keen bronze.' Need I say more than these extracts say for themselves? What commonness and what distinction, what puerility of effort and what repose in energy!

Then there is Scott's feeling for nature. The feeling was deep and genuine, and in a conversation with Washington Irving Scott expressed it more poignantly than he has ever done in his verse. 'When,' he said, 'I have been for some time in the rich scenery about Edinburgh, which is like ornamented garden land, I begin to wish myself back again among my own honest grey hills; and if I did not see the heather at least once a year, *I think I should die!*' There is a great deal of landscape painting in Scott's verse, and it has many good prose qualities: it is very definite, it is written 'with the eye on the object,' it is always sincere, in a certain sense; it is always felt sincerely. But it is not felt deeply, and it becomes either trite or generalised in its rendering into words. Take the description of Loch Katrine in the third canto of the 'Lady of the Lake,' the final passage which Ruskin quotes for special praise in that chapter of 'Modern Painters' which is devoted to a eulogy of Scott as the master of 'the modern landscape' in verse. It gives a pretty and, no doubt, accurate picture, but with what vagueness, triteness, or conventionality of epithet! We get one line in which there is no more than a statement, which may have its place in poetry: —

> 'The grey mist left the mountain side.'

In the next line we get a purely conventional rendering of

SIR WALTER SCOTT

what has evidently been both seen clearly and felt sympathetically: —

'The torrent showed its glistening pride.'

How false and insincere that becomes in the mere putting into words! And what a *cliché* is the simile for the first faint shadows on the lake at dawn: —

'In bright uncertainty they lie,
Like future joys to Fancy's eye.'

Even in better landscape work, like the opening of the first introduction to 'Marmion,' how entirely without magic is the observation, how superficial a notation of just what every one would notice in the scenery before him! To Ruskin, I know, all this is a part of what he calls Scott's unselfishness and humility, 'in consequence of which Scott's enjoyment of Nature is incomparably greater than that of any other poet I know.' Enjoyment, perhaps; but we are concerned, in poetry, with what a poet has made out of his enjoyment. Scott puts down in words exactly what the average person feels. Now it is the poet's business to interpret, illuminate, or at the least to evoke in a more exquisite form, all that the ordinary person is capable of feeling vaguely, by way of enjoyment. Until the poet has transformed enjoyment into ecstasy there can be no poetry. Scott's genuine love of nature, so profound in feeling, as his words to Washington Irving testify, was never able to translate itself into poetry; it seemed to become tongue-tied in metre.

And, also, there was in Scott a love of locality, which was perhaps more deeply rooted in him than his love of nature, just as his love of castles and armour and the bricabrac of mediævalism which filled his brain and his house was more deeply rooted than his love of the Middle Ages. 'If,' said Coleridge to Payne Collier, 'I were called upon to form an opinion of Mr. Scott's poetry, the first thing I would do would be to take away all his names of old castles, which rhyme very prettily, and read very picturesquely; next, I would exclude the mention of all nunneries, abbeys, and priories, and I should then see what would be the residuum — how much poetry would remain.' In all these things there was personal sincerity; Scott was following his feeling, his bias; but it has to be determined how far, and in how many instances, when he said nature he meant locality, and when he said chivalry or romance, he meant that 'procession of my furniture, in which old swords, bows, targets, and lances made a very conspicuous show,' on the way to Abbotsford.

Ruskin's special praise of Scott, in his attitude toward nature, is that Scott did not indulge in 'the pathetic fallacy' of reading one's own feelings into the aspect of natural things. This, in the main, is true, in spite of those little morals which Scott attaches to what he sees. But it is hardly more than a negative merit, at the best; and it is accompanied by no intimacy of insight, no revealing passion; aspects are described truthfully, and with sympathy, and that is all.

Throughout the whole of his long poems, and throughout almost the whole of his work in verse, Scott remains an improviser in rhyme, not a poet. But in a few of the songs contained in the novels, songs written after he had practically given up writing verse, flickering touches of something very like poetry are from time to time seen. In one song of four stanzas, 'Proud Maisie,' published in 1818 in the 'Heart of Midlothian,' Scott seems to me to have become a poet. In this poem, which is like nothing else he ever wrote, some divine accident has brought all the diffused poetical feeling of his nature to a successful birth. Landor, who seems to have overlooked this perfect lyric, thought there was one line of genuine poetry in Scott's verse, which he quotes from an early poem on Helvellyn. But I cannot feel that this line is more than a pathetic form of rhetoric. In 'Proud Maisie' we get, for once, poetry.

For the rest, all Scott's verse is written for boys, and boys, generation after generation, will love it with the same freshness of response. It has adventure, manliness, bright landscape, fighting, the obvious emotions; it is like a gallop across the moors in a blithe wind; it has plenty of story, and is almost as easily read as if it were prose. The taste for it may well be outgrown with the first realisation of why Shakespeare is looked upon as the supreme poet. Byron usually follows Scott in the boy's head, and drives out Scott, as that infinitely greater, though imperfect, force may well do. Shelley often completes the disillusion. But it is well, perhaps, that there should be a poet for boys, and for those grown-up people who are most like boys; for those, that is, to whom poetry appeals by something in it which is not the poetry.

JAMES MONTGOMERY (1771-1854) [1]

THROUGHOUT Montgomery's too copious work, which varies from being almost or quite good to being scarcely existent, there is a thin but natural stream of poetical feeling, not enough to make him a considerable poet, but setting him apart from such versifiers as his namesake, Robert Montgomery, and other pious companions, such as Kirke White. It was part of Montgomery's pride to realise that he had not merely aimed at being a poet, and it is to the credit of his sincerity that he should have realised the fact as well as the intention. All through his life he was a fighter, not only in his poems, on behalf of freedom and justice. His poem on 'The West Indies,' though indignation, as he admitted, 'gave to the versification the character of loud public speaking,' is as fervid as Whittier; and the later 'Climbing Boy's Soliloquies,' had they been much shorter, would have had real merit of a

[1] (1) *The Ocean*, 1805. (2) *The Wanderer of Switzerland*, 1806.
(3) *The West Indies*, 1809. (4) *The World before the Flood*, 1812.
(5) *Greenland*, 1819. (6) *The Pelican Island*, 1826. (7) *Hymns*, 1853.
(8) *Selected Works*, 1841.

natural human kind. It was Montgomery who edited 'The Chimney-Sweepers' Annual,' to which Lamb sent Blake's poem as well as his own. It is with truth that he says of these and other poems: 'It appealed to universal principles, to imperishable affections, to primary elements of our common nature.' He says further: 'My small plot of ground is no more than Naboth's vineyard to Ahab's Kingdom; but it is my own, it is no copyhold; I borrowed it, I leased it, from none. . . . The secret of my moderate success, I consider to have been the right direction of my abilities to right objects.'

Now here there is perhaps a certain confusion in the mind between what concerns a right object and a successful poem. And is this small plot of ground so entirely unmortgaged as we are assured? Various influences are to be seen: the influences of Cowper, of Wordsworth's 'Lyrical Ballads,' of whatever was best in Southey. The simple humour of such a poem as the 'Soliloquy of a Water-Wagtail' suggests Southey; the fine qualities of 'The Common Lot' are akin, by the prose side, to Wordsworth, of whom it has the grave speech, without the unaccountable poetry. There are other such poems which may well still have their appeal to the audience from whom he looked for remembrance, 'the young, the fair, and the devout'; poems which are as full of pleasant thought and fancy as the dialogues of 'Birds,' and at times with something of the prim meditation of Matthew Arnold. Thought, of a carefully religious kind, there always is, and it is genuine, touched with a sense of beauty and meaning in visible things, to which he is sometimes able to give adequate expression in a lyric, but which is lost or diluted in the long poems on which he probably supposed that his fame would rest: 'The World before the Flood,' 'Greenland,' 'The Pelican Island.' Much of the moralising has come to weary us, and the smooth cadences seem to have been picked out on the keyboard of an early pianoforte. There is something in the whole form, easy and natural as it generally is, that has a little the air of a thing remembered rather than newly made. Here, for instance, is the typical Montgomery: —

> 'The Dead are like the stars by day;
> Withdrawn from mortal eye,
> But not extinct, they hold their way
> In glory through the sky.'

Thus, it is with no surprise that we find his most satisfying work in his translation of the Psalms in the form of hymns. They have been adopted, I believe, for congregational singing by the churches of all denominations. Nothing could be better suited for the purpose than, for instance, the version of Psalm LXXVI, 'Hail to the Lord's anointed.' I do not say that anything like justice is done to the great poetry of the original, as we read it in the incomparable prose of the English Bible. The greatest of English poets never has done and never will do that. But, in such renderings as these, done for singing, there is a swiftness, an easy flow, together with a real fidelity to the original, which it is unusual to find in professedly pious work. To see how easily the attempt to deal with Biblical material, whether in the form of translation or adaptation, can turn to rhetoric, make-believe, or some other sort of insincerity, we need only look at the experiments of Moore and all but the best of Byron's. Montgomery does his useful pedestrian work competently.

MRS. TIGHE (1772-1810) [1]

MRS. TIGHE was one of the most famous of the women poets of her period. She is chiefly remembered now because the very early Keats seems to have thought her a poet almost worth imitating. But not long after he could say: 'Mrs. Tighe and Beattie once delighted me — now I see through them and can find nothing in them or weakness, and yet how many they still delight.' Her chief and most popular composition was a

[1] *Psyche; or the Legend of Love*, 1805, 1811.

'Psyche,' done at a great distance after Apuleius, but not without a kind of fanciful female prettiness. The luxury of her picture-painting, the smoothness of her Spenserian stanzas, her fluent feeling, —

> 'And all that can the female heart delight,'

had a natural attraction for an audience which began with Moore and ended with Mrs. Hemans.

HENRY FRANCIS CARY (1772–1844) [1]

HENRY FRANCIS CARY, a busy man of letters in his time, is remembered by only one of his many excellent translations, the still unsurpassed version of the Divine Comedy of Dante. But there is real merit in the translation of the 'Birds' of Aristophanes, which, for its speed and its good homely burlesque English words, has its place somewhere between Mitchell and Frere. Better still are the translations from 'Early French Poets,' from Marot to Gringoire, for the most part in the metres of the original. The book has not been replaced since, and should be reprinted for its choice anthology, in French and English, and its well aware and sympathetic narrative of poets who are hardly better known now than then. Cary shows the true translator's energy, agility, and quick sense of words and rhythms, and without being exactly a poet he conveys from one language to another a great deal more than mere substance or mere form. Who, before Rossetti, could have done Villon so well into English verse?

> 'Where is Heloise the wise,
> For whom Abelard was fain,
> Mangled in such cruel wise,
> To turn a monk instead of man?'

[1] (1) *Ode to Lord Heathfield*, 1787. (2) *Poems*, 1788. (3) *Sonnets and Odes*, 1788. (4) *Ode to General Kosciusko*, 1797. (5) *Inferno of Dante*, 1805. (6) *The Vision; or Hell, Purgatory, and Paradise, of Dante Alighieri*, 3 vols., 1814. (7) *Pindar*, 1824. (8) *Birds of Aristophanes*, 1824. (9) *The Early French Poets*, 1846.

The only lines which he attempts from another ballad have the strong, direct, faithful quality of his Dante. I give the best of them: —

'As to our flesh, which once too well we fed,
That now is rotten quite, and mouldered;
And we, the bones, do turn to dust and clay.
None laugh at us that are so ill bested,
But pray ye God to do our sins away.'

Cary published the first part of his translation of what he called 'The Vision; or, Hell, Purgatory, and Paradise,' in 1805, and the whole trilogy in 1814. To translate Dante is an impossible thing, for to do it would demand, as the first requirement, a concise and luminous style equal to Wordsworth at his best, as when he said (it should have been said of Dante): —

'Thy soul was like a star, and dwelt apart.'

The style and cadence of Dante were beyond the best skill of Cary; but what he did was to turn the Italian poem into an English one, to a certain degree Miltonic, but faithful to the simplicity of the words and turns of speech in the original. Only the complete version of Cary, and the daring experiment of Dr. Shadwell, who has rendered the 'Purgatorio' into the metre of Marvell's great ode, have succeeded in the one thing most necessary: that a poem should not cease to be a poem on being transferred into another language. Cary's great task, which he fulfilled, was to do this service to Dante and to England.

SAMUEL TAYLOR COLERIDGE (1772–1834) [1]

IN one of Rossetti's invaluable notes on poetry, he tells us that to him 'the leading point about Coleridge's work is its human love.' We may remember Coleridge's own words: —

[1] (1) *The Fall of Robespierre*, 1794. (2) *Poems on Various Subjects* (together with four poems by Charles Lamb), 1796. (3) *Ode on the Departing Year*, 1796. (4) *Poems by S. T. Coleridge*, Second Edition (together

'To be beloved is all I need,
And whom I love I love indeed.'

Yet love, though it is the word which he uses of himself, is not really what he himself meant when using it, but rather an affectionate sympathy, in which there seems to have been little element of passion. Writing to his wife, during that first absence in Germany, whose solitude tried him so much, he laments that there is 'no one to love.' 'Love is the vital air of my genius,' he tells her, and adds: 'I am deeply convinced that if I were to remain a few years among objects for whom I had no affection, I should wholly lose the powers of intellect.'

With this incessant, passionless sensibility, it was not unnatural that his thirst for friendship was stronger than his need of love; that to him friendship was hardly distinguishable from love. Throughout all his letters there is a series of causeless explosions of emotion, which it is hardly possible to take seriously, but which, far from being insincere, is really, no doubt, the dribbling overflow of choked-up feelings, a sort of moral leakage. It might be said of Coleridge, in the phrase which he used of Nelson, that he was 'heart-starved.' Tied for life to a woman with whom he had not one essential sympathy, the whole of his nature was put out of focus; and perhaps nothing but 'the joy of grief,' and the terrible and fettering power of luxuriating over his own sorrows, and tracing them to first principles, outside himself or in the depths of his subconsciousness, gave him the courage to support that long ever-present divorce.

with Poems by Charles Lamb and Charles Lloyd), 1797. (5) *Fears in Solitude*, 1798. (6) *The Piccolomini*, or the First Part of *Wallenstein*. Translated from the German of Friedrich von Schiller, 1800. (7) *Poems*. Third Edition, 1803. (8) *Remorse*, 1813. (9) *Christabel: Kubla Khan, a Vision: The Pains of Sleep*, 1816. (10) *Sibylline Leaves*: a Collection of Poems, 1817. (11) *Zapolya*, 1817. (12) *Poetical Works*, 3 vols., 1828, 1829, 1834. (13) *Poems*, 1848. (14) *Poems*, edited by Derwent and Sara Coleridge, 1852 (1870). (15) *Dramatic Works*, 1852. (16) *Poetical and Dramatic Works*, 4 vols., 1877. (17) *Poetical Works*, edited by J. Dykes Campbell, 1899.

Both for his good and evil, he had never been able to endure emotion without either diluting or intensifying it with thought, and with always self-conscious thought. He uses identically the same words in writing his last, deeply moved letter to Mary Evans, and in relating the matter to Southey. He cannot get away from words; coming as near to sincerity as he can, words are always between him and his emotion. Hence his over-emphasis, his rhetoric of humility. In 1794 he writes to his brother George: 'Mine eyes gush out with tears, my heart is sick and languid with the weight of unmerited kindness.' Nine days later he writes to his brother James: 'My conduct towards you, and towards my other brothers, has displayed a strange combination of madness, ingratitude, and dishonesty. But you forgive me. May my Maker forgive me! May the time arrive when I shall have forgiven myself!'. Here we see both what he calls his 'gangrened sensibility' and a complete abandonment to the feelings of the moment. It is always a self-conscious abandonment, during which he watches himself with approval, and seems to be saying: 'Now that is truly "feeling"!' He can never concentrate himself on any emotion; he swims about in floods of his own tears. With so little sense of reality in anything, he has no sense of the reality of direct emotion, but is preoccupied, from the moment of the first shock, in exploring it for its universal principle, and then flourishes it almost in triumph at what he has discovered. This is not insincerity; it is the metaphysical, analytical, and parenthetic mind in action. 'I have endeavoured to feel what I ought to feel,' he once significantly writes.

Coleridge had many friends, to some of whom, as to Lamb, his friendship was the most priceless thing in life; but the friendship which meant most to him, not only as a man, but as a poet, was the friendship with Wordsworth and with Dorothy Wordsworth. 'There is a sense of the word Love,' he wrote to Wordsworth in 1812, 'in which I never felt it but to you and one of your household.' After his quarrel in that year he has 'an agony of weeping.' 'After fifteen years of such religious, almost superstitious idolatry and self-sacrifice!' he laments. Now it was during his first, daily companionship with the Wordsworths that he wrote almost all his greatest work. The 'Ancient Mariner' and 'Christabel' were both written in a kind of rivalry with Wordsworth; and the 'Ode on Dejection' was written after four months' absence from him, in the first glow and encouragement of a return to that one inspiring comradeship. Wordsworth was the only poet among his friends whom he wholly admired, and Wordsworth was more exclusively a poet, more wholly absorbed in thinking poetry and thinking about poetry, and in a thoroughly practical way, than almost any poet who has ever lived. It was not only for his solace in life that Coleridge required sympathy; he needed the galvanising of continual intercourse with a poet, and with one to whom poetry was the only thing of importance. Coleridge, when he was by himself, was never sure of this; there was his *magnum opus*, the revelation of all philosophy; and he sometimes has doubts of the worth of his own poetry. Had Coleridge been able to live uninterruptedly in the company of the Wordsworths, even with the unsympathetic wife at home, the opium in the cupboard, and the *magnum opus* on the desk, I am convinced that we should have had for our reading to-day all those poems which went down with him into silence.

What Coleridge lacked was what theologians call a 'saving belief' in Christianity, or else a strenuous intellectual immorality. He imagined himself to believe in Christianity, but his belief never realised itself in effective action, either in the mind or in conduct, while it frequently clogged his energies by weak scruples and restrictions which were but so many internal irritations. He calls upon the religion which he has never firmly apprehended to support him under some misfortune of his own making; it does not support him, but he finds excuses for his weakness in what seem to him its promises of help. Coleridge was not strong enough to be a Christian, and he was not strong enough to rely on the impulses of his own nature, and to turn his failings into a very actual kind of success. When Blake said, 'If the fool would persist in his folly he would become wise,' he expressed a profound truth which Nietzsche and others have done little more than amplify. There is nothing so hopeless as inert or inactive virtue: it is a form of life grown putrid, and it turns into poisonous, decaying matter in the soul. If Coleridge had been more callous towards what he felt to be his duties, if he had not merely neglected them, as he did, but justified himself for neglecting them, on any ground of intellectual or physical necessity, or if he had merely let them slide without thought or regret, he would have been more complete, more effectual, as a man, and he might have achieved more finished work as an artist.

To Coleridge there was as much difficulty in belief as in action, for belief is itself an action of the mind. He was always anxious to believe anything that would carry him beyond the limits of time and space, but it was not often that he could give more than a speculative assent to even the most improbable of creeds. Always seeking fixity, his mind was too fluid for any anchor to hold in it. He drifted from speculation to speculation, often seeming to forget his aim by the way, in almost the collector's delight over the curiosities he had found in passing. On one page of his letters he writes earnestly to the atheist Thelwall in defence of Christianity; on another page we find him saying, 'My Spinosism (if Spinosism it be, and i' faith 't is very like it)'; and then comes the solemn assurance: 'I am a Berkeleyan.' Southey, in his rough, uncomprehending way, writes: 'Hartley was ousted by Berkeley, Berkeley by Spinoza, and Spinoza by Plato; when last I saw him Jacob Behmen had some chance of coming in. The truth is that he plays with systems'; so it seemed to Southey, who could see no better. To Coleridge all systems were of importance, because in every system there was its own measure of truth. He was always setting his mind to think about itself, and felt that he worked both hard and well if he had gained a clearer glimpse into that dark cavern. 'Yet I have not been altogether idle,' he writes in December, 1800, 'having in my own conceit gained great light into several parts of the human mind which have hitherto remained either wholly unexplained or most falsely explained.' In March, 1801, he declares that he has 'completely extricated the notions of time and space.' 'This,' he says, 'I have *done ;* but I trust that I am about to do more — namely, that I shall be able to evolve all the five senses, and to state their growth and the causes of their difference, and in this evolvement to solve the process of life and consciousness.' He hopes that before his thirtieth year he will 'thoroughly understand the whole of Nature's works.' 'My opinion is this,' he says, defining one part at least of his way of approach to truth, 'that deep thinking is attainable only by a man of deep feeling, and that all truth is a species of revelation.' On the other hand, he assures us, speaking of that *magnum opus* which weighed upon him and supported him to the end of his life, 'the very object throughout from the first page to the last [is] to reconcile the dictates of common sense with the conclusions of scientific reasoning.'

This *magnum opus,* 'a work which should contain all knowledge and proclaim all philosophy, had,' says Mr. Ernest Coleridge, 'been Coleridge's dream from the beginning.' Only a few months before his death, we find him writing to John Sterling: 'Many a fond dream have I amused myself with, of your residing near me, or in the same house, and of preparing, with your and Mr. Green's assistance, my whole system for the press, as far as it exists in any *systematic* form; that is, beginning with the Propyleum, On the Power and Use of Words, comprising Logic, as the Canons of *Conclusion,* as the criterion of *Premises,* and lastly as the discipline and evolution of Ideas (and then the Methodus et Epochee, or the Disquisition on

God, Nature, and Man), the two first grand divisions of which, from the Ens super Ens to the *Fall*, or from God to Hades, and then from Chaos to the commencement of living organization, containing the whole of the Dynamic Philosophy, and the deduction of the Powers and Forces, are complete.' Twenty years earlier, he had written to Daniel Stuart that he was keeping his morning hours sacred to his 'most important Work, which is printing at Bristol,' as he imagined. It was then to be called 'Christianity, the one true Philosophy, or Five Treatises on the Logos, or Communicative Intelligence, natural, human, and divine.' Of this vast work only fragments remain, mostly unpublished: two large quarto volumes on logic, a volume intended as an introduction, a commentary on the Gospels and some of the Epistles, together with 'innumerable fragments of metaphysical and theological speculation.' But out of those fragments no system was ever to be constructed, though a fervent disciple, J. H. Green, devoted twenty-eight years to the attempt. 'Christabel' unfinished, the *magnum opus* unachieved: both were but parallel symptoms of a mind 'thought-bewildered' to the end, and bewildered by excess of light and by crowding energies always in conflict, always in escape.

Coleridge's search, throughout his life, was after the absolute, an absolute not only in thought, but in all human relations, in love, friendship, faith in man, faith in God, faith in beauty; and while it was this profound dissatisfaction with less than the perfect form of every art, passion, thought, or circumstance, that set him adrift in life, making him seem untrue to duty, conviction, and himself, it was this also that formed in him the double existence of the poet and the philosopher, each supplementing and interpenetrating the other. The poet and the philosopher are but two aspects of one reality; or rather, the poetic and the philosophic attitudes are but two ways of seeing. The poet who is not also a philosopher is like a flower without a root. Both seek the same infinitude;

one apprehending the idea, the other the image. One seeks truth for its beauty; the other finds beauty, an abstract, intellectual beauty, in the innermost home of truth. Poetry and metaphysics are alike a disengaging, for different ends, of the absolute element in things.

In Coleridge, metaphysics joined with an unbounded imagination, in equal flight from reality, from the notions of time and space. Each was an equal denial of the reality of what we call real things; the one experimental, searching, reasoning; the other a 'shaping spirit of imagination,' an embodying force. His sight was always straining into the darkness; and he has himself noted that from earliest childhood his 'mind was habituated to the Vast.' 'I never regarded my senses,' he says, 'as the criteria of my belief'; and 'those who have been led to the same truths step by step, through the constant testimony of their senses, seem to want a sense which I possess.' To Coleridge only mind existed, an eternal and an eternally active thought; and it was as a corollary to his philosophical conception of the universe that he set his mind to a conscious re-building of the world in space. His magic, that which makes his poetry, was but the final release in art of a winged thought fluttering helplessly among speculations and theories; it was the song of release.

De Quincey has said of Coleridge: 'I believe it to be notorious that he first began the use of opium, not as a relief from any bodily pains or nervous irritations — for his constitution was strong and excellent — but as a source of luxurious sensations.' Hartley Coleridge, in the biographical supplement to the 'Biographia Literaria,' replies with what we now know to be truth: 'If my Father sought more from opium than the mere absence of pain, I feel assured that it was not luxurious sensations or the glowing phantasmagoria of passive dreams; but that the power of the medicine might keep down the agitations of his nervous system, like a strong hand grasping the strings of some shattered lyre.' In 1795, that is, at the age of twenty-three, we find him taking laudanum; in 1796, he is taking it in large doses; by the late spring of 1801 he is under the 'fearful slavery,' as he was to call it, of opium. 'My sole sensuality,' he says of this time, 'was not to be in pain.' In a terrible letter addressed to Joseph Cottle in 1814 he declares that he was 'seduced to the *accursed* habit ignorantly'; and he describes 'the direful moment, when my pulse began to fluctuate, my heart to palpitate, and such a dreadful falling abroad, as it were, of my whole frame, such intolerable restlessness, and incipient bewilderment . . . for my case is a species of madness, only that it is a derangement, an utter impotence of the volition, and not of the intellectual faculties.' And, throughout, it is always the pains, never the pleasures, of opium that he registers. Opium took hold of him by what was inert in his animal nature, and not by any active sensuality. His imagination required no wings, but rather fetters; and it is evident that opium was more often a sedative than a spur to his senses.

The effect of opium on the normal man is to bring him into something like the state in which Coleridge habitually lived. The world was always a sufficiently unreal thing to him, facts more than remote enough, consequences unrelated to their causes; he lived in a mist, and opium thickened the mist to a dense yellow fog. Opium might have helped to make Southey a poet; it left Coleridge the prisoner of a cobweb-net of dreams. What he wanted was some astringent force in things, to tighten, not to loosen, the always expanding and uncontrollable limits of his mind. Opium did but confirm what the natural habits of his constitution had bred in him: an overwhelming indolence, out of which the energies that still arose intermittently were no longer flames, but the escaping ghosts of flame, mere black smoke.

At twenty-four, in a disinterested description of himself for the benefit of a friend whom he had not yet met, he declares, 'The walk of the whole man indicates *indolence capable of energies.*' It was that walk which Carlyle afterwards described, unable to keep to either side of the garden-path. 'The moral obligation is to me so very strong a stimulant,' Coleridge writes to Crabb Robinson, 'that in nine cases out of ten it acts as a narcotic. The blow that should rouse, *stuns* me.' He plays another variation on the ingenious theme in a letter to his brother: 'Anxieties that stimulate others infuse an additional narcotic into my mind. . . . Like some poor labourer, whose night's sleep has but imperfectly refreshed his over-wearied frame, I have sate in drowsy uneasiness, and doing nothing have thought what a deal I have to do.' His ideal, which he expressed in 1797 in a letter to Thelwall, and, in 1813, almost word for word, in a poem called 'The Night-Scene,' was, 'like the Indian Vishnu, to float about along an infinite ocean cradled in the flower of the Lotus, and wake once in a million years for a few minutes just to know that I was going to sleep a million years more.' Observe the effect of the desire for the absolute, reinforced by constitutional indolence, and only waiting for the illuminating excuse of opium.

From these languors, and from their consequences, Coleridge found relief in conversation, for which he was always ready, while he was far from always ready for the more precise mental exertion of writing. 'Oh, how I wish to be talking, not writing,' he cries in a letter to Southey in 1803, 'for my mind is so full, that my thoughts stifle and jam each other.' And, in 1816, in his first letter to Gillman, he writes, more significantly, 'The stimulus of conversation suspends the terror that haunts my mind; but when I am alone, the horrors that I have suffered from laudanum, the degradation, the blighted utility, almost overwhelm me.' It was along one avenue of this continual escape from himself that Coleridge found himself driven (anywhere, away from action) towards what grew to be the main waste of his life. Hartley Coleridge, in the preface to 'Table-Talk,' has told us eloquently how, 'throughout a long-drawn summer's day, would this man talk to you in low, equable, but clear and musical tones, concerning things human and divine'; we know that Carlyle found him 'unprofitable, even tedious,' and wished 'to worship him, and toss him in a blanket'; and we have the vivid reporting of Keats, who tells us that, on his one meeting with Coleridge, 'I walked with him at his alderman-after-dinner pace, for near two miles, I suppose. In those two miles he broached a thousand things. Let me see if I can give you a list—nightingales — poetry— on poetical sensation — metaphysics — different genera and species of dreams — nightmare — a dream accompanied with a sense of touch — single and double touch — a dream related — first and second consciousness — the difference explained between will and volition — so say metaphysicians from a want of smoking — the second consciousness — monsters — the Kraken — mermaids — Southey believes in them — Southey's belief too much diluted — a ghost story — Good-morning — I heard his voice as he came towards me — I heard it as he moved away — I had heard it all the interval — if it may be called so.' It may be that we have had no more wonderful talker, and, no doubt, the talk had its reverential listeners, its disciples; but to cultivate or permit disciples is itself a kind of waste, a kind of weakness; it requires a very fixed and energetic indolence to become, as Coleridge became, a vocal utterance, talking for talking's sake.

But beside talking, there was lecturing, with Coleridge a scarcely different form of talk; and it is to this consequence of a readiness to speak and a reluctance to write that we owe much of his finest criticism, in the imperfectly recorded 'Lectures on Shakespeare.' Coleridge as a critic is not easily to be summed up. What may first surprise us, when we begin to look into his critical opinions, is the uncertainty of his judgements in regard to his own work, and to the work of his friends; the curious bias which a feeling or an idea, affection or a philosophical theory, could give to his mind. His admiration for Southey, his consideration for Sotheby, perhaps in a less degree his unconquerable esteem for Bowles, together with something very like adulation of Wordsworth, are all instances of a certain loss of the sense of proportion. He has left us no penetrating criticisms of Byron, of Shelley, or of Keats; and in a very interesting letter about Blake, written in 1818, he is unable to take the poems merely as poems, and chooses among them with a scrupulous care 'not for the want of innocence in the poem, but from the too probable want of it in many readers.'

Lamb, concerned only with individual things, looks straight at them, not through them, seeing them implacably. His notes to the selections from the Elizabethan dramatists are the surest criticisms that we have in English; they go to the roots. Coleridge's critical power was wholly exercised upon elements and first principles; Lamb showed an infinitely keener sense of detail, of the parts of the whole. Lamb was unerring on definite points, and could lay his finger on flaws in Coleridge's work that were invisible to Coleridge; who, however, was unerring in his broad distinctions, in the philosophy of his art.

'The ultimate end of criticism,' said Coleridge, 'is much more to establish the principles of writing than to furnish rules how to pass judgement on what has been written by others.' And for this task he had an incomparable foundation: imagination, insight, logic, learning, almost every critical quality united in one; and he was a poet who allowed himself to be a critic. Those pages of the 'Biographia Literaria' in which he defines and distinguishes between imagination and fancy, the researches into the abstract entities of poetry in the course of an examination of Wordsworth's theories and of the popular objections to them, all that we have of the lectures on Shakespeare, into which he put an illuminating idolatry, together with notes and jottings preserved in the 'Table-Talk,' 'Anima Poetæ,' the 'Literary Remains,' and on the margins of countless books, contain the most fundamental criticism of literature that has ever been attempted, fragmentary as the attempt remains. 'There is not a man in England,' said Coleridge with truth, 'whose thoughts, images, words, and erudition have been published in larger quantities than *mine;* though I must admit, not *by*, nor *for*, myself.' He claimed, and rightly, as his invention, a 'science of reasoning and judging concerning the productions of literature, the characters and measures of public men, and the events of nations, by a systematic subsumption of them, under principles deduced from the nature of man,' which, as he says, was unknown before the year 1795. He is the one philosophical critic who is also a poet, and thus he is the one critic who instinctively knows his way through all the intricacies of the creative mind.

Most of his best criticism circles around Shakespeare; and he took Shakespeare almost as frankly in the place of Nature, or of poetry. He affirms, 'Shakespeare knew the human mind, and its most minute and intimate workings, and he never introduces a word, or a thought, in vain or out of place.' This granted (and to Coleridge it is essential that it should be granted, for in less than the infinite he cannot find space in which to use his wings freely) he has only to choose and define, to discover and to illuminate. In the 'myriad-minded man,' in his 'oceanic mind,' he finds all the material that he needs for the making of a complete æsthetic. Nothing with Coleridge ever came to completion; but we have only to turn over the pages about Shakespeare, to come upon fragments worth more than any one else's finished work. I find the whole secret of Shakespeare's way of writing in these sentences: 'Shakespeare's intellectual action is wholly unlike that of Ben Jonson or Beaumont and Fletcher. The latter see the totality of a sentence or passage, and then project it entire. Shakespeare goes on creating, and evolving B out of A, and C out of B, and so on, just as a serpent moves, which makes a fulcrum of its own body, and seems forever twisting and untwisting its own strength.' And here are a few axioms: 'The grandest efforts of poetry are where the imagination is called forth, not to produce a distinct form, but a strong working of the mind'; or, in other words, 'The power of poetry is, by a single word perhaps, to instil that energy into the mind which compels the imagination to produce the picture.' 'Poetry is the identity of all other knowledges,' 'the blossom and fragrance of all human knowledge, human thoughts, human passions, emotions, language.' 'Verse is in itself a music, and the natural symbol of that union of passion with thought and pleasure, which constitutes the essence of all poetry'; 'a more than usual state of emotion, with more than usual order,' as he has elsewhere defined it. And, in one of his spoken counsels, he says: 'I wish our clever young poets would remember my homely definitions of prose and poetry; that is, prose — words in their best order; poetry — the best words in the best order.'

Unlike most creative critics, or most critics who were creative artists in another medium, Coleridge, when he was writing criticism, wrote it wholly for its own sake, almost as if it were a science. His prose is rarely of the finest quality as prose writing. Here and there he can strike out a phrase at red-heat, as when he christens Shakespeare 'the one Proteus of the fire and flood'; or he can elaborate subtly, as when he notes the judgement of Shakespeare, observable in every scene of the 'Tempest,' 'still preparing, still inviting, and still gratifying, like a finished piece of music'; or he can strike us with the wit of the pure intellect, as when he condemns certain work for being 'as trivial in thought and yet enigmatic in expression, as if Echo and the Sphinx had laid their heads together to construct it.' But for the most part it is a kind of thinking aloud, and the form is wholly lost in the pursuit of ideas. With his love for the absolute, why is it that he does not seek after an absolute in words considered as style, as well as in words considered as the expression of thought? In his finest verse Coleridge has the finest style perhaps in English; but his prose is never quite reduced to order from its tumultuous amplitude or its snake-like involution. Is it that he values it only as a medium, not as an art? His art is verse, and this he dreads, because of its too mortal closeness to his heart; the prose is a means to an end, not an end in itself.

The poetry of Coleridge, though it is closely interwoven with the circumstances of his life, is rarely made directly out of those circumstances. To some extent this is no doubt explained by a fact to which he often refers in his letters, and which, in his own opinion, hindered him not only from writing about himself in verse, but from writing verse at all. 'As to myself,' he writes in 1802, 'all my poetic genius . . . is gone,' and he attributes it 'to my long and exceedingly severe metaphysical investigations, and these partly to ill-health, and partly to private afflictions which rendered any subjects, immediately connected with feeling, a source of pain and disquiet to me.' In 1818 he writes: 'Poetry is out of the question. The attempt would only hurry me into that sphere of acute feelings from which abstruse research, the mother of self-oblivion, presents an asylum.' But theory worked with a natural tendency in keeping him for the most part away from any attempt to put his personal emotions into verse. 'A sound promise of genius,' he considered, 'is the choice of subjects very remote from the private interests and circumstances of the writer himself.' With only a few exceptions, the wholly personal poems, those actually written under a shock of emotion, are vague, generalised, turned into a kind of literature. The success of such a poem as the almost distressingly personal 'Ode on Dejection' comes from the fact that Coleridge has been able to project his personal feeling into an outward image, which becomes to him the type of dejection; he can look at it as at one of his dreams which become things; he can sympathise with it as he could never sympathise with his own undeserving self. And thus one stanza, perhaps the finest as poetry, becomes the biography of his soul: —

'There was a time when, though my path was rough,
  This joy within me dallied with distress,
And all misfortunes were but as the stuff
  Whence Fancy made me dream of happiness:
For hope grew round me, like the twining vine,
And fruits, and foliage, not my own, seemed mine.
But now afflictions bow me down to earth:
Nor care I though they rob me of my mirth;
  But oh! each visitation
Suspends what nature gave me at my birth,
  My shaping spirit of Imagination.
For not to think of what I needs must feel,
  But to be still and patient all I can,
And haply by abstruse research to steal
  From my own nature all the natural man —
  This was my sole resource, my only plan:
Till that which suits a part infects the whole,
And now is almost grown the habit of my soul.'

Elsewhere, in personal poems like 'Frost at Midnight,' and 'Fears in Solitude,' all the value of the poem comes from the delicate sensations of natural things which mean so much more to us, whether or not they did to him, than the strictly personal part of the matter. You feel that there he is only using the quite awake part of himself, which is not the essential one. He requires, first of all, to be disinterested, or at least not overcome by emotion; to be without passion but that of abstract beauty, in nature, or in idea; and then to sink into a quite lucid sleep, in which his genius came to him like some attendant spirit.

In the life and art of Coleridge, the hours of sleep seem to have been almost more important than the waking hours. 'My dreams became the substance of my life,' he writes, just after the composition of that terrible poem on 'The Pains of Sleep,' which is at once an outcry of agony, and a yet more disturbing vision of the sufferer with his fingers on his own pulse, his eyes fixed on his own hardly awakened eyes in the mirror. In an earlier letter, written at a time when he is trying to solve the problem of the five senses, he notes: 'The sleep which I have is made up of ideas so connected, and so little different from the operations of reason, that it does not afford me the due refreshment.' To Coleridge, with the help of opium, hardly required, indeed, there was no conscious division between day and night, between not only dreams and intuitions, but dreams and pure reason. And we find him, in almost all his great poems, frankly taking not only his substance, but his manner from dreams, as he dramatises them after a logic and a passion of their own. His technique is the transposition into his waking hours of the unconscious technique of dreams. It is a kind of verified inspiration, something which came and went, and was as little to be relied upon as the inspiration itself. On one side it was an exact science, but on the other a heavenly visitation. Count and balance syllables, work out an addition of the feet in the verse by the foot-rule, and you will seem to have traced every miracle back to its root in a natural product. Only, something, that is, everything, will have escaped you. As well dissect a corpse to find out the principles of life. That elusive something, that spirit, will be what distinguishes Coleridge's finest verse from the verse of, well, perhaps of every conscious artist in our language. For it is not, as in Blake, literally unconscious, and wavering on every breath of that unseen wind on which it floats to us; it is faultless; it is itself the wind which directs it, it steers its way on the wind, like a seagull poised between sky and sea, and turning on its wings as upon shifted sails.

This inspiration comes upon Coleridge suddenly, without warning, in the first uncertain sketch of 'Lewti,' written at twenty-two: and then it leaves him, without warning, until the great year 1797, three years later, when 'Christabel' and the 'Ancient Mariner' are begun. Before and after, Coleridge is seen trying to write like Bowles, like Wordsworth, like Southey, perhaps, to attain 'that impetuosity of transition and that precipitancy of fancy and feeling, which are the *essential* qualities of the sublimer Ode,' and which he fondly fancies that he has attained in the 'Ode on the Departing

Year,' with its one good line, taken out of his note-book. But here, in 'Lewti,' he has his style, his lucid and liquid melody, his imagery of moving light and the faintly veiled transparency of air, his vague, wildly romantic subject-matter, coming from no one knows where, meaning one hardly knows what; but already a magic, an incantation. 'Lewti' is a sort of preliminary study for 'Kubla Khan'; it, too, has all the imagery of a dream, with a breathlessness and awed hush, as of one not yet accustomed to be at home in dreams.

'Kubla Khan,' which was literally composed in sleep, comes nearer than any other existing poem to that ideal of lyric poetry which has only lately been systematised by theorists like Mallarmé. It has just enough meaning to give it bodily existence; otherwise it would be disembodied music. It seems to hover in the air, like one of the island enchantments of Prospero. It is music not made with hands, and the words seem, as they literally were, remembered. 'All the images,' said Coleridge, 'rose up before me as *things*, with a parallel production of the correspondent expressions.' Lamb, who tells us how Coleridge repeated it 'so enchantingly that it irradiates and brings heaven and elysian bowers into my parlor when he says or sings it to me,' doubted whether it would 'bear daylight.' It seemed to him that such witchcraft could hardly outlast the night. It has outlasted the century, and may still be used as a touchstone; it will determine the poetic value of any lyric poem which you place beside it. Take as many poems as you please, and let them have all the merits you please, their ultimate merit as poetry will lie in the degree of their approach to the exact, unconscious, inevitable balance of qualities in the poetic art of 'Kubla Khan.'

In the 'Ancient Mariner,' which it seems probable was composed before, and not after 'Kubla Khan,' as Coleridge's date would have us suppose, a new supernaturalism comes into poetry, which, for the first time, accepted the whole responsibility of dreams. The impossible, frankly accepted, with its own strict, inverted logic; the creation of a new atmosphere, outside the known world, which becomes as real as the air about us, and yet never loses its strangeness; the shiver that comes to us, as it came to the wedding-guest, from the simple good faith of the teller; here is a whole new creation, in subject, mood, and technique. Here, as in 'Kubla Khan,' Coleridge saw the images ' as *things* '; only a mind so overshadowed by dreams, and so easily able to carry on his sleep awake, could have done so; and, with such a mind, 'that willing suspension of disbelief for a moment, which constitutes poetic faith,' was literally forced upon him. 'The excellence aimed at,' says Coleridge, 'was to consist in the interesting of the affections by the dramatic truth of such emotions, as would naturally accompany such situations,' those produced by supernatural agency, 'supposing them real. And real in this sense they have been to every human being who, from whatever sense of delusion, has at any time believed himself under supernatural agency.' To Coleridge, whatever appealed vitally to his imagination was real; and he defended his belief philosophically, disbelieving from conviction in that sharp marking off of real from imaginary which is part of the ordinary attitude of man in the presence of mystery.

It must not be forgotten that Coleridge is never fantastic. The fantastic is a playing with the imagination, and Coleridge respects it. His intellect goes always easily as far as his imagination will carry it, and does not stop by the way to play tricks upon its bearer. Hence the conviction which he brings with him when he tells us the impossible. And then his style, in its ardent and luminous simplicity, flexible to every bend of the spirit which it clothes with flesh, helps him in the idiomatic translation of dreams. The visions of Swedenborg are literal translations of the imagination, and need to be retranslated. Coleridge is equally faithful to the thing seen and to the laws of that new world into which he has transposed it.

The 'Ancient Mariner' is the most sustained piece of imagination in the whole of English poetry; and it has almost every definable merit of imaginative narrative. It is the only poem I know which is all point and yet all poetry; because, I suppose, the point is really a point of mystery. It is full of simple, daily emotion, transported, by an awful power of sight, to which the limits of reality are no barrier, into an unknown sea and air; it is realised throughout the whole of its ghastly and marvellous happenings; and there is in the narrative an ease, a buoyancy almost, which I can only compare with the music of Mozart, extracting its sweetness from the stuff of tragedy; it presents to us the utmost physical and spiritual horror, not only without disgust, but with an alluring beauty. But in 'Christabel,' in the first part especially, we find a quality which goes almost beyond these definable merits. There is in it a literal spell, not acting along any logical lines, not attacking the nerves, not terrifying, not intoxicating, but like a slow, enveloping mist, which blots out the real world, and leaves us unchilled by any 'airs from heaven or blasts from hell,' but in the native air of some middle region. In these two or three brief hours of his power out of a lifetime, Coleridge is literally a wizard. People have wanted to know what 'Christabel' means, and how it was to have ended, and whether Geraldine was a vampire (as I am inclined to think) or had eyes in her breasts (as Shelley thought). They have wondered that a poem so transparent in every line should be, as a whole, the most enigmatical in English. But does it matter very much whether 'Christabel' means this or that, and whether Coleridge himself knew, as he said, how it was to end, or whether, as Wordsworth declared, he had never decided? It seems to me that Coleridge was fundamentally right when he said of the 'Ancient Mariner,' 'It ought to have had no more moral than the Arabian Nights' tale of the merchant's sitting down to eat dates by the side of a well, and throwing the shells aside, and lo! a genie starts up, and says he *must* kill the aforesaid merchant, because one of the date-shells had, it seems, put out the eye of the genie's son.' The 'Ancient Mariner,' if we take its moral meaning too seriously, comes near to being an allegory. 'Christabel,' as it stands, is a piece of pure witchcraft, needing no further explanation than the fact of its existence. Rossetti called Coleridge the Turner of poets, and indeed there is in Coleridge an aerial glitter which we find in no other poet, and in Turner only among painters. With him colour is always melted in atmosphere, which it shines through like fire within a crystal. It is liquid colour, the dew on flowers, or a mist of rain in bright sunshine. His images are for the most part derived from water, sky, the changes of weather, shadows of things rather than things themselves, and usually mental reflections of them. 'A poet ought not to pick Nature's pocket,' he said, and it is for colour and sound, in their most delicate forms, that he goes to natural things. He hears

'the merry nightingale
That crowds and hurries and precipitates
With fast thick warble his delicious notes';

and an ecstasy comes to him out of that natural music which is almost like that of his own imagination. Only music or strange effects of light can carry him swiftly enough out of himself, in the presence of visible or audible things, for that really poetic ecstasy. Then all his languor drops off from him, like a clogging garment.

The first personal merit which appears in his almost wholly valueless early work is a sense of colour. In a poem written at twenty-one he sees Fancy

'Bathed in rich amber-glowing floods of light,'

and next year the same colour reappears, more expressively, in a cloud,

'wholly bright,
With a rich and amber light.'

The two women in 'The Two Graves,' during a momentous pause, are found discussing whether the rays of the sun are green or amber; a valley is

> 'Tinged yellow with the rich departing light';

seen through corn at evening,

> 'The level sunshine glimmers with green light';

and there is the carefully observed

> 'western sky
> And its peculiar tint of yellow green.'

The 'Ancient Mariner' is full of images of light and luminous colour in sky and sea; Glycine's song in 'Zapolya' is the most glittering poem in our language, with a soft glitter like that of light seen through water. And Coleridge is continually endeavouring, as later poets have done on a more deliberate theory, to suffuse sound with colour or make colours literally a form of music; as in an early poem

> 'Where melodies round honey-dropping flowers,
> Footless and wild, like birds of Paradise,
> Nor pause, nor perch, hovering on untamed wing.'

With him, as with some of them, there is something pathological in this sensitiveness, and in a letter written in 1800 he says: 'For the last month I have been trembling on through sands and swamps of evil and bodily grievance. My eyes have been inflamed to a degree that rendered reading scarcely possible; and, strange as it seems, the act of mere composition, as I lay in bed, perceptibly affected them, and my voluntary ideas were every minute passing, more or less transformed into vivid spectra.'

Side by side with this sensitiveness to colour, or interfused with it, we find a similar, or perhaps a greater, sensitiveness to sound. Coleridge shows a greater sensitiveness to music than any English poet except Milton. The sonnet to Linley records his ecstatic responsiveness to music; Purcell's music, too, which he names with Palestrina's ('some madrigals which he heard at Rome') in the 'Table-Talk.' 'I have the intensest delight in music,' he says there, 'and can detect good from bad'; a rare thing among poets. In one of his letters he notes: 'I hear in my brain . . . sensations . . . of various degrees of pain, even to a strange sort of uneasy pleasure. . . . I hear in my brain, and still more in my stomach.' There we get the morbid physical basis of a sensitiveness to music which came to mean much to him. In a note referring to 'Christabel,' and to the reasons why it had never been finished, he says: 'I could write as good verse now as ever I did, if I were perfectly free from vexations, and were in the *ad libitum* hearing of fine music, which has a sensible effect in harmonizing my thoughts, and in animating and, as it were, lubricating my inventive faculty.' 'Christabel,' more than anything of Coleridge, is composed like music; you might set at the side of each section, especially of the opening, *largo, vivacissimo,* and, as the general expression signature, *tempo rubato.* I know no other verse in which the effects of music are so precisely copied in metre. Shelley, you feel, sings like a bird; Blake, like a child or an angel; but Coleridge certainly writes music.

The metre of the 'Ancient Mariner' is a re-reading of the familiar ballad-metre, in which nothing of the original force, swiftness or directness is lost, while a new subtlety, a wholly new music, has come into it. The metre of 'Christabel' is even more of an invention, and it had more immediate consequences. The poem was begun in 1797, and not published till 1816; but in 1801 Scott heard it recited, and in 1805, reproduced what he could of it in 'The Lay of the Last Minstrel' and the other metrical romances which, in their turn, led the way to Byron, who himself heard 'Christabel' recited in 1811. But the secret of Coleridge's instinct of melody and science of harmony was not discovered. Such ecstasy and such collectedness, a way of writing which seems to aim at nothing but the most precisely expressive simplicity, and yet sets the whole brain dancing to its tune, can hardly be indicated more exactly than in Coleridge's own words in reference to the Italian lyrists of the fifteenth and sixteenth centuries. They attained their aim, he says, 'by the avoidance of every word which a gentleman would not use in dignified conversation, and of every word and phrase which none but a learned man would use; by the studied position of words and phrases, so that not only each part should be melodious in itself, but contribute to the harmony of the whole, each note referring and conducing to the melody of all the foregoing and following words of the same period or stanza; and, lastly, with equal labour, the greater because unbetrayed, by the variation and various harmonies of their metrical movement.' These qualities we may indeed find in many of Coleridge's songs, part Elizabethan, part eighteenth century, in some of his infantile jingles, his exuberant comic verse (in which, however, there are many words 'which a gentleman would not use') and in a poem like 'Love,' which has suffered as much indiscriminate praise as Raphael's Madonnas, which it resembles in technique and sentiment, and in its exquisite perfection of commonplace, its *tour de force* of an almost flawless girlishness. But in 'Christabel' the technique has an incomparable substance to work upon; substance at once simple and abnormal, which Coleridge required, in order to be at his best.

It has been pointed out by the profoundest poetical critic of our time that the perfection of Coleridge's style in poetry comes from an equal balance of the clear, somewhat matter-of-fact qualities of the eighteenth century with the remote, imaginative qualities of the nineteenth century. 'To please me,' said Coleridge in 'Table-Talk,' ' a poem must be either music or sense.' The eighteenth-century manner, with its sense only just coupled with a kind of tame and wingless music, may be seen quite by itself in the early song from 'Robespierre': —

> 'Tell me, on what holy ground
> May domestic peace be found.'

Here there is both matter and manner, of a kind; in 'The Kiss' of the same year, with its one exquisite line, —

> 'The gentle violence of joy,'

there is only the liquid glitter of manner. We get the ultimate union of eighteenth and nineteenth century qualities in 'Work without Hope,' and in 'Youth and Age,' which took nine years to bring into its faultless ultimate form. There is always a tendency in Coleridge to fall back on the eighteenth-century manner, with its scrupulous exterior neatness, and its comfortable sense of something definite said definitely whenever the double inspiration flags, and matter and manner do not come together. 'I cannot write without a *body of thought*,' he said, at a time before he had found himself or his style; and he added: 'Hence my poetry is crowded and sweats beneath a heavy burden of ideas and imagery! It has seldom ease.' It was an unparalleled ease in the conveying of a 'body of thought' that he was finally to attain. In 'Youth and Age,' think how much is actually said, and with a brevity impossible in prose; things, too, far from easy for poetry to say gracefully, such as the image of the steamer, or the frank reference to 'this altered size'; and then see with what an art, as of the very breathing of syllables, it passes into the most flowing of lyric forms. Besides these few miracles of his later years, there are many poems, such as the Flaxman group of 'Love, Hope, and Patience supporting Education,' in which we get all that can be poetic in the epigram softened by imagination, all that can be given by an ecstatic plain thinking. The rarest magic has gone, and he knows it; philosophy remains, and out of that resisting material he is able, now and again, to weave, in his deftest manner, a few garlands.

ROBERT SOUTHEY (1774–1843) [1]

I

LANDOR, whose praise, but for Byron's immortalising onslaught, would be Southey's chief claim to remembrance, said in all good faith: 'Interest is always excited by him, enthusiasm not always. If his elegant prose and harmonious verse are insufficient to excite it, turn to his virtues.' While Southey was living, his virtues benefited many; with his death they ceased to concern the world; only his legacy remained. It is that legacy, of verse and prose, which we have to consider in any attempt to estimate his position in English literature; and it is only to confuse two distinct worlds of activity, to put forward, as so many of his admirers and apologists have done, 'his virtues,' 'the beauty of his life,' or even 'the magnitude and variety of his powers, the field which he covered in literature,' as in any sense a compensation for his lack of the virtues and beauty of great poetry, the magnitude and variety of great prose.

Byron said of Southey that he was 'the only existing entire man of letters'; and in the preface to the first volume of his collected poems Southey names, as 'what has been the greatest of all advantages, that I have passed more than half my life in retirement, conversing with books rather than men, con-

---

[1] (1) *Fall of Robespierre* (with Coleridge and Lovell), 1794. (2) *Poems* (by Robert Lovell and Robert Southey), 1795. (3) *Poems by Bion and Moschus*, 1795. (4) *Joan of Arc*, 1796. (5) *Minor Poems*, 2 vols., 1797. (6) *Thalaba the Destroyer*, 2 vols., 1801. (7) *Metrical Tales*, 1805. (8) *Madoc*, 1805. (9) *The Curse of Kehama*, 1810. (10) *Roderick, the Last of the Goths*, 1814. (11) *Carmen Triumphale*, 1814. (12) *Carmen Aulica*, 1814. (13) *Odes to the Regent*, 1814. (14) *The Lay of the Laureate : Carmen Nuptiale*, 1816. (15) *The Poet's Pilgrimage to Waterloo*, 1816. (16) *Wat Tyler*, 1817. (17) *Princess Charlotte's Epithalamion*, 1817. (18) *A Vision of Judgement*, 1821. (19) *A Tale of Paraguay*, 1825. (20) *All for Love*, and *The Pilgrim to Compostella*, 1829. (21) *Oliver Newman* (posthumous), 1845. (22) *Robin Hood*, 1847.

stantly and unweariedly engaged in literary pursuits.' There, in what made him so capable a man of letters, was what made him no poet; 'books made out of books pass away.' He gives us a conscientious list of 'the obligations which I am conscious of owing either to my predecessors, or my contemporaries'; and assures us that 'the taste which has been acquired in that school' (some of his masters were among the best) 'was not likely to be corrupted afterwards.' It matters little how far that taste was or was not corrupted; what mattered was, that there was no native genius for the best taste in the world to set in motion; and that such impulse as there was, the genuine will to write, was never wholly unencumbered by second thoughts, or by recollections of what had been written and printed by poets. Southey had no new vision of the world; he came with no new music.

To himself, it is true, he seemed to have made a new heaven and a new earth, and to have perfected a rare and unfamiliar music. He went to the East, or to Spain, or to heaven itself, for the scene of his 'works of greater extent'; he followed Dr. Sayers in the use of unrhymed metres, and produced English hexameters of his own. He is forever insisting that he will 'sing as he pleases,' imagining that a new metre means a new music, and that the desire to be novel brings with it the power to be new. It seems to him a self-evident corollary that by 'following his own sense of propriety' he was 'thereby obtaining the approbation of that fit audience, which, being contented that it should be few, I was sure to find.' And it is with complete confidence that, thirty years after 'Kehama' had been published, he reminds us that, at the time of writing, 'it appeared to me, that here neither the tone of morals, nor the strain of poetry, could be pitched too high; that nothing but moral sublimity could compensate for the extravagance of the fictions.' That moral sublimity, he never doubted that it was within his grasp; that strain of poetry, he never doubted that he could pitch it as high as he had the mind to. Untroubled by a suspicion that he might not be a poet, he was conscious that he could write in verse very much as he wanted to write. All his knowledge of literature, which was not even sufficient to make him a fine critic, availed him nothing when he came to look at his own work in verse. The criticism, severe but just, of Jeffrey and the others, seemed to him 'malice' which he need only disregard. 'The reader will be as much amused as I was,' he says, in quoting that admirable letter of Jeffrey to Hogg: 'For Southey, I have, as well as you, great respect, and, when he will let me, great admiration; but he is a most provoking fellow, and at least as conceited as his neighbour Wordsworth.' He quotes many unfavourable criticisms in his prefaces, always with lofty scorn; but time has sided with the critics.

Southey loved books with the chief passion of his life; and Rogers, who notes acutely that 'he was what you call a cold man,' declares that he was never happy 'except when reading a book or making one.' He lived always in the midst of books, considered that 'it is to literature, humanly speaking, that I am beholden, not only for the means of subsistence, but for every blessing which I enjoy'; and, as the mind died out of him in his last years, still loved to handle and caress the books which he could no longer read. He was probably what is called the 'best read' of English writers; he had taste and memory; and in all he has written about books there is prodigious knowledge and for the most part ready, or as he would have called it, catholic sympathy. But he said, really meaning the lamentable thing which he said: 'Your true lover of books is never fastidious.' He read everything, and he read with an enthusiasm which was never sharpened into divination; when he took the right view, as he more often did than not, he never said the essential thing; of what has been called the *vraie vérité* of things he had no conception: never does he come upon it even by accident.

So, though he quotes the 'Mad Song' of Blake with admiration, he calls it 'painful,' and Blake an 'insane and erratic genius'; and though he praises Drayton, can say nothing more to the point, when he has finished a judicious commendation of the 'Polyolbion,' than that 'some of his minor poems have merit enough in their execution to ensure their preservation.' One discovery he made, the discovery of Landor, whom he praised gallantly, and by whom he was rewarded beyond his deserts. He was the friend of Wordsworth, and at one time the friend of Coleridge; Coleridge he once praised, though without discernment, and Wordsworth to his full deserts, or beyond them. But of Coleridge, at his death, he said: 'He has long been dead to me,' and, if Moore is to be believed, he said that Coleridge died 'lamented by few, and regretted by none.' 'He builds up kingdoms and pulls them down,' he had said, in 1810, 'just as children serve their card houses; aiming at nothing permanent, and incapable of producing anything that can be so.' 'His habits have continued, and so have mine,' he says in another letter, not realising the irony of what he says; and then, for twenty years, there is silence, and not even a relenting towards the dead. Byron was never on civil terms with him, and he allowed morals and politics to turn him into a traducer of Byron; he seemed never to have suspected the genius of Shelley and of Keats; he could go out of his way to call Leigh Hunt 'wrong-headed, foolish, impudently conceited'; he was the friend of Lamb, but he did nothing for him until he was already famous, and beyond need of his help. He edited, it is true, the first collected edition of the works of Chatterton; but he edited also the worthless remains of Henry Kirke White, announcing him as 'one whose early death is not less to be lamented as a loss to English literature.' 'And whose virtues were as admirable as his genius,' he adds; and there, in that fixed idea, that persistent confusion of virtue with genius, we may distinguish part, the deliberate part, of the reason why he was not more certain, why he could not be more disinterested, as a critic.

What renders Southey so irritating as a man, for all his virtues, is his conscious rectitude. Virtue may or may not be its own reward to most people, but it certainly was to Southey, and he is at no pains to disguise the fact, or the virtue. His biographer sees 'the wisdom of the heart' in a letter written to his wife in absence, in which he says: 'Though not unhappy (my mind is too active and too well disciplined to yield to any such criminal weakness) still without you I am not happy.' Can moderation show itself in a more contemptible light? It is the same spirit of conscious rectitude that shows itself in the second 'Letter concerning Lord Byron' of 1824, where, speaking of Shelley, he says: 'When I had ceased to regard him with hope, he became to me an object for sorrow and awful commiseration.' What man has the right to speak in that tone of another man, whose opinions do not happen to be identical with his? And of a man of genius? But Southey had no reverence for the individuality of genius; he could recognise the divine only when it came to him in the full regimentals of his own creed; he demanded a universal moral conformity, a universal uniformity of belief. It is not that he is Christian: he is parochial.

And so I find in Southey, high-minded, generous, and helpful as he could be, a disloyalty more serious than any personal disloyalty, such as Coleridge's, a disloyalty to genius; an immorality more hurtful than Byron's, the immorality of the intellect, which shuts its eyes to truth when truth comes to it under some disguise of evil; together with a vindictive moral sense which not only perverted his judgement, but soured his whole nature. He could refer to Byron as 'one, whose baseness is such as to sanctify the vindictive feeling that it provokes, and upon whom the act of taking vengeance, is that of administering justice.' Byron's 'Don Juan' he thought a 'flagitious production, by which he will be remembered for lasting infamy.' It seemed to him 'a work in which mockery was mingled with horrors, filth with impiety, profligacy with sedition and slander.' And he affirmed: 'I have fastened his name upon the gibbet, for reproach and ignominy, as long as it shall endure. Take it down who can!'

Well, the name of Byron has long since been taken down from that forgotten gibbet, and all that anybody now remembers is that Byron, justly or unjustly, pilloried Southey into fame, in a 'Vision of Judgment' named after its victim's. Where the moral right or wrong was, no one cares: a great work of satiric genius has crushed out a little and mediocre work of careful talent. 'Don Juan,' a great imperfect work, in which there is much that is gross, and trivial, and unworthy, has come to be recognised as Byron's masterpiece, the masterpiece of a great and imperfect writer. What to Southey seemed all-important, seems to us now not worth lingering over. Only what was great in it has survived.

In his 'Table-Talk' Coleridge is reported to have spoken of Southey's English prose as 'next door to faultless.' It is that, and it has most negative merits; but it is, like his verse, uninspired, without any great or exquisite qualities; without magic. It has ease and flexibility; it is, as he said of it, contrasting it scornfully with Coleridge's, 'perspicuous and to the point.' As a style of all work it is incomparable; as Southey is the ideal of the 'well-read' man, so his style is the ideal of the 'readable' style. His 'Life of Wesley' is remarkable as a psychological study, and that, like the 'Life of Nelson,' is a marvel of clear, interesting, absorbing narrative. We remember it, not for any page or passage, but as a whole, for its evenness, proportion, and easy mastery of its subject. But in that unique subject, which gave him the opportunity of his life, a subject absolutely 'made to his hand,' can it be said that Southey found, any more than in his criticism of literature, the *vraie vérité*, the essential thing? The portrait of Wesley he gives us, but does he give us anywhere the secret of Wesley?

In one of his books, 'The Doctor,' which was published

anonymously, volume by volume, Southey has tried for once to give us what he could of the secret of himself. It is his most personal work in prose; and it is personal partly for this reason, that it is a compilation, a collection of curiosities, a farrago, yet thrown together, one realises, by a man of order, who lets nothing escape him unawares, tells just what he chooses to tell. Poe, who thought Southey could not have written it, imagined that it had been written 'with a sole view (or nearly with the sole view) of exciting inquiry and comment.' 'I see in "The Doctor,"' wrote Southey, who, in the course of his book, refers, rather more often than is necessary for purposes of disguise, to Southey, 'Southey and Wordsworth' (never 'Wordsworth and Southey'), 'a little of Rabelais, but not much; more of Tristram Shandy, somewhat of Burton, and perhaps more of Montaigne; but methinks the *quintum quid* predominates.' The influences are there, it is true, and the personal quality; but can the book, with all its quaintness, pleasantness and variety, bear the least of these comparisons, or stand by itself with any firmness? Perhaps the best thing in it is the nursery story of 'The Three Bears,' and that is one of Southey's real successes, one of his successes in comedy; but how few of the other more serious pages leave so deep an impression on the memory as this piece of engaging nonsense?

II

As a writer of verse Southey had a small but genuine talent of a homely and grotesque order; and if he had had less ambition, and a keener sense of his own limitations, he might have appealed with more likelihood of final satisfaction to 'that Court of Record' which, sooner or later, as he says, with his imperturbable self-confidence, 'pronounces unerringly upon the merits of the case.' But he was revolutionary, where no revolt was needed; original, at his own expense; an inventor of systems, not a discoverer of riches. And first in regard to metre. Southey wrote one or two clever pieces, such as 'The Cataract of Lodore,' to show how easily and effectively he could rhyme, but it was one of his theories that better verse could be written in English without rhyme than with it. A certain Dr. Sayers ('the German critics observed a resemblance between Sayers and Gray') had published in 1790 some 'Dramatic Sketches of Northern Mythology'; and, much later, writing about him in the 'Quarterly,' Southey tells us that 'Sayers was not of the school of Shakespeare,' whereas 'the simplest of the Greek dramas are not so simple in their construction as these dramatic sketches.' They were written in blank verse mingled with choruses in unrhymed lyrical verse. 'Unrhymed lyrical measures,' Southey tells us, 'had been tried by Milton with unhappy success; and his failure would have deterred any ordinary mind from repeating the experiment; but in reality that failure proved only that the experiment had been ill made. There are parts in the choruses of the "Samson Agonistes" wherein it is difficult to discover any principle of rhythm.' Where Milton, however, had failed, 'Dr. Sayers committed no such error.' And Southey reminds his readers that Dr. Sayers had been followed to good purpose. 'If blank verse,' he says, 'be much more difficult than couplets or stanzas, that measure is itself not so difficult as the verse of Sayers' choruses. The poet who rejects the aid of uniformity takes upon himself a task of more arduous execution. Sayers has been followed by Mr. Southey in the metre of "Thalaba" and of many minor poems: he would have found more followers if the model had been as easy as it may appear to those who have had no experience in composition.' In 1792 Dr. Sayers published a short poem which he called 'Oswald, a Monodrama,' and in his preface he tells us: 'The Monodrama is a species of Play, which has not yet, as far as I am able to discover, been attempted by English writers.' In a year's time there is another monodrama in English; it is Southey's; and who knows if we may not trace to Dr. Sayers, through Southey, the beginnings in modern English of a form which Landor made Greek and Browning made alive and his own? If so, it would not be the only instance in which Southey found out new ways for better walkers. In the 'English Eclogues' of 1799, with their deliberate realism of tone and detail, their careful English local colour, I cannot but see the origin of those 'English Idylls' of Tennyson, which travel along a hardly higher road, for the most part, but of which it could not be said, as Lamb justly said of Southey's, that they are 'as poetical as the subject requires, which asks no poetry.'

Dr. Sayers' unrhymed measures attempt less than Southey attempted, and are even further from being good verse. But we see them, carefully tended by Taylor of Norwich, in an elegant volume of remains, suggesting a ghastly heredity for later *vers libristes*, classical or impressionistic. It is almost in the words of Mr. Bridges that Southey explains to us how Dr. Sayers 'constructed his verses so that they required no humouring from an indulgent reader, but that in the easy and natural pronunciation of the words, the accent should necessarily fall where the harmony of the line required it.' There, certainly, we have the principle of all good verse not written to a known tune; but the tune, 'the harmony of the tune,' if that should be absent, of what avail are all the theories?

If we wish to find an infallible test of Southey's ear for rhythm, we shall find it in the 'short passages of Scripture rhythmically arranged or paraphrased' which are printed among his 'poetical remains.' One example will suffice. Here is the text as we find it in Jeremiah: 'Give glory unto the Lord your God, before he cause darkness, and before your feet stumble upon the dark mountains, and, while ye look for light, he turn it into the shadow of death, and make it gross darkness.' And this is what seemed to Southey a finer rhythmical arrangement: —

> 'Give glory to the Lord your God!
> Lest, while ye look for light,
> He bring the darkness on,
> And the feet that advanced
> With haughty step,
> Marching astray in their pride,
> Stumble and fail
> In the shadow of death.'

Just as we see him deliberately, and with complete unconsciousness of what he is doing, turning a solemn and measured prose into unevenly jigging verse, so, in his vast metrical romances, 'Thalaba' and 'Kehama,' we find him turning his own clear and graceful prose into verse as inexplicably cadenced as this: —

> 'Reclined against a column's broken shaft,
> Unknowing whitherward to bend his way,
> He stood, and gazed around.
> The Ruins closed him in;
> It seem'd as if no foot of man
> For ages had intruded there.'

It is hardly possible for a thing to be said with more complete dissonance between sound and sense, meaning and measure, than the thing which is said in these lines.

Then, Southey was not only an innovator in regard to metre, but in regard to the subject-matter of poetry. His great ambition was to write epics, and he wrote five or six immense narratives, of which the two most characteristic were founded on Arabian and Indian mythology. Southey once brought down on himself the wrath of Lamb for calling the 'Ancient Mariner' 'a Dutch attempt at German sublimity.' A phrase in the same letter precisely defines that quality of 'the material sublime' which was all that Southey himself ever captured: 'Thalaba' and 'Kehama' are 'fertile in unmeaning miracles.' It still puzzles the mind that any one who had read Coleridge and also 'Sakuntala' could have constructed these empty frameworks, gaudy with far-fetched rags of many colours, which collapse at a touch or breath;

empty of the magic of Coleridge, and of the wisdom of 'Sakuntala.' A quiet home-keeping temper of mind is seen moving about in worlds not realised, in which for every reader, as for Lamb, 'the imagination goes sinking and floundering.' We see him reaching wildly after the local colour of the East, and yet, while trying to weave an Eastern pattern, boasting that 'there was nothing Oriental in the style.' It is as if a traveller brought back foreign fripperies from far countries, and hung himself all over with them, not in manner native to them, or to him. For all his deliberate heapings up of horror and amazement, his combinations of violence without heat and adventures without vital motion, Southey was no born romantic, but the solitary seeker after romance, writing among his books, and seeking in them the atmosphere, and in his subjects the imagination, which he should have brought with him, for they are to be found in no books and in no subjects. His incidents are impossible, but have none of that strangeness which is one of the properties of beauty; his seminary of sorcerers, his Glendoveers and Azyoruca, his demons and deities of Indian and Arabian mythology, have no power over the mind or the senses; in the horrors of his slaughtering and suffering immortals there is no thrill. A shadow on the wall, a footstep on an empty road, is enough material for the true master of terrors to chill the soul with. Southey wrecks many heavens and many hells, and does not quicken a pulse.

In one of his letters defending 'Kehama' against some one who had not admired it, Southey says: 'It is just as impossible to give a taste for works of imagination as it is to give a taste for music. . . . This is their use: to take us out of ourselves, to carry us into the world of unrealities, to busy us with something which is not immediately connected with flesh and blood, to elevate rather than to affect, and to make us perceive our imaginative power, instead of constantly referring us to ordinary feelings.' In thus writing Southey made the twofold mistake of supposing that he had imagination, and that imagination could only or could ever live in a world of unrealities. The fundamental criticism of Southey as a poet is to be found in an entry in Crabb Robinson's diary, in the year 1812. 'Wordsworth when alone,' he says, 'speaking of Southey, said he is one of the cleverest men now living. At the same time he justly denies him ideality in his works. He never enquires, says Wordsworth, on what idea his poem is to be wrought; what feeling or passion is to be excited; but he determines on a subject, and then reads a good deal, and combines and connects industriously; but he does not give anything which impresses the mind strongly, and is recollected in solitude.'

Take, for instance, 'Roderick, the Last of the Goths,' the latest and perhaps the best of the epics. The narrative is told with simplicity, with dignity; there is, as Lamb says, 'firm footing' in it; the verse is quiet, and might contain good poetry, if it were not presented as a substitute for it. It is the rarest thing for a narrative poem, unless the narrative is an excuse and not an object, to be anything but prose disguised; here the narrative is everything, and we can but wonder why it has been written in blank verse rather than in prose. No unexpected beauty, light or music, ever comes into it; but one reads on, placidly interested, as if one were reading history. 'I have often said,' Southey once wrote to Landor, 'that I learnt how to see, for the purposes of poetry, from Gebir'; and there are, in 'Roderick,' a few things seen in Landor's manner; as thus:—

 'and when she stoopt
Hot from the chase to drink, well pleased had seen
Her own bright crescent, and the brighter face
It crowned, reflected there.'

But there is not in the whole long poem a single line by which one could recognise it at sight as poetry; not a line of the quality of two at least in a single passage, quoted loyally but unwisely from 'Count Julian,' in the footnotes to this version of the same story. One is the line on him who stands and sees the flames above the towers —

'Spire, with a bitter and severe delight';

and the other on him

'whose hills
Touch the last cloud upon the level sky.'

In those lines something speaks, which is not the voice of prose; but in all 'Roderick', (can we say in all Southey?) nothing which is not the voice of prose.

When I ask myself if there is not in all Southey's work in verse anything which might not as well have been written in prose, I find myself hesitating a little over one section of that work, a section in which homely quaintness is sometimes combined with a grotesque or ironical humour. 'Take my word for it, Sir,' said Mr. Edgworth to Southey, 'the bent of your genius is for comedy'; and I think Mr. Edgworth was right. There is real metrical fun in 'The Cataract of Lodore,' and in 'The Old Woman of Berkeley' a real mastery of the gruesome. In the verses on 'The Holly Tree' there is a certain measure, and in the verses written in his library there is more, of a pungent homeliness, through which for once the real man seems to speak, and to speak straight. But better than any of these, because it combines in one the best of their qualities, is 'The Battle of Blenheim,' where the irony is at once naïve and profound, and where the extreme simplicity of the form is part of the irony. All the other poems may be compared with other better things of the same kind, as 'The Cataract of Lodore' with 'The Bells' and 'The Old Woman of Berkeley' with 'The Witch of Fyfe'; but in this poem Southey is himself, and no one has done a better poem of the kind. It is a poem of the pedestrian sort, but it is good of its sort. Southey's talent was pedestrian, and it was his misfortune that he tried to fly, with wings made to order, and on his own pattern, and a misfit.

ROBERT TANNAHILL (1774–1810) [1]

ROBERT TANNAHILL was born at Paisley in 1774, and worked at the loom all his life, making up his songs as he worked, and fitting new words to old tunes. Ill-health and disappointment seem to have turned him melancholy-mad, and after burning all his manuscripts he drowned himself in the river in the year 1810. He left a local fame which has spread, although the editor of his poems says naïvely: 'They do not interest the readers so much as he seems to have expected.' His own attitude was unnecessarily humble, and he apologised for his work as 'the effusions of an unlettered mechanic, whose hopes, as a poet, extend no further than to be reckoned respectable among the minor bards of his country.' His songs are written spontaneously, often with real felicities of phrase, and almost always with a natural knack for that almost inarticulate jingle and twinkle which goes with the genuine gallop of the Scottish tongue. Like all writers who are neither lettered nor unlettered he is not always sure of his own limits, and does not realise what he loses by leaving his 'bonnie woods and braes' for an unrealised world where 'Vengeance drives his crimson car.' The sentimentality of the moment, sad or joyous, rarely goes deep enough to retain any permanent heat in songs, improvised with natural skill, and never better than when they are savoured with petulance or homely humour.

CHARLES LAMB (1775–1834) [2]

'I RECKON myself a dab at prose — verse I leave to my betters,' Lamb once wrote to Wordsworth; and, in a letter to Charles

[1] (1) *Poems*, 1807. (2) *Works*, 1838, 1873.
[2] (1) *Blank Verse*, by Charles Lloyd and Charles Lamb, 1798. (2) *John Woodvil*, 1802. (3) *Works*, 2 vols., the first containing collected poems, 1818. (4) *Album Verses*, 1830. (5) *Poetical Works*, 1836.

Lloyd, he tells him, by way of praise, 'your verses are as good and as wholesome as prose.' 'Those cursed Dryads and Pagan trumperies of modern verse have put me out of conceit of the very name of poetry,' he has just said. At the age of twenty-one he talks of giving up the writing of poetry. 'At present,' he writes to Coleridge, 'I have not leisure to write verses, nor anything approaching to a fondness for the exercise. . . . The music of poesy may charm for awhile the importunate teasing cares of life; but the teased and troubled man is not in a disposition to make that music.' Yet, as we know, Lamb, who had begun with poetry, returned to the writing of poetry at longer or shorter intervals throughout his whole life: was this prose-writer, in whom prose partook so much of the essence of poetry, in any real or considerable sense a poet?

The name of Lamb as a poet is known to most people as the writer of one poem. 'The Old Familiar Faces' is scarcely a poem at all; the metre halts, stumbles, there is no touch of magic in it; but it is speech, naked human speech, such as rarely gets through the lovely disguise of verse. It has the raw humanity of Walt Whitman, and almost hurts us by a kind of dumb helplessness in it. A really articulate poet could never have written it; here, the emotion of the poet masters him as he speaks; and you feel, with a strange thrill, that catch in his breath which he cannot help betraying. There are few such poems in literature, and no other in the work of Lamb.

For Lamb, with his perfect sincerity, his deliberate and quite natural simplicity, and with all that strange tragic material within and about him (already coming significantly into the naïve prose tale of 'Rosamund Gray'), was unable to work directly upon that material in the imaginative way of the poet, unable to transform its substance into a creation in the form of verse. He could write about it, touchingly sometimes, more or less tamely for the most part, in a way that seems either too downright or too deliberate. 'Cultivate simplicity, Coleridge,' he wrote, with his unerring tact of advice, 'or rather, I should say, banish elaborateness; for simplicity springs spontaneous from the heart, and carries into daylight its own modest buds and genuine, sweet, and clear flowers of expression. I allow no hot-beds in the gardens of Parnassus.' This simplicity, which was afterwards to illuminate his prose, is seen in his verse almost too nakedly, or as if it were an end rather than a means.

Lamb's first master was Cowper, and the method of Cowper was not a method that could ever help him to be himself. But, above all, verse itself was never as much of a help to him as it was a hindrance. Requiring always, as he did, to apprehend reality indirectly, and with an elaborately prepared ceremony, he found himself in verse trying to be exactly truthful to emotions too subtle and complex for his skill. He could but set them down as if describing them, as in most of that early work in which he took himself and his poetry most seriously. What was afterwards to penetrate his prose, giving it that savour which it has, unlike any other, is absent from his almost saltless verse. There is the one inarticulate cry, 'The Old Familiar Faces,' and then, for twenty years and more, only one or two wonderful literary exercises, like the mad verses called 'A Conceipt of Diabolical Possession,' and the more intimate fantasy of the 'Farewell to Tobacco' ('a little in the way of Withers'), with one love-song, in passing, to a dead woman whom he had never spoken to.

The Elizabethan experiments, 'John Woodvil,' and, much later, 'The Wife's Trial,' intervene, and we see Lamb under a new aspect, working at poetry with real ambition. His most considerable attempt, the work of his in verse which he would most have liked to be remembered, was the play of 'John Woodvil.' 'My tragedy,' he wrote to Southey, at the time when he was finishing it, 'will be a medley (as I intend it to be a medley) of laughter and tears, prose and verse, and in some places rhyme, songs, wit, pathos, humour, and, if possible, sublimity; at least, it is not a fault in my intention if it does not comprehend most of these discordant colours.' It was meant, in short, to be an Elizabethan play, done, not in the form of a remote imitation, but with 'a colloquial ease and spirit, something like' Shakespeare, as he says. As a play, it is the dream of a shadow. Reading it as poetry, it has a strange combination of personal quality with literary experiment: an echo, and yet so intimate; real feelings in old clothes. The subject probably meant more to Lamb than people have usually realised. I do not doubt that he wrote it with a full consciousness of its application to the tragic story which had desolated his own household, with a kind of generous casuistry, to ease a somewhat uneasy mind, and to be a sort of solace and defence for Mary. The moral of it is:—

> 'And not for one misfortune, child of chance,
> No crime, but unforeseen, and sent to punish
> The less offence with image of the greater,
> Thereby to work the soul's humility.'

And when John Woodvil, after his trial, begins 'to understand what kind of creature Hope is,' and bids Margaret 'tell me if I over-act my mirth,' is there not a remembrance of that mood which Lamb had confessed to Coleridge, just after his mother's funeral, when he says, 'I was in danger of making myself too happy?' Some touch of this poignant feeling comes into the play here and there, but not vividly enough to waken it wholly out of what Southey called its 'lukewarm' state. The writing has less of the Elizabethan rhetoric and more of the quaint directness, the kindly nature, the eager interest in the mind, which those great writers whom Lamb discovered for the modern world had to teach him, than any play written on similar models. I am reminded sometimes of Heywood, sometimes of Middleton; and even when I find him in his play 'imitating the defects of the old writers,' I cannot but confess with Hazlitt that 'its beauties are his own, though in their manner.' Others have written more splendidly in the Elizabethan manner, but no one has ever thought and felt so like an Elizabethan.

After one much later and slighter experiment in writing plays 'for antiquity,' Lamb went back to occasional writing, and the personal note returns with the 'Album Verses' of 1830. Lamb's album verses are a kind of amiable task-work, done easily, he tells us, but at the same time with something painfully industrious, not only in the careful kindness of the acrostic. The man of many friends forgets that he is a man of letters, and turns amateur out of mere geniality. To realise how much he lost by writing in verse rather than in prose, we have only to compare these careful trifles with the less cared for and infinitely more exquisite triflings of the letters. The difference is that between things made to please and things made for pleasure. In the prose he is himself, and his own master; in the verse he is never far enough away from his subject to do it or himself justice; and, tied by the metre, has rarely any fine freak or whimsical felicity such as came to him by the way in the mere turn of a sentence in prose.

More than of any poet we might say that a large part of his poems were recreations. We might indeed, but with a different meaning, say as much of Herrick. To Herrick his art was his recreation, but then his recreation was his art. He has absolute skill in the game, and plays it with easy success. Lamb seems to find playing a task, or allows himself to come but indifferently through it. His admiration for 'Rose Aylmer' was not surprising, for there, in that perfectly achieved accident, was what he was forever trying to do.

Yet, at times, the imprisoned elf within him breaks forth, and we get a bubble of grotesque rhymes, as cleverly done as Butler would have done them, and with a sad, pungent jollity of his own; or, once at least, some inspired nonsense, in parody of himself, the

'Angel-duck, Angel-duck, winged and silly,
Pouring a watering-pot over a lily;'

together with, at least once, in the piece of lovely lunacy called 'The Ape,' a real achievement in the grotesque. His two task-masters, 'Work' and 'Leisure,' both inspire him to more than usual freedom of fancy. And it is among the 'Album Verses' that we find not only those 'whitest thoughts in whitest dress,' which, for the Quakeress, Lucy Barton,

> 'best express
> Mind of quiet Quakeress,'

but also the solemn fancy of the lines 'In My Own Album,' in which a formal and antique measure is put to modern uses, and the jesting figure of 'My soul, an album bright,' is elaborated with serious wit in the manner of the 'metaphysical' poets. And it is under the same covers, and as if done after the same pattern, that we find the most completely successful of his poems, the lines 'On an Infant Dying as Soon as Born.' The subject was one which could not but awaken all his faculties, stirring in him pity, compassionate wonder, a tender whimsicalness; the thought of death and the thought of childhood being always sure to quicken his imagination to its finest utterance. There is good poetical substance, and the form, though not indeed original, is one in which he moves with as natural an air as if he were actually writing two hundred years ago. It was in this brief, packed, 'matterful' way, full of pleasant surprises, that his favourite poets wrote; the metre is Wither's, with some of the woven subtleties of Marvell.

With Lamb, more than with most poets, the subject-matter of his work in verse determines its value. He needs to 'load every rift with ore,' not for the bettering, but for the mere existence, of a poem. In his pleasant review of his own poems he protests, in the name of Vincent Bourne, against 'the vague, dreamy, wordy, *matterless* poetry of this empty age,' and finds satisfaction in Bourne's Latin verses because 'they fix upon *something*.' For him that 'something' had to be very definite, in the subject-matter of his own verse; and it was not with the mere humility of self-depreciation that he wrote to Coleridge in 1796: 'Not that I relish other people's poetry less — their's comes from 'em without effort, mine is the difficult operation of a brain scanty of ideas, made more difficult by disuse.' He was a poet to whom prose was the natural language, and in verse he could not trust himself to rove freely, though he had been born a gipsy of the mind.

Even in his best work in verse Lamb has no singing voice. The poetry of those lines 'On an Infant Dying as Soon as Born' is quite genuine, and it has made for itself a form adequate to its purpose; but the verse, after all, is rather an accompaniment than a lifting; and 'la lyre,' it has been rightly said, 'est en quelque manière un instrument ailé.' He speaks in metre, he does not sing; but he speaks more delicately in metre than any one else not born a singer.

CHARLES LLOYD (1775–1839) [1]

'YOUR verses are as good and wholesome as prose,' Lamb wrote to Lloyd in the autumn of 1823, long after he had ceased to see him. They have indeed a great resemblance to prose, but are by no means as good as good prose. In his first book of verse, 'Poems on Various Subjects,' 1795, through which he met Coleridge, there is an Ode to Simplicity, and a sonnet 'occasioned by a Domestic's tears at parting from the Author.' These, as well as a sorry address to a beggar woman, seem to have anticipated the unconscious humour of the beginnings of Lamb, Wordsworth and Coleridge. None of the

---

[1] (1) *Poems on Various Subjects*, 1795. (2) *Poems by S. T. Coleridge*, second edition, to which are now added *Poems by Charles Lamb and Charles Lloyd*, 1797. (3) *Blank Verse by Charles Lloyd and Charles Lamb*, 1798. (4) *Lines suggested by the Fast, appointed on Wednesday, February 27*, 1799, 1799. (5) *The Tragedies of Vittorio Alfieri*, 3 vols., 1815. (6) *Desultory Thoughts in London, Titus and Gissippus, with other Poems*, 1821. (7) *The Duke of Ormond, a Tragedy*, and *Beritola, a Tale*, 1822. (8) *Poems*, 1823.

three, however, not Southey even, arrived at the pitch of this last stanza, with its inconceivable conclusion: —

> 'Ah! what shall I do, I am poor
>   Gentle maid!
> And nip'd by chill misery's breath —
> Yet my last penny take,
> It may buy a small cake,
> And preserve thee a moment from death,
>   Well-a-day!'

Coleridge, who was afterward to mock Lloyd, Lamb, and himself for these dangerous qualities, was soon writing a sonnet addressed 'To a Friend who asked, How I felt when the Nurse first presented my Infant to me.' In 1797 there appeared a volume of 'Poems by S. T. Coleridge, second edition, to which are now added Poems by Charles Lamb and Charles Lloyd.' 'My Coleridge, take the wanderer to thy heart,' he writes, in the muling manner of the moment; but the gloom is already overshadowing him, and we find Poems on 'The Melancholy Man' and 'The Maniac': —

> 'Poor Maniac, I envy thy state
> When with sorrow and anguish I shrink;
> When shall I *be wise* — and forget!
> For his *madness* to feel and to think!'

The Quaker appears in the next book of 'blank Verse' written by Lloyd and Lamb, and from this time we get moral musings against 'this evil spirit misnamed Liberty,' together with more wailing of this sort: —

> 'But what have I done that I'm thus forsaken?
> Whom have I injured that I'm thus neglected?'

Coleridge and Lamb, no doubt, would be meant, with whom he had quarrelled. The 'desultory Thoughts on London,' written in ottava rima, wandered in a certainly desultory manner, from 'the inefficacy of all worldly objects,' to 'reflection on unfortunate feelings' (of quite a kindly character) and on 'the reformation produced in Newgate by Mrs. Fry.' A tragedy in verse came next, dull and heavy, with notes and prefaces sometimes as amusing as this: 'It was not until the following Tragedy had gone through the press to nearly the middle of the fourth act, that it struck the author that the feelings of some more *serious friends* might be hurt by it.' Three volumes of translations from Alfieri had preceded this volume, and it was followed in 1823 by 'Poems,' about which Lamb wrote his criticism. Lamb also said: 'Your lines are not to be understood reading on one leg.'

JOSEPH BLANCO WHITE (1775-1840) [1]

JOSEPH BLANCO WHITE was a Spaniard by birth and an Irishman by nationality. He was ordained a priest in Spain, but he abandoned the Catholic Church and came to London as the editor of a Spanish newspaper, afterwards taking orders in the Anglican Church, and finally relapsing into Unitarianism. He is remembered in English literature for a single sonnet, of great beauty, which Coleridge and Leigh Hunt praised with enthusiasm: Coleridge defining it as 'the finest and most grandly conceived sonnet in our language.' The last line suggests Coleridge, in its imaginative philosophy —

'If Light conceals so much, wherefore not Life?'

and an earlier line has a single flash of rhetorical splendour:

'Hesperides with the host of heaven came.'

[1] *Life of Rev. Joseph Blanco White*, edited by J. H. Thorn, 3 vols., 1845.

THOMAS DERMODY (1775–1802) [1]

Thomas Dermody was a lyric poet whose best verses were concerned with himself, from the time of the 'Poems written between the thirteenth and sixteenth years of his age,' bidding

> 'No Satan come, with sawcer eyes,
>   In shape of Fellows!'

to the later years when he wrote odes to himself: —

> 'Thou prince of jovial fellows,
>   Whose little span
> Is spent 'twixt poetry and ale house.'

Dermody died at the age of twenty-seven in a wretched hovel, shivering over a few embers; an insatiable thirst for drink, together 'with habits so eccentric, principles so wild, and passions so perverted,' had ruined his life, and left him to die with a 'Hudibras' on the table by his side, and the cynical words on his life: 'You see I am merry to the last.' He wrote with immense facility: his knowledge, from a boy, was astonishing; at fourteen he had acquired Greek, Latin, French, Italian, and a little Spanish. His poems are crude, coarse, vigorous, with a genuine lyrical swing, after this manner: —

> 'Some folks there are, gay, trim and fine,
>   In silk and sattins, idly flaming;
> But she I love is all divine,
>   Their artful toil and dresses shaming.'

He calls himself 'a giant of genius,' and writes ('oddest of odd compositions') his own epitaph: —

> 'Unnoticed for talents he had, and forgot,
>   But most famously noticed for faults he had not.'

[1] (1) *Poems*, consisting of Essays, Lyric, Elegiac, etc., by Thomas Dermody, written between the thirteenth and sixteenth years of his age, 1792. (2) *The Harp of Erin*, 2 vols., 1807

DR. JOHN LEYDEN (1775-1811)[1]

In the kindly, vivid, and critical account of the life and work of John Leyden, Sir Walter Scott, after praising him as a scholar, for his early knowledge of Latin, Greek, French, Spanish, Italian, German, Icelandic, Hebrew, Arabic and Persian, and the ease with which he acquired and put aside all sciences and kinds of knowledge, completes the picture by adding that he was 'a fearless player at single-stick, a formidable boxer, a distinguished adept at leaping, running, walking, climbing, and all exercises which depend on animal spirits and muscular effort.' His appearance in society, where he imitated the manners and assumed the tone of a Borderer of former times, was, it seems, 'somewhat appalling to persons of low animal spirits.' 'Elasticity and ardour of genius' are the epithets by which Scott characterises him in the first sentence of his memoir, and no words could be more explicit. 'An ardent and unutterable longing for information of every description' was added to 'an irresistible thirst for discovery,' and in order to accompany an expedition to India he qualified himself in six months for his degree in medicine and surgery. There, after many 'adventures to outrival the witch of Endor,' given up five times by the doctors, and living 'as happy as the day was long,' he set himself, in the Indian heats, and in the intervals of his duty in Indian hospitals, to learn Hindustani, Mahratta, Tamal, Telinga, Canara, Sanscrit, Malayalam, Malay, Maldivian, Mapella and Armenian. It was the incessant labour of an abnormal and indefatigable brain that killed him; and he died 'as devoted a martyr in the cause of science as ever died in that of religion,' as Scott said of him in his just and generous way.

As a poet Leyden had, in another of Scott's acute phrases,

[1] (1) *Poetical Remains*, edited by James Morton, 1819. (2) *Poems and Ballads*, edited by Robert White, with Memoir by Sir Walter Scott, 1858.

'more genius than taste,' though there is taste, as well as personal feeling, in a sonnet on 'The Sabbath Morning' which deserves a place in anthologies. Much of his earlier verse was written with too easy a facility, and in the manner of his time. There is little originality even in the ballad of 'The Mermaid,' of which Scott made the extraordinary statement that the opening of it 'exhibits a power of numbers, which, for the mere melody of sound, has seldom been excelled in English poetry.' 'Lord Soulis,' a ballad of wizardy, is incomparably finer, and best of all are his Malay poems, the feverish address to his green agate-handled kriss, the 'Dirge of the Departed Year,' together with the 'Finland Mother's Song,' the 'Arab Warrior,' and 'The Fight of Praya,' a Malay dirge. There are a few others, technically finer, such as 'The Battle of Assaye,' which was probably suggested, in its ringing metrical effect, by Campbell's battle-songs, but it is, in any case, on a level with all but the finest of them. Here is one of the vigorous stanzas:

> 'But, when we first encountered man to man,
> Such odds came never on,
> Against Greece or Macedon,
> When they shook the Persian throne
> Mid the old barbaric pomp of Ispahan.'

Eastern colour, and a kind of ferocity, is to be found in the best of Leyden's poems, together with something of that battling and indomitable temperament which was life and death to him. It would be incorrect to call him a scholarly poet, but there was a wild flicker of poetry in the heart of a scholar.

WALTER SAVAGE LANDOR (1775–1864) [1]

LANDOR has said, not speaking of himself: —

> 'Wakeful he sits, and lonely, and unmoved,
> Beyond the arrows, views, or shouts of men.'

[1] (1) *Poems*, 1795. (2) *A Moral Epistle*, 1795. (3) *Gebir*, 1798; second edition with Latin version, 1803. (4) *Poems from the Arabic and Persian.*

And of himself he has said, in perhaps his most memorable lines: —

> 'I strove with none, for none was worth my strife;
> Nature I loved, and, next to Nature, Art;
> I warmed both hands before the fire of life;
> It sinks, and I am ready to depart.'

In the preface to the 'Heroic Idyls' he writes: 'He who is within two paces of the ninetieth year may sit down and make no excuses; he must be unpopular, he never tried to be much otherwise, he never contended with a contemporary, but walked alone on the far eastern uplands, meditating and remembering.' He remains alone in English literature, to which he brought, in verse and prose, qualities of order and vehemence, of impassioned thinking and passionless feeling, not to be found combined except in his own work. And in the man there was a like mingling of opposites: nobility and tenderness, haste and magnanimity, courtesy and irresponsible self-will, whatever is characteristically English and whatever is characteristically Roman, with the defects of every quality. Landor is monumental by the excess of his virtues, which are apt to seem, at times, a little too large for the stage and scenery of his life. He desired to live with grandeur; and there is grandeur in the outlines of his character and actions. But some gust of the will, some flurry of the nerves, was always at hand, to trouble or overturn this comely order. The ancient

1800. (5) *Poetry by the Author of 'Gebir,'* 1802. (6) *Simonidea,* 1806. (7) *Ad Gustavum Regem, Ad Gustavum exsulem,* 1810. (8) *Count Julian,* 1812. (9) *Idyllia Heroica,* 1814. (10) *Idyllia Heroica decem,* 1820. (11) *Gebir, Count Julian, and other Poems,* 1831. (12) *Terry Hogan,* 1835. (13) *Pentalogia* (included in the *Pentameron*), 1837. (14) *A Satire on Satirists and Admonition to Detractors,* 1837. (15) *Andrea of Hungary and Giovanni of Naples,* 1839. (16) *Fra Rupert,* 1840. (17) *The Siege of Ancona,* 1842. (18) *Collected Works,* 2 vols., 1846. (19) *Poemata et Inscriptiones,* 1847. (20) *The Hellenics of Walter Savage Landor,* 1847; revised and enlarged edition, 1859. (21) *Italics,* 1848. (22) *Five Scenes in Verse on Beatrice Cenci* in *The Last Fruit off an Old Tree,* 1853. (23) *Scenes for the Study,* 1856. (24) *Dry Sticks fagoted by W. S. Landor,* 1858. (25) *Heroic Idyls,* 1863.

Roman becomes an unruly child, the scholar flings aside cap and gown and leaps into the arena.

Landor began to write verse when he was a schoolboy, and it is characteristic of him that poetry came to him first as a school exercise, taken for once seriously. Latin was to him, it has been well said, 'like the language of some prior state of existence, rather remembered than learned.' His first book, published at the age of twenty, contains both Latin and English verse, together with a defence, in Latin, of the modern use of that language. When, a few years later, he began to work upon his first serious poem, 'Gebir,' he attempted it both in Latin and in English, finally decided to write it in English, and, later on, turned it also into Latin.

'Gebir' was published in 1798 the year of the 'Lyrical Ballads,' and, in its individual way, it marks an epoch almost as distinctly. No blank verse of comparable calibre had appeared since the death of Milton, and, though the form was at times actually reminiscent both of Milton and of the Latin structure of some of the portions as they were originally composed, it has a quality which still remains entirely its own. Cold, sensitive, splendid, so precise, so restrained, keeping step with such a stately music, scarcely any verse in English has a more individual harmony, more equable, more refreshingly calm to the ear. It contains those unforgettable lines, which can never be too often repeated: —

> 'But I have sinuous shells of pearly hue
> Within, and they that lustre have imbibed
> In the sun's palace-porch, where when unyoked
> His chariot-wheel stands midway in the wave:
> Shake one and it awakens, then apply
> Its polisht lips to your attentive ear,
> And it remembers its august abodes,
> And murmurs as the ocean murmurs there.'

There are in it single lines like,—

> 'The sweet and honest avarice of love';

and there are lines marching like these: —

> 'the feast
> Was like the feast of Cepheus, when the sword
> Of Phineus, white with wonder, shook restrain'd,
> And the hilt rattled in his marble hand.'

Has not that the tread of the Commander in 'Don Juan'? And there are experiments in a kind of naïveté: —

> 'Compared with youth
> Age has a something like repose.'

Tennyson is anticipated here: —

> 'On the soft inward pillow of her arm
> Rested her burning cheek';

Mr. Swinburne here: —

> 'The silent oars now dip their level wings,
> And weary with strong stroke the whitening wave.'

But where the most intimately personal quality of Landor is seen is in the lofty homeliness of speech which is always definite, tangible, and about definite, tangible things. The Gadites are building, and Landor, remembering the workmen he has seen in the streets of Warwick, notes: —

> 'Dull falls the mallet with long labour fringed.'

Gebir is wrestling with the nymph, who sweats like any mortal; Landor does not say so, but he sets her visibly before us, —

> 'now holding in her breath constrain'd,
> Now pushing with quick impulse and by starts,
> Till the dust blackened upon every pore.'

We are far enough from Milton here; not so far, perhaps, from the Latin precision of statement; but certainly close to reality. And it is reality of a kind new to English poetry, — painter's, sculptor's, reality, — discovered, as we have seen, at precisely the moment when Wordsworth was discovering for himself the reality of simple feeling, and Coleridge the reality of imaginative wonder.

A few years after 'Gebir,' Landor published two poems, 'Chrysaor' and 'The Phocæans,' and then, for many years, at long intervals, wrote, and occasionally published, other poems in Latin and English, which were eventually to make up the 'Idyllia Heroica' and the 'Hellenics.' They are, to use a word which Browning was to invent (having learned the thing, perhaps from Landor), dramatic idyls. The most perfect of them, 'The Death of Artemidora,' is only nineteen lines long; 'The Last of Ulysses' fills fifty-five pages in the edition of 1847. Landor never ceased to shift their places, and to add, reject, and, above all, rewrite. The two essentially different texts are those of 1847 and 1859; and it is necessary to compare these with each other, and both with such as exist also in Latin, if we would trace with any care the diligent and never quite final labour which Landor gave to his verse.

In the poems which Landor twice translated from his own Latin, it is not often that either form of the English is quite as good as the Latin, and it is not always easy to choose between the two versions, of which the first is usually more easy and fluent, while the second, though more Latin, is often more personal to Landor. Often the second version is nearer to the original, as in the opening of 'Coresus and Callirrhoë,' where the two lines, —

> 'Impulit adstantem lascivior una ministram,
> Irrisitque pedi lapso passisque capillis,' —

are first rendered: —

> 'A playful one and mischievous pusht on
> Her who stood nearest, laughing as her foot
> Tript and her hair was tangled in the flowers';

and afterwards: —

> 'A wanton one pusht forward her who stood
> Aside her; when she stumbled they all laught
> To see her upright heels and scattered hair.'

Sometimes the earlier version is the more literal, but the later one gains by condensation. Thus the first eight lines of 'Cupid and Pan' follow closely the first six lines of 'Cupido et Pan,' while the version of 1859, reduced to six lines, omits, without loss, a line of the Latin which had filled nearly three lines of the English. This process of condensation will be seen in lines 140–141 of 'Coresus et Callirrhoë,'

> 'gelidaeque aspergine lymphae,
> Et, manibus lapso in resonantia marmora, ferro';

rendered literally in 1847 : —

> 'At the cold sprinkling of the sacred lymph
> Upon her temples, and at (suddenly
> Dropt, and resounding on the floor) the sword';

and in 1859 condensed into the single line, —

> 'And the salt sprinklings from the sacred font.'

The aim is always at adding more weight, in the clearing away of mere detail, with only an occasional strong addition, as, a few lines lower, 'Less mournfully than scornfully said he,' for the mere 'inquit' of the original. The style stiffens into harder marble in its 'rejection of what is light and minute.'

Alike from what is gained and from what is lost in this recasting we see how uncertain, with all his care, was Landor's touch on English verse, how a Latin sound dominated his ears when he was writing English, and how his final choice of form was almost invariably of the nature of a compromise, like that of one to whom his native tongue was foreign. Compare the two versions of lines 30–34 of 'Veneris Pueri': —

> 'At neque propositum neque verba superba remittit,

> ' Ut Chaos antiquum flamma radiante subegit,
> Ut tenebras pepulit coelo, luctantiaque astra
> Stare, vel aeterno jussit prodire meatu,
> Ut pelago imposuit domito confinia rupes.'

In 1847 'The Children of Venus' reads: —

> 'But neither his proud words did he remit
> Nor resolution: he began to boast
> How with his radiant fire he had reduced
> The ancient Chaos; how from heaven he drove
> The darkness that surrounded it, and drew
> Into their places the reluctant stars,
> And made some stand before him, others go
> Beyond illimitable space; then curb'd
> The raging sea and chain'd with rocks around.'

In 1859 'The Boys of Venus' reads: —

> 'Still neither would he his intent forego
> Nor moderate his claim, nor cease to boast
> How Chaos he subdued with radiant fire,
> How from the sky its darkness he dispell'd,
> And how the struggling planets he coerced,
> Telling them to what distance they might go,
> And chain'd the raging Ocean down with rocks.'

Both versions are fine, though the second, trying to follow the Latin more closely line for line, abandons the freer cadences of the first; but is either wholly without a certain constraint, which we do not feel in even those passages of Milton most like Latin? And is there not, when we read the lines in Latin, a sense, not due to mere knowledge of the fact, that we are reading an original after a translation?

Yet it is to this fact, partly, to this Latin savour in English, that not only those poems of Landor which were first written in Latin, but others also, never written in anything but English, owe their exceptional, evasive, almost illegitimate charm. What, we find ourselves saying, is this unknown, exquisite thing, which yet seems to be not quite poetry, or is certainly unlike anything else in English poetry? A perfume clings about it, as if it had been stored for centuries in cedar chests, and among spices. Nor does it fail to respond to its own appeal: —

> 'We are what suns and winds and waters make us.'

I have read the 'Hellenics,' lying by the seashore, on warm, quiet days when I heard nothing but the monotonous repetition of the sea at my feet, and they have not seemed out of key. The music is never full-throated or organ music, but picked out note by note on a reed-pipe, a slender sound with few intervals. And it is with truth that Landor says, in the preface to the edition of 1859, 'Poetry, in our day, is oftener prismatic than diaphanous: this is not so: they who look into it may see through. If there be anywhere a few small air-bubbles, it yet leaves to the clear vision a wide expanse of varied scenery.'

In his first preface, in 1847, Landor had written: 'It is hardly to be expected that ladies and gentlemen will leave on a sudden their daily promenade, skirted by Turks and shepherds and knights and plumes and palfreys, of the finest Tunbridge manufacture, to look at these rude frescoes, delineated on an old wall high up, and sadly weak in colouring. As in duty bound, we can wait. The reader (if there should be one) will remember that Sculpture and Painting have never ceased to be occupied with the scenes and figures which we venture once more to introduce into poetry, it being our belief that what is becoming in two of the Fine Arts is not quite unbecoming in a third, the one which indeed gave birth to them.' The 'Hellenics' are all in low relief; you can touch their surface, but not walk round them. Some are moulded in clay, some carved in marble; all with the same dispassionate and energetic skill of hand, the same austere sense of visible beauty. They do not imitate the variety and movement of life; they resemble the work of Flaxman rather than the work of Greek sculpture, and have the careful charm of the one rather than the restrained abundance of the other. They wish to be taken for what they are, figures in relief, harmoniously arranged, not without a reasonable decorative likeness to nature. The contours which have arrested them are suave, but a trifle rigid; the design has proportion, purity, rarely breadth or intensity. The planes are never obscured or unduly heightened; no figure, suddenly starting into life, throws disarray among the firmly stationed or sedately posed figures around.

With all his care, Landor rarely succeeds in seeming spontaneous; the fastidiousness of the choice is too conspicuous, and wounds the susceptibilities of the mind, as one who too obviously 'picks and chooses' wounds the susceptibilities of a host or a friend. His touch, above all things sensitive, sometimes misses the note; in evading the brutality of statement, he sometimes leaves his meaning half expressed.

> 'The shore was won; the fields markt out; and roofs
> Collected the dun wings that seek house-fare;
> And presently the ruddy-bosom'd guest
> Of winter knew the doors; then infant cries
> Were heard within; and lastly, tottering steps
> Pattered along the image-stationed hall.'

It is not without some intent deciphering that any one will realise from these hints that the passage of three years is meant to be indicated in them. Landor prefers to give you a sort of key, which he expects you to fit in the lock, and turn there; there is disdain in his way of stopping short, as with a half-courteous and half-contemptuous gesture. For the most part he hints at what has happened by mentioning an unimportant, but visible, consequence of it.

Landor's chief quality is sensitiveness; and this is seen equally in his touch on verse and in the temper of his daily life. The root of irritability is sensitiveness; and sensitiveness is shown by Landor when he throws the cook out of the window upon the flower-bed, and not only when he remembers that he has 'forgotten the violets.' All his prejudices, unreasons, the occasional ungentlemanliness of his enraged caprices, come from this one source. We trace it in his attitude of angry contempt toward Byron: ' "Say what you will," once whispered a friend of mine, "there are things in him strong as poison, and original as sin." ' We trace it in his refusal to call on Shelley, when the poet, whom he admired profoundly, was his neighbour in Pisa. He marries precipitately, at the sight of 'the nicest girl in the room,' at a provincial ball, and leaves his wife in Jersey, to cross over to France, alone in an open boat, because she has reminded him before her sister that he is older than she is. Throughout life his bluster was the loud, assumed voice of a sensitive nature, hurt to anger by every imperfection that disconcerted his taste.

And sensitiveness makes his verse shrink away from any apparent self-assertion, all in little shivers, like the nymph's body at the first cold touch of the river. He heard a music which seemed to beat with too definite a measure, and he often draws back his finger from the string before he has quite sounded the note, so fearful is he lest the full twang should be heard. The words pause half uttered; what they say is never more than a part of what they mean, as the tune to which they say it always supposes a more ample melody completing it behind the silence. In that familiar ending of 'The Death of Artemidora,' —

> 'and now a loud deep sob
> Swell'd thro' the darken'd chamber: 't was not hers,' —

we find this shy reticence, which from an idiosyncrasy has become almost a method.

Landor was a scholar of beauty, and it was with almost too disinterested an homage, too assured at once and too shy, that he approached the Muses. 'The kingdom of heaven suffereth violence,' and poetry wants to be wooed by life. Landor was not a strong man; he was a loud weak man; in his life we see the tumult, and only in his verse 'the depth and not the tumult of the soul.' His work is weakness made marmoreal; the explosive force tamed, indeed, but tamed too well, showing the lack of inner fire, so busy with rocks and lava on the surface. That is why it becomes tedious after a little; because life comes and goes in it but capriciously, like the shooting flames of his life; it is not warmed steadily throughout.

Something of this may have been in Coleridge's mind when he said, in the 'Table-Talk' of January 1, 1834, 'What is it that Mr. Landor wants, to make him a poet? His powers are certainly very considerable, but he seems to be totally deficient in that modifying faculty which compresses several units into one whole. The truth is, he does not possess imagination in its highest form, — that of stamping *il più nell' uno*. Hence his poems, taken as wholes, are unintelligible; you have eminences excessively bright, and all the ground around and between them in darkness.' And he adds, 'Besides which, he has never learned, with all his energy, how to write simple and lucid English.'

Is it, really, imagination which he lacks? In some lines addressed to Barry Cornwall, Landor states his own theory: —

> 'Imagination's paper kite,
> Unless the string is held in tight,
> Whatever fits and starts it takes,
> Soon bounces on the ground, and breaks.'

Landor holds in the string so tight that the kite never soars to the end of its tether. In one of his many fits of 'the pride that apes humility,' he writes: —

> 'And yet, perhaps, if some should tire
> Of too much froth or too much fire,
> There is an ear that may incline
> Even to words so dull as mine.'

He was, indeed, averse to both froth and fire, and there is nothing of either in his temperate and lofty work. Yet there are times when he lets his Muse grow a little thin on an Arab fare, dates and water, in his dread of letting her enter 'Literature's gin-palaces.'

It is in Landor's dramatic work that we see, perhaps more clearly than elsewhere, the point beyond which he could not go, though nowhere else in his work do we see more clearly his nobility of attitude and his command of grave and splendid verse. Landor's method in dialogue is a logical method; the speeches are linked by a too definite and a too visible chain; they do not spring up out of those profound, subconscious affinities, which, in the work of the great dramatists, mimic Nature with all her own apparent irregularity. Coleridge, writing of 'The Tempest,' has noticed in Shakespeare, with deep insight: 'One admirable secret of his art is, that separate speeches frequently do not appear to have been occasioned by those which preceded, and which are consequent upon each other, but to have arisen out of the peculiar character of the speaker.' How minutely Landor follows the mechanical regularity of logic and association of ideas will be seen if we turn to almost any page of his dramas. In the second scene of the second act of 'Count Julian,' one speech of Julian's ends: 'Remember not our country'; and Covilla echoes: —

'Not remember!
What have the wretched else for consolation?'

She dwells on her desire of her own country, and Julian continues, rather than replies: —

'Wide are the regions of our far-famed land.'

Covilla responds in the same key, and ends her speech with the words: —

'Outcast from virtue, and from nature, too.'

It is now Julian who becomes the echo: —

' Nature and virtue! they shall perish first.'

His long speech ends with a reflection that the villagers, if they came among them, —

'Would pity one another less than us,
In injury, disaster, or distress.'

Covilla instantly catches the word 'pity,' and replies: —

'But they would ask each other whence our grief,
That they might pity.'

Landor, to forestall criticism, tells us that 'Count Julian' is 'rather a dialogue than a drama'; but it adopts the dramatic form, and even the form of French drama, in which the entrance of a new speaker begins a new scene. It could very well be presented by marionettes with sonorous voices, speaking behind the scenes. Landor never sees his people; they talk unmoved, or enunciate a sudden emotion with unnatural abruptness. The verse is too strict and stern, within measured Miltonic limits, for dramatic speech, or even for lifelike dialogue; thus:—

> 'If strength be wanted for security,
> Mountains the guard, forbidding all approach
> With iron-pointed and uplifted gates,
> Thou wilt be welcome too in Aguilar,
> Impenetrable, marble-turreted.'

Yet there are moments when the Miltonic speech becomes, as it can become, nakedly dramatic:—

> 'Heaven will inflict it, and not I . . . but I
> Neither will fall alone nor live despised.'

To Landor his own people were very real; and he says, 'I brought before me the various characters, their forms, complexions, and step. In the daytime I laboured, and at night unburdened my mind, shedding many tears.' But between this consciousness of a step heard in the mind, and a working knowledge of the movement of an actor across the stage, there is a great gulf; and Landor never crossed it. He aimed at producing the lofty effect of Greek tragedy, but in reading Sophocles he seems never to have realised the unerring, the infinitely ingenious playwright, to whom speech is first of all the most direct means of setting his characters to make his plot. Landor endows each of his characters with a few unvarying sentiments, and when several characters meet in action they do but give dignified expression, each as if speaking by himself, to those sentiments. The clash of wills, which makes drama, may be loud enough somewhere off the stage, but here it is but 'recollected in tranquillity.'

Landor is a great master of imagery, and in 'Count Julian' there are many lines like these:—

> 'Gryphens and eagles, ivory and gold,
> Can add no clearness to the lamp above;
> Yet many look for them in palaces
> Who have them not, and want them not, at home.'

Note how precise, how visual (in his own remote, sumptuous way), is the image; and how scrupulous the exactitude of the thought rendered by the image. But the image is, after all, no more than just such an ornamentation of 'gryphens and eagles, ivory and gold' to a thought separately clear in itself. The image is not itself the most vital part of the speech. Take, again, the speech of Julian to Roderigo, in which an image is used with more direct aim at dramatic effect: —

> 'I swerve not from my purpose: thou art mine,
> Conquer'd; and I have sworn to dedicate,
> Like a torn banner on my chapel's roof,
> Thee to the power from whom thou hast rebelled.'

In my copy of the first collected edition of Landor's poems some one has marked these last two lines; and they are striking lines. But let us open Shakespeare, and read, say, this: —

> 'He was a queen's son, boys:
> And though he came our enemy, remember
> He was paid for that: though mean and mighty, rotting
> Together, have one dust, yet reverence,
> That angel of the world, doth make distinction
> Of place 'twixt high and low.'

Here the superb epithet, 'that angel of the world,' which seems to interrupt a straightforward speech, heightens it with meaning. The 'torn banner on the chapel's roof' is only a decoration; it shows self-consciousness in the speaker, who thinks aside, in an unlikely way, and for effect.

In the later plays and scenes, in 'The Siege of Ancona,' and in the 'Beatrice Cenci,' most notably, Landor seems to have more nearly mastered the dramatic method, partly by limiting himself to briefer and less complicated action; and he has finally adopted a style which is at once more flexible and more beautiful. In 'The Siege of Ancona' there is a note of almost homely heroism which comes to one with a direct thrill; in 'Beatrice Cenci' there is both pity and terror; a deep tenderness in the scene between Beatrice and Margarita, and, in the last scene, where the citizens, 'at a distance from the scaffold,' hear the groans of Beatrice under torture, and suffer indignant agonies with each groan, a profound and almost painful beauty, at times finding relief in such lines as these: —

> 'She always did look pale,
> They tell me; all the saints, and all the good
> And all the tender-hearted, have looked pale.
> Upon the Mount of Olives was there one
> Of dawn-red hue even before that day?
> Among the mourners under Calvary
> Was there a cheek the rose had rested on?'

In some of the briefer scenes, those single conversations in which Landor could be so much more himself than in anything moving forward from scene to scene, there are lines that bite as well as shine; such lines as those of the drunken woman who has drowned her child: —

> '*Febe.* I sometimes wish 't were back again.
> *Griselda.* To cry?
> *Febe.* Ah! it *does* cry ere the first sea-mew cries;
> It wakes me many mornings, many nights,
> And fields of poppies could not quiet it.'

It is, after all, for their single lines, single speeches, separate indications of character (the boy Cæsarion in 'Antony and Octavius,' the girl Erminia in 'The Siege of Ancona,' a strain of nobility in the Consul, of honesty in Gallus, Inez de Castro at the moment of her death), that we remember these scenes. If we could wholly forget much of the rest, the 'rhetoric-roses,' not always 'supremely sweet,' though 'the jar is full,' the levity without humour, and, for the most part, without grace, the 'giggling' women (he respects the word, and finds it, in good Greek, in Theocritus), the placid arguing about emotions, his own loss of interest, it would seem, in some of these pages as he wrote them, we might make for ourselves in Landor what Browning in a friendly dedication calls him, 'a great dramatic poet,' and the master of a great and flawless dramatic style. There is another whole section of Landor's work, consisting of epigrams and small poems, more numerous, perhaps, than any English poet since Herrick has left us. Throughout his life he persistently versified trifles, as persistently as Wordsworth, but with a very different intention. Wordsworth tries to give them a place in life, so to speak, talking them, as anecdotes or as records of definite feelings; while Landor snatches at the feeling or the incident as something which may be cunningly embalmed in verse, with almost a funereal care. Among these poems which he thus wrote there are immortal successes, such as 'Dirce' or 'Rose Aylmer,' with many memorable epitaphs and epitomes, and some notable satires. By their side there is no inconsiderable number of petty trivialities, graceful nothings, jocose or sentimental trifles. With a far less instinctive sense of the capacities of his own language than Herrick, Landor refused to admit that what might make a poem in Latin could fail to be a poem in English. He won over many secrets from that close language; but the ultimate secrets of his own language he never discovered. Blake, Shelley, Keats, Coleridge, Wordsworth, among his contemporaries, could all do something that he could not do, something more native, more organically English, and therefore of a more absolute beauty as poetry. He reads Pindar for his 'proud complacency and scornful strength. If I could,' he says, 'resemble him in nothing else, I was resolved to be as compendious and as exclusive.' From Catullus he learned more, and his version of one of the lighter poems of Catullus has its place to-day, as if it were an original composition, among the mass of his collected lyrics, where it is not to be distinguished from the pieces surrounding it. Yet, if you will compare any of Landor's translations, good as they are, with the original Latin, you will see how much of the energy has been smoothed out, and you will realise that, though Catullus in Landor's English is very like Landor's English verse, there is something, of infinite importance, characteristic alike of Catullus and of poetry, which has remained behind, uncapturable.

Is it that, in Coleridge's phrase, 'he does not possess imagination in its highest form'? Is it that, as I think, he was lacking in vital heat?

No poet has ever been a bad prose-writer, whenever he has cared to drop from poetry into prose; but it is doubtful whether any poet has been quite so fine, accomplished, and persistent a prose-writer as Landor. 'Poetry,' he tells us, in one of his most famous passages, 'was always my amusement, prose my study and business. I have published five volumes of "Imaginary Conversations": cut the worst of them thro' the middle, and there will remain in this decimal fraction quite enough to satisfy my appetite for fame. I shall dine late; but the dining-room will be well lighted, the guests few and select.' Without his prose Landor is indeed but half, if he is half, himself. His verse at its best has an austere nobility, a delicate sensitiveness, the qualities of marble or of onyx. But there is much also which is no more than a graceful trifling, the verse of a courtly gentleman, who, as he grows older, takes more and more assiduous pains in the shaping and polishing of compliments. It is at its best when it is most personal, and no one has written more nobly of himself, more calmly, with a more lofty tenderness for humanity seen in one's small, private looking-glass. But the whole man never comes alive into the verse, body and soul, but only as a stately presence.

He has put more of himself into his prose, and it is in the prose mainly that we must seek the individual features of his soul and temperament. Every phrase comes to us with the composure and solemnity of verse, but with an easier carriage under restraint. And now he is talking, with what for him is an eagerness and straightforwardness in saying what he has to say,—the 'beautiful thoughts' never 'disdainful of sonorous epithets.' And you discover that he has much more to say than the verse has quite fully hinted at: a whole new hemisphere of the mind becomes visible, completing the sphere. And in all his prose, though only in part of his verse, he has the qualities which he attributes to Pindar: 'rejection of what is light and minute, disdain of what is trivial, and selection of those blocks from the quarry which will bear strong strokes of the hammer and retain all the marks of the chisel.' He wrote far more prose than verse, concentrating his maturest years upon the writing of prose. Was it, then, that his genius was essentially a prose genius, and that it was only when he turned to prose that, in the fullest sense, he found himself? I do not think it can be said that the few finest things in Landor's verse are excelled by the best of the many fine things in his prose; but the level is higher. His genius was essentially that of the poet, and it is to this quality that he owes the greater among the excellences of his prose. In the expression of his genius he was ambidextrous, but neither in prose nor in verse was he able to create life in his own image. No one in prose or in verse has written more finely about things; but he writes about them, he does not write them.

JAMES SMITH (1775-1839) AND HORATIO SMITH (1779-1849) [1]

JAMES and HORATIO SMITH were collaborators in one of the most perfect collections of parodies that exist, the 'Rejected Addresses,' published in 1812, in answer to a public appeal from the manager of Drury Lane Theatre for 'an Address to be spoken upon the opening of the Theatre,' after its rebuilding. The volume contained twenty-one parodies

[1] (1) *Rejected Addresses*, 1812. (2) *Horace in London*, 1813. (3) *Amarynthus, the Nympholept* (by Horace), 1821. (4) *Gaieties and Gravities*, 2 vols., 1825. (5) *Memoirs, Letters, and Comic Miscellanies, in Prose and Verse*, of the late James Smith, edited by his br other Horace Smith, 2 vols., 1840. (6) *Poetical Works of Horace*, 2 vols., 1846.

of living poets, done with equal skill, wit, and ingenuity by the two brothers. The success was immediate, and, for such a book, enormous, and very little of its savour has gone out of it after a century. Some of the parodies which must have been among the most amusing at a time when the Hon. William Spencer was commonly confused with an older poet of similar name, can scarcely appeal to us as they did to those familiar with the verses parodied. But the Wordsworth, the Coleridge, the Scott ('I certainly must have written this myself' said 'that fine-tempered man' to one of the authors), the Southey, all these remain a perpetual delight, unsurpassed by any later parodist. The words of Shelley, used of one, might well be applied to both, who, if they laughed inordinately, laughed without 'a sting in the tail of the honey.' Here is Shelley's summing up in verse: —

> 'Wit and sense,
> Virtue and human knowledge; all that might
> Make the dull world a business of delight,
> Are all combined in Horace Smith.'

And in talk he defined him as one who 'writes poetry and pastoral drama, and yet knows how to make money, and does make it, and is still generous.' The pastoral drama meant 'Amarynthus, the Nympholept,' which he published anonymously in 1821, in a little book containing, among some sonnets, one to Shelley, 'bold herald of announcements high.' The play overflows with fancy: —

> 'For now the clouds, in tufts of fleecy hue,
> Wander, like flocks of sheep, through fields of blue,
> Cropping the stars for daisies, while the moon
> Sits smiling on them as a shepherdess';

and

> 'The Spring time gushes
> For us as in the lusty grass and bushes,'

says or sings Amarynthus, who for some reason hears rills or streams in the strange and six-times repeated act of 'guggling.' For its sylvan gaiety, 'bathing in leafy greenness,' and full of the sap and savour of 'the jolly Spring,' this pastoral deserves a place, somewhere half-hidden, between Leigh Hunt and Keats. It has more sincerity than the one and less rich ardour than the other, but it shows us the approved wit in a new and not less delightful aspect. Some of the poems in his collected 'Poetical Works' are remarkable in other ways, sometimes lightly humorous, sometimes full of strange meditation, like the 'Address to a Mummy,' sometimes, as in 'The Murderer's Confession,' as grotesquely horrible as Hood.

THOMAS CAMPBELL (1775-1844)[1]

CAMPBELL shares with Longfellow the position of the favourite poet in elementary schools, where verse is learnt by heart as an exercise. There his good poems and his bad poems are equally appreciated: 'Lord Ullin's Daughter' neither more nor less than 'Hohenlinden,' and 'The Harper' than the 'Battle of the Baltic.' In his own lifetime Byron could say, meaning what he said: 'We are all wrong except Rogers, Crabbe, and Campbell.' It could be said, without apparent extravagance, by Campbell's not too considerate biographer, Cyrus Redding, that one of his long poems, 'Gertrude of Wyoming,' 'combines in itself the best characteristics of the classic and romantic styles, in that just medium which forms the truest principle for modern poetry'; and of the other equally famous long poem, 'The Pleasures of Hope,' that it belonged to 'that species of poetical composition which can alone be expected to attain in the eyes of true taste a classical and healthy longevity.' He was blamed for his too conscious and

[1] (1) *The Pleasures of Hope*, 1799. (2) *Gertrude of Wyoming*, 1809. (3) *O'Connor's Child*, 1810. (4) *Theodoric*, 1824. (5) *Miscellaneous Poems*, 1824. (6) *The Pilgrim of Glencoe*, 1842.

too deliberate art, for 'the smell of the lamp' which clung about his verse. To-day his audience is found on the lower benches of day-schools; that audience has been faithful to him for at least two generations; but it has never heard of 'Gertrude of Wyoming' or of 'The Pleasures of Hope,' in which Campbell's contemporaries saw 'intimations' for him 'of immortality.'

The problem is curious, and there are complications in it; for, while all the bookish and ambitious verse has been forgotten, some of the simple verse which has remained popular is not less worthless, while some of it, a very little, has qualities more or less unique in English poetry. How are we to explain these compromises and caprices of posterity?

Campbell lived his whole life at a great distance from reality, always believing what he wanted to believe and denying what he did not want to believe. He was not a dreamer who could transpose the worlds and be content in either; he was fitful, essentially unreal, a faint-hearted evader of reality. In a conversation which might have come direct out of 'The Egoist,' he is seen defending Mrs. Siddons against a criticism whose justice he does not actually dispute, by saying pettishly: 'I won't admit her want of excellence in anything. She is an old friend of mine.' Himself a persistent critic of his own work, he forgave no other critic, and refused to correct an error which had been discovered by any one but himself. He despised his own 'Hohenlinden,' which he called a 'damned drum and trumpet thing,' and only printed to please Scott. The famous false rhyme in the last stanza — 'sepulchre' for what should be sounded 'sepulchry' — he neither admitted nor denied, neither blamed nor defended. We see him wondering whether such a word as 'sepulchry' ever existed, half wishing that it did, yet refusing to adopt it, and concluding weakly that the word as it is 'reads well alone, if we forget that there should be a concinnity with the preceding lines.' He was fastidious without taste, full of alarmed susceptibility; so that when he was editing Colburn's 'New Monthly' he disliked his best contributor, the one who brought him most that was new, Hazlitt, and was with difficulty persuaded to accept the epical essay on the prize-fight.

The truth is that Campbell was a sentimental egoist, the Sir Willoughby Patterne of poets. His incapability of realising things as they are, until the realisation was forced upon him by some crisis, explains that unreality, that vague rosy tinge, which we find in almost all of his poetry which professes to deal with actual life. In life, as in poetry, the real force of things was not to be wholly evaded. There is a story told of how a stranger repeated to him the words of an old Welsh bard: 'My wife is dead, my son is mad, my harp is unstrung,' and how Campbell burst into tears, for the burden of the triad might have been his own. These profound distresses, it is true, he never met fairly. He tried to forget them, in what his biographers call 'convivial company,' in change of abode, even in unnecessary hack-work. He regarded, we are told, 'poetical composition as a labour,' and the inclination for it 'came upon him only at rare intervals.' It may be that 'his slowness of composition was,' as he says of Carew, 'evidently that sort of care in the poet which saves trouble to his reader.' But not only did he write with labour; poetry was never to him a means of self-expression.

It was the age when poets set themselves tasks in verse, and to Campbell as a young man Rogers' 'Pleasures of Memory,' itself descended from Akenside's 'Pleasures of Imagination,' presented itself as a model of what should be attempted. He found it easy, in 'The Pleasures of Hope,' to surpass his models, but, though one of its lines is continually on our lips to-day,

' 'T is distance lends enchantment to the view,'

the smooth meandering of verse, with its Micawber-like cheerfulness, becomes drearier and more dismal as we read; and when we have reached

> 'Come, bright Improvement, on the car of Time,
> And rule the spacious world from clime to clime,'

we begin to wonder by what cottage-side poetry has gone to live in the land. With Wordsworth, perhaps, whose 'Lyrical Ballads' have just been published, to the derision of a polite public which applauds 'The Pleasures of Hope!'

Tastes change, they say, and tastes do change, though taste does not. But there is one touchstone which may be applied, apart from all technical qualities, all rules of metre or fashions of speech, whenever verse has a plain thing to say. The verse which takes what has already been finely and adequately said in prose, and makes of it something inferior in mere directness and expressiveness of statement, cannot be good verse. This is what Campbell found in the Bible: 'And the king was much moved, and went up to the chamber over the gate, and wept: and as he went, thus he said: "O my son Absalom, my son, my son Absalom! would God I had died for thee, O Absalom, my son, my son!"' And this is what Campbell made of it in 'The Pleasures of Hope': —

> '"My Absalom!" the voice of Nature cried,
> "O that for thee thy father could have died!
> For bloody was the deed, and rashly done,
> That slew my Absalom! — my son! — my son!"'

In this poem one seems to catch the last gasp of the eighteenth century; in 'Gertrude of Wyoming,' published ten years later, we are in the century of 'Childe Harold' and the romantic tales. 'Gertrude' is a tepid romance, such as school-girls may dream after reading books of improving travel; a thing all feminine and foppish, written by the man, 'dressed sprucely,' whom Byron calls up for us: 'A blue coat becomes him — so does his new wig.' The blue coat and the new wig are never far away from these Pennsylvanian forests, with their panthers, palm-trees, and flamingoes of the tropics. Unreality is in every languid line.

> 'So finished he the rhyme (howe'er uncouth)
> That true to nature's fervid feelings ran
> (And song is but the eloquence of truth)'

says Campbell, vaguely; and I suppose he believed himself to have been 'true to nature's fervid feelings' in his record of the respectable loves of Gertrude and Waldegrave. 'Never insensible to female beauty,' says the commentator, Cyrus Redding, 'and fond of the society of women, it was singular that Campbell, the poet of sentiment and imagery, should have written little or nothing breathing of ardent affection.' Campbell's was, in his own affected phrase,

> 'The heart that vibrates to a feeling tone';

and here as elsewhere one can imagine him to have been genuinely touched by what, in his way of telling it, fails to touch us. When people read 'Gertrude of Wyoming' they had acquired a taste for poetical narratives; since Rousseau, the virtues of forest folk were esteemed; and the poem, no doubt, responded to some occasion in the public mind. I have tried to find a single line of genuine poetry in its thin trickle of verse, but I have found none. There is in it a little more of what used to be called 'fancy' than in the much later, wholly unsuccessful 'Theodoric'; but it is not appreciably nearer to poetry. 'The pearly dew of sensibility,' which Hazlitt discovered in its recesses, has not, as he thought it would, 'distilled and collected, like the diamond in the mine'; nor does 'the structure of his fame,' according to the singular metaphor, 'rest on the crystal columns of a polished imagination.'

Yet other props and embellishments must be knocked away from the structure of Campbell's fame before we can distinguish what is really permanent in it. There is, first of all, the series of romantic ballads. In 'Lord Ullin's Daughter' and the rest Campbell writes with a methodical building up of circumstantial emotion which in the end becomes ludicrous, from its 'more than usual order.' Few escape absurdity, but

I doubt whether any parodist has ever equalled the quite serious conclusion of 'The Ritter Bann': —

> 'Such was the throb and mutual sob
> Of the Knight embracing Jane.'

Here and there, in a homelier story, Campbell seems to be trying to imitate Wordsworth, as in the foolish 'Child and Hind' and the less foolish 'Napoleon and the British Sailor'; and once, in 'The Parrot of Mull: a Domestic Anecdote,' he seems to have almost caught the knack, and the piece might take its place, not unworthily, among Wordsworth's second-rate work in that kind.

Another sort of work which Campbell attempted with much immediate success, and for which he is still remembered in the schoolroom, is a kind of pathetic ballad which appeals almost indecently to the emotions: I mean such pieces as 'The Exile of Erin,' 'The Harper,' 'The Wounded Hussar.' There is emotion in them, but the emotion, when it is not childish, is genteel. I scarcely know whether the misfortunes of 'poor dog Tray' or of the 'wounded hussar' are to be taken the less seriously; the latter, perhaps, by just the degree in which it aims at a more serious effect. 'And dim was that eye, once expressively beaming': it is of the soldier he speaks, not of the dog. But it is in a better poem, 'The Exile of Erin,' that we see most clearly the difference and the cause of the difference between Campbell's failures and successes in precisely what he could do best in the expression of patriotic feeling. 'The Exile of Erin' is one of those many poems, written, often, by men who would have died for the convictions expressed in them, but written with so hackneyed and commonplace a putting of that passion into words that the thing comes to us lifeless, and stirs in us no more of a thrill than the casual street-singer's 'Home, Sweet Home,' drawled out for pence and a supper.

Conviction, it should always be remembered, personal sincerity, though it is an important ingredient in the making of a patriotic or national poem, is but one ingredient among many; and there is one of these which is even more important: poetical impulse, which is a very different thing from personal impulse. I have no doubt that the personal impulse of 'The Exile of Erin' was at least as sincere as that of 'Hohenlinden'; I should say it was probably much more deeply felt; but here the poetical energy lags behind the energy of conviction; the effort to be patriotic and to draw an affecting moral is undisguised; the result is a piece of artistic insincerity. In 'Hohenlinden' some wandering spark has alighted; the wind has carried it, and one knows not from whence; only, a whole beacon is ablaze.

'Hohenlinden' is a poem made wholly out of very obvious materials, and made within very narrow limits, to which it owes its intensity. Campbell had precisely that mastery of the obvious which makes rememberable lines, such as 'Distance lends enchantment to the view,' or 'Coming events cast their shadows before,' which we remember as we remember truisms, almost ashamed at doing so. They contain no poetic suggestion, they are no vital form of poetic speech; but they make statements to which verse lends a certain emphasis by its limiting form or enclosure. Very often Campbell uses this steady emphasis when no emphasis is needed, as in this kind of verse, for instance: —

> 'I mark his proud but ravaged form,
> As stern he wraps his mantle round,
> And bids, on winter's bleakest ground,
> Defiance to the storm.'

This is merely meant for the picture of the friendless man, not a Byronic Corsair; and here the emphasis is above all a defect of the visual sense: he cannot see simply with the mind's eye. In such poems as the powerful and unpoetical 'Last Man' the emphasis is like a conscious rigidity of bearing on parade, a military earnestness of rhetoric. The lines march with feet keeping time with the drill-master; and the wonder and terror which should shake in the heart of the poem are frozen at the source. In the genuine success of 'Hohenlinden' every line is a separate emphasis, but all the emphasis is required by the subject, is in its place. The thud and brief repeated monotony of the metre give the very sound of cannonading; each line is like a crackle of musketry. What is obvious in it, even, comes well into a poem which depends on elements so simple for its success; indeed, its existence.

The one fixed passion in Campbell's shifting soul seems to have been the passion for liberty. The dust from Kosciusko's grave, cast by a Polish patriot into the grave of Campbell in Westminster Abbey, was a last appropriate homage to one who had always been 'the sanguine friend of freedom.' He was the patriot of all oppressed countries, and his love for his own country was only part of that wider human enthusiasm. His love of England was quickened, or brought to poetic heat, by a love of the sea, and by a curiously vivid appreciation of the life and beauty of warships. In his controversy with Bowles, as to the place of nature and of art in poetry, his most effective argument was drawn from a warship. 'Those who have ever witnessed the spectacle of the launching of a ship of the line will perhaps forgive me for adding this to the examples of the sublime objects of artificial life. Of that spectacle I can never forget the impression, and of having witnessed it reflected from the faces of ten thousand spectators. . . . It was not a vulgar joy, but an affecting national solemnity.' Something of this 'mental transport,' as he elsewhere describes it, this sense of the beauty and grandeur of the actual circumstances of sea-fighting, came, along with the patriotic fervour, into his two naval odes, 'Ye Mariners of England', and 'The Battle of the Baltic,' his two really great poems.

'Ye Mariners of England' has a finer poetic substance than 'Hohenlinden' and a more original metrical scheme, here, as there, curiously well adapted to its subject. The heavy pauses and loud rushes: 'And sweep through the deep,' with its checked flow and onset; 'When the stormy winds do blow,' twice repeated, with a vehement motion, and an exultation as of wind and water: conscious art has here, for once, caught hands with a fiercer impulse, and wrought better than it knew. Even here, however, the impulse is on the wane before the last stanza is over; and that last stanza has been made for logic's sake rather than for any more intimate need.

And even in 'The Battle of the Baltic,' where Campbell reaches his highest height, there are flaws, weaknesses, trifling perhaps, but evident here and there; touches of false poetising, like the line in the last stanza: 'And the mermaid's song condoles.' But the manliness, haughty solemnity, the blithe courage and confidence of the poem, and also the invention of the metre (an afterthought, as we know, introduced when the poem was cut down from twenty-seven stanzas of six lines each into eight stanzas of nine) are things unique in English. The structure, with its long line moving slowly to the pause, at which the three heavily weighted, yet, as it were, proudly prancing syllables fall over and are matched by the three syllables which make the last line, the whole rhythmical scheme, unlike anything that had been done before, has left its mark upon whatever in that line has been done finely since: upon Browning in 'Hervé Riel,' upon Tennyson in 'The Revenge.' And if any one thinks that this kind of masterpiece is hardly more than the natural outcome of a fervid patriotic impulse, let him turn to others of Campbell's poems full of an even lustier spirit of patriotism, to poems as bad as the 'Stanzas on the Threatened Invasion,' 1803, or as comparatively good as 'Men of England,' and he will see just how far the personal impulse will carry a poet of uncertain technique in the absence of adequate poetic impulse and adequate poetic technique.

In much of Campbell's work there is a kind of shallow elegance, a turn of phrase which is neat, but hardly worth doing at all if it is done no better. Read the little complimentary verses to ladies, and think of Lovelace; read 'The Beech-Tree's Petition,' with its nice feeling and words without atmosphere, and think of Marvell's garden-verses, in which every line has perfume and radiance. The work is so neat, so rounded and polished; like waxen flowers under glass shades; no nearer to nature or art.

In the 'Valedictory Stanzas to Kemble' there is a definition of 'taste,' which shows us something of Campbell's theory and aim in art: —

> 'Taste, like the silent dial's power,
> That, when supernal light is given,
> Can measure inspiration's hour,
> And tell its height in heaven.'

And he defines the mind of the actor as 'at once ennobled and correct.' Always labouring to be 'at once ennobled and correct,' Campbell is never visited by any poetic inspiration, except in those few poems in which he has not been more sincere, or chosen better, than usual, but has been more lucky, and able to carry an uncertain technique further. That, and not emotion, or sincerity, or anything else, is what distinguishes what is good from what is bad in his work, even in those poems which have given our literature its greatest war-songs.

THOMAS MOORE (1779–1852) [1]

MOORE as a poet is the Irishman as the Englishman imagines him to be, and he represents a part of the Irish temperament;

[1] (1) *Odes from Anacreon,* 1800. (2) *The Poetical Works of the Late Thomas Little,* 1801. (3) *Epistles, Odes, and other Poems,* 1806. (4) *Irish Melodies, with Music by Sir James Stevenson,* i, 1807; ii, 1807; iii, 1810; iv, 1811; v, 1813; vi, 1815; vii, 1818; viii, 1821; ix, 1824; x, 1834. (5) *Corruption and Intolerance,* 1808. (6) *The Sceptic.* (7) *Intercepted Letters, or The Two-penny Post Bag,* 1813. (8) *Sacred Songs,* 1816, 1824. (9) *Lalla Rookh,* 1817. (10) *National Airs,* 1818, 1826. (11) *The Fudge*

but not the part which makes for poetry. All the Irish quicksilver is in him; he registers change with every shift in the weather. He has the spirits of a Dublin mob; and it is the voice of the mob, prettily refined, sweetened, set to a tune, which we hear in his songs. But the voice of the peasant is not in him; there is in him nothing of that uneasy, listening conscience which watches the earth for signs, and is never alone in solitude. He is without imagination, and his fun and his fancy are but the rising and sinking of the quicksilver, and mean no more than a change in the weather. The imagination, which made the great Irish legends, is still awake in the peasant; education has not yet robbed him of the best part of his birthright; and in Mr. Yeats, and in A. E., and in Dr. Douglas Hyde, we see the Irish imagination again creating nobly after its kind. Moore prattled of 'the harp that once through Tara's halls the soul of music shed'; but the harp to which his ears really listened was modern and gilded, and played by a young lady in a drawing-room. He sang to it with an agreeable voice, and he delighted his contemporaries.

In considering the question of any individual popularity, it is needful, I think, to take into account the general level of taste which can be distinguished in the public which has created that popularity. Sophocles was popular in his time, and if we scrutinise all that is known of the Athenian public which appreciated his plays, we shall see that the general level of that public's taste was very high, and we shall not be surprised by the popularity of so great a poet and so severe an artist. The public which delighted in Shakespeare was the public which had a more vivid appreciation of strange and

Family in Paris, 1818. (12) *The Loves of the Angels*, 1823. (13) *Fables for the Holy Alliance*, 1823. (14) *Evenings in Greece*, 1826, 1832. (15) *Odes upon Cash, Corn, Catholics, and other Matters*, 1828. (16) *Legendary Ballads*, 1828. (17) *The Summer Fête*, 1831. (18) *Vocal Minstrelsy*, 1834, 1835. (19) *The Fudges in England*, 1835. (20) *Alciphron* (added to a new edition of *The European*, a prose romance), 1839. (21) *Poetical Works*, 10 vols., 1840-41.

stirring things, a more lively sense of personal adventure, and a more friendly and intimate love and cultivation of music, than the public of any other century in England. What, then, was the general level of taste in art at the time when Thomas Moore was (in the words of Byron's dedication of 'The Corsair') 'the poet of all circles and the idol of his own'? Blake was living, and, when known, known only to be mocked, when Moore's career as a poet was practically over; the 'Lyrical Ballads' appeared two years before the 'Odes of Anacreon' and three years before the 'Poetical Works of the Late Thomas Little, Esq.,' and Wordsworth and Coleridge were probably little more than uncouth names, just known enough to be scorned, to the 'princely' circles in which Moore was an idol and the world-wide circles of whom he was the poet; Keats and Shelley, both younger men, died thirty years before Moore, and we find Shelley in the year of his death, speaking of 'Hellas' (he might have spoken for 'Lamia' as well) as 'the last of my orphans,' and asking a friend if it was he who was 'introducing it to oblivion, and me to my accustomed failure.' Scott, an older man, and Byron, a younger man, were Moore's only serious rivals in the affection of the public; and Byron was loved more for his defects than for his qualities, and Scott, as a poet, was scarcely less overrated than Moore. What, then, can be said of the general level of taste of the public which Moore intoxicated? Can we argue from what we know of it that Moore's popularity was greatly to his credit?

'It is Moore's great distinction,' we are told by his biographer, 'that he gave real pleasure to all sorts and conditions of men.' That is true, and it gave to his fame a pleasant flavour: 'my friendly fame,' he calls it. He pleased by his songs and by his singing of them: how is it that the songs to-day seem to us like last season's fashions, melancholy in their faded prettiness? He gave pleasure, but the quality of that pleasure must be considered, and it will be seen that it was not the quality of poetic pleasure.

Moore, it may be said, wrote to please, not out of any deep inner need; yet, if he wrote what pleased others, it was mainly because it had pleased himself. No; what is poetry can be distinguished from what is not poetry by none of these tests, which are tests of probability, at the utmost; it can be distinguished only by the presence or absence in it of the qualities common to all genuine poetry: some quality of strangeness in its beauty, some gravity or gaiety beyond the mere sound or message of its words in the ear, and, in its sincerity to a mood, an emotion, or a sensation,

'One grace, one thought, one wonder, at the least,
Which into words no virtue can digest.'

Herrick wrote drinking songs, and he left in them some of the mournful ecstasy of the vine. But, in the drinking songs of Tom Moore, only the lees are left.

In the preface to his early poems we find Moore wishing himself Catullus. But did he ever quite realise what was said in that naked speech, that word like a flame of live coal, of the great lover and the great hater? It does not seem so, for he praises him for his 'exquisite playfulness,' his 'warm yet chastened description.' Even in Rochester and Sedley, whom he professes to have learnt from, he sees only the 'graceful levity,' and this as a mere 'dissipation of the heart,' set off by 'those seductive graces by which gallantry almost teaches it to be amiable.' What counts in Rochester is not that, but the sting; and the sting comes from some quintessential expression of a nature which at least paid the price of sincerity. Do Mr. Thomas Little's 'ten or twenty kisses,' however counted or however multiplied, fill up the millionth interval of Rochester's 'live-long minute' of fidelity, or even Sedley's regret that he cannot 'change each hour'?

It is to the Cavalier Lyrics, no doubt, that Moore at his best comes nearest; never within recognisable distance of any Elizabethan work, and never near enough to the good work of the

Restoration for the comparison to be seriously made. He has their fluency, but none of their gentlemanly restraint; touches of their crudity, but none of their straightforwardness; and of their fine taste, nothing, and nothing of the quality of mind which lurks under all their disguises. In Moore's songs there is no 'fundamental brain-work'; they have no base in serious idea or in fine emotion. The sensations they render are trivial in themselves, or become so in the rendering; there is a continual effervescence, but no meditation and no ecstasy. Between this faint local heat of the senses and the true lyric rapture there is a great gulf. Moore brims over with feeling, and his feeling is quick, honest, and generous. But he never broods over his feeling until he has found his way down to its roots: the song strikes off from the surface like the spurt of a match; there is no deep fire or steady flame. He never realised the dignity of song or of the passions. In his verse he was amorous, but a foolish lover; shrewd, but without wisdom; honest, but without nobility; a breeder of easy tears and quick laughter. He sang for his evening, not his day; and he had his reward, but must go without the day's wages.

In his 'Book of Irish Verse,' Mr. Yeats has made a cruel and just test of the essential quality of Moore's lyrical work by printing, one after the other, a song of Moore: —

> 'You who would try
> The terrible track';

Théophile Gautier's close and heightened translation: —

> 'Vous qui voulez courir
> La terrible carrière';

and Mr. Robert Bridges' translation back into English from Gautier: —

> 'O youth whose hope is high,
> Who dost to truth aspire,'

in which, as he rightly says, the lines are at last lifted 'into the rapture and precision of poetry.' A similar test might be made by looking from the lines of Dante which Moore paraphrases in his 'Dream of the Two Sisters' to the tripping triviality of his version. Three lines will sufficiently show the havoc.

> 'Giovane e bella in sogno mi parea,
> Donna vedere andar per una landa,
> Cogliendo fiori; e cantando dicea.'

So far Dante: this is what Moore thought Dante meant: —

> 'Methought at that sweet hour
> A nymph came o'er the lea,
> Who, gath'ring many a flow'r,
> Thus said and sung to me.'

But if these comparisons seem too lofty, I have a very legitimate one in reserve, and I am not sure that it is not the most convincing. There is an 'Irish Melody' of Moore which begins: —

> 'Oh! had we some bright little isle of our own,
> In a blue summer ocean, far off and alone,
> Where a leaf never dies in the still blooming bowers,
> And the bee banquets on through a whole year of flowers.'

The idea has been repeated by another Irishman, Mr. Yeats, and his poem begins: —

> 'I will arise and go now, and go to Innisfree,
> And a small cabin build there, of clay and wattles made;
> Nine bean-rows will I have there, a hive for the honey-bee,
> And live alone in the bee-loud glade.'

No two poems could be more exactly comparable; the resemblances are as striking as the differences; and the differences might teach in one lesson all that distinguishes what is poetry from what is not poetry.

And further, if you will compare the versification of these two poems, or indeed any other poems of the two writers, you will see how cheap, for the most part, were Moore's rhythmical effects, how continually he sacrificed the accent of the sense to the accent of the rhythm, and how little he made even out of those rhythms which he is believed to have introduced into English. Those who still claim for Moore some recognition as a poet claim it mainly on account of his skill in metre, and on account of his tact in writing words for singing. With a good poet, good music can make good songs; with a bad poet, the best of all music cannot do as much, and Moore, in putting words to his 'Irish Melodies,' did not always give the tunes a chance. We are told: 'He based his work upon Irish tunes, composed in the primitive manner, before poetry was divorced from music. One may say, virtually, that in fitting words to these tunes he reproduced in English the rhythms of Irish folk-song.' But we are told further, and then the case is altered: 'The thing was not done completely: for instance, in the first number of the "Melodies," the song "Erin, the smile and the tear in thine eye," is to the tune of "Eileen Aroon," and the Irish words . . . do not correspond in metre with Moore's. He has varied the tune, and is consequently using a different stanza.' If, further, one may judge from Dr. Hyde's translations in his beautiful book, 'The Love Songs of Connacht,' Moore has come very far short of having 'reproduced in English the rhythms of Irish folk-song.' Certain cadences he has caught, like that cadence of

'At the mid hour of night, when stars are weeping, I fly,'

which we are told is 'a metrical effect wholly new in English.' To have introduced a new cadence into English is quite a creditable thing to have done, even without writing a good poem by its aid. And, though the poem beginning with this line may be 'the most beautiful lyric that Moore ever wrote,' I do not think it can be accepted as really a good poem. To be 'exquisite,' or to attain 'high poetry,' requires qualities which Moore never possessed, and neither in this nor in another popular lyric, 'The Light of Other Days,' graceful and plaintive as they are, can I find an exception to those qualities of strictly second-rate skill in verse-writing which he did possess. I find in both poems a facility which carries the tune and the sense smoothly and quickly along; a prettiness, alike of sentiment and form; a certain elegance, yet a thin elegance, which covers nothing vital; and the sincerity of a superficial emotion which I can neither respect nor share, for it is fancy playing the part of feeling.

Moore's trot, gallop, and jingle of verse has, no doubt, its skill and its merit; but its skill is not seldom that of the circus-rider, and its merit no more than to have gone the due number of times round the ring without slackening speed. It entertains the most legitimately when it carries mere folly on its back. But Moore had ideals and ideas, and only the same trained nag to carry them. 'Almost without knowing it,' says his biographer, 'he wrote primarily for his own countrymen'; and it was to his countrymen that he said: 'There exists no title of honour or distinction to which I could attach half so much value as that of being called your poet, — the poet of the people of Ireland.' First, and for long, he sang his patriotism to the strains of his own barrel-organ; and makes pity and anger jig to the same measures as 'endearing young charms.' Gradually he gave up writing verse, and wrote prose, controversial prose, and was looked upon as 'the champion of the liberties of Ireland.' It is significant of the whole man, and of how small a segment of him was an artist, that for Moore to become really serious meant giving up verse. Only in prose could he conceive of people being quite serious, and writing nobly.

ROBERT EYRES LANDOR (1781–1869) [1]

THE style and language of Robert Landor's plays were more interesting and original than the matter of them. In the preface to 'The Count Arezzi' he says that 'it was written de-

[1] (1) *The Count Arezzi*, 1824. (2) *The Impious Feast*, 1828. (3) *The Earl of Brecon, Faith's Fraud, The Ferryman*, 1841.

signedly with those qualities which were to render it unfit for representation.' We can read with pleasure: —

> 'Be merry,
> Sing like some April cuckoo all day long
> The same dull note, for rustic fools to mock at —
> Their jest, their weariness.'

More clothed speech is to be found in: —

> 'Five-hooped stoops
> Are empty ere they well have laid the dust
> Of such fierce dog-day drouth and sultriness.'

Here, and elsewhere, too careful a search after metaphor and elaborate speech tends to absorb the emotion, which is lofty, and to get in the way of the drama, which is not dramatic. In a narrative poem, 'The Impious Feast,' there is a wild imaginative extravagance, and the experiment is not unsuccessful of 'a rhyme occasionally so close and so frequent as to rescue the stanza; or it may be rendered so lax as to have all the freedom of blank verse.' But it is in his prose that Landor excels, in 'The Fawn of Sertorius? and especially in 'The Fountain of Arethusa.' That fantastic romance, written to personify a strange philosophy, is the invention of a moralist and a poet. The style has something of the purity of his brother's, but is at times touched with eccentricity, in its expression of a calm persuasive satire. 'Figures of speech, which were originally intended to explain our reasons and opinions, like unpractised performers in a new dance, jostle against their partners, and confuse the rest': how like Landor that is! But here is the brother: 'Since it is much more pleasurable to carry the whip in your hand than to feel it upon your shoulder, who would not be a critic if he could, as the herring would be a shark, the rabbit a stoat, and the oyster an alderman?' The outlines of the narrative are ingeniously contrived, not without humour in its picture of a world peopled by dead Romans who had survived death, and remained critics of the living. Their arguments against a conventional Christianity are uncommon and irrefutable; against these Britons, who 'cannot have shown so much courage in subduing the world as in defying its Creator.'

EDWARD, BARON THURLOW (1781-1829)[1]

ONE of Lord Thurlow's sonnets, the only good one, is known because Lamb praised and quoted it in a note to his essay on Sidney's Sonnets on the first appearance of that essay in the 'London Magazine.' He called it a sonnet which 'for quiet sweetness and unaffected morality has scarcely its parallel in our language.' If any reader goes further, and turns over the chill and elegant pages where there are other sonnets, addressed to 'very illustrious noblemen,' with pastorals done after old patterns, and Tasso tepidly imitated, he must remember that in a letter to Wordsworth Lamb himself complained of the fatigue of 'going through a volume of fine words by Lord Thurlow,' and that he was glad to turn from the 'excellent words' to Vincent Bourne, 'his diction all Latin and his thoughts all English.'

EBENEZER ELLIOTT (1781-1849)[2]

A GREAT deal too much space in the collected poems of Ebenezer Elliott is filled with a series of rhymed and blank verse narrative and 'epical' productions, filled with fervid talk, not without vigour and a kind of rough eloquence, but result-

[1] (1) *Verses on Several Occasions*, 1812. (2) *Ariadne*, 1814. (3) *Carmen Britannicum*, 1814. (4) *The Doge's Daughter*, 1814. (5) *Select Poems*, 1821. (6) *Angelica*, 1822.
[2] (1) *The Vernal Walk*, 1798. (2) *Night*, 1818. (3) *Love, a Poem*, 1823. (4) *The Village Patriarch*, 1829. (5) *Corn-Law Rhymes*, 1831. (6) *The Splendid Village, etc.*, 3 vols., 1833-35. (7) *Poetical Works*, 1840, 1846.

ing in so much definite waste of a special talent, which could only work satisfactorily within certain limits. It is amusing to see the seriousness with which he measures himself, in his 'Spirits and Men,' against 'all that is transcendent in genius'. which has dealt with similar material, — Milton, Byron, Moore, and Montgomery. In 'The Village Patriarch' he is nearer to a suitable subject, and begins to express, though not yet with due concentration, his own message. He says of himself: —

> 'But distempered, if not mad,
> I feed on Nature's bane and mess with scorn.
> I would not, could not if I would, be glad,
> But, like shade-loving plants, am happiest sad.
> My heart, once soft as woman's tear, is gnarled
> With gloating on the ills I cannot cure.'

He proceeds to compare himself with 'Arno's bard,' whose music, he says, 'snarled.' That is but one instance of a radical lack of critical sense in literature, which leads him to dedicate his earliest compositions to Lord Lytton and to 'my great master, Robert Southey, who condescended to teach me the art of poetry,' and to characterise Byron as

> 'thrice a Ford, twice an Euripides,
> And half a Schiller.'

His energy of speech in verse was natural to him from the first, and as soon as he began to subdue its buoyancy and give it that alloy, of prose perhaps, in a sense, which it required for due hardness, the work begins to become interesting. Realism has never perhaps been made more pardonable in verse than in some of Elliott's harsh but vivid, violent but pungent, delineations of country scenes and situations. In his earlier manner it is, like Crabbe, hurried, a little unceremoniously, into a quicker pace, and a more warm and ready observation. By 1848, 'The Year of Seeds,' the style in these would-be sonnets has turned into a more ragged but more muscular activity, coarsely and wonderfully alive. It is all improvised, on one indignant impulse after another, but there is always, as in a Dutch picture, atmosphere.

The actual 'Corn-Law Rhymes,' after which Ebenezer Elliott is commonly named, are only fifteen in all, and only one or two of them are among his best work. The song, 'Child, is Thy Father dead?' can be compared with Hood, but just fails to touch us so much or so completely to satisfy the ear. The 'Battle Song' has justly found its way into anthologies, though too Byronic in its emphasis for really fine kind of lyric poetry. But there are other pieces, which might be called labour poems, in which there is sometimes a quality that has analogies both with Hood and with Wordsworth; as in the lines called 'Sabbath Morning,' which bring a clear, ringing, exultant melody out of the mere appeal to a 'young mechanic' to go into the open air on a Sunday.

> 'Then let me write for immortality
> One honest song,'

he prayed; and there is an ardour in the honesty of many of his shorter pieces which lifts them out of mere oratory, even when they are concerned with matters of politics, and oddly decorated with words like 'Free Trade.' A poem of twelve tiny lines, like that which ends, —

> 'Then, the thoughtful look for thunder,'

has gnomic weight, like some rhymed saying of the Middle Ages. Thought is hammered by emotion into poetry. The fact is, that he is only concerned with a few great rights and wrongs, and that these temporary names are mere labels for them. His feeling is fierce and swift, and often snatches up a wild open-air poetry as it goes, or drops to a deep, thrilling note, as in the strange poem 'A Shadow,' in which thought shudders on unknown verges. This particular quality is seen at its best in a haunting poem, written on one rhyme, and with the refrain of 'the land which no one knows,' a poem which is marred only by the intrusion of one uncouth, moralising stanza, where the prose of the thought naturally brings with it the single jarring inversion in an otherwise delicately modulated harmony.

'I am sufficiently rewarded,' he said, 'if my poetry has led one poor despairing victim of misrule from the alehouse to the fields'; and the chief quality which goes, in his verse, with a fierce indignant sympathy with the poor is a continual sense of nature, very simply apprehended, and coming to us like the bright refreshing air of English lanes. English landscape is felt as perhaps no one else has quite felt it, for the rest and solace that it can give; so that the last lines which he dictated before dying were a prayer that the autumn primrose and the robin's song might come back to him.

There is much in Ebenezer Elliott's work which is merely spasmodic, merely oratorical, merely prose of one kind or another. But his poetical impulse is unquestionable, and there is in it a solid part of individuality, in which tenderness and irony are combined. He can find in 'rain, steam, and speed' not indeed all that Turner found in them, but that —

'Streams trade with clouds, seas trade with heaven,
Air trades with light, and is forgiven.'

And he can concern himself with many subtle riddles, finding poetry in the dark corners of conduct and conscience. Sometimes we are reminded of Donne, sometimes of crabbed and coloured ingenuities of the later Elizabethans, in these strangely assorted compositions. And, in spite of his many earnest purposes, his best verse has an accidental character, comes from and renders a mood, as lyrical verse is rarely allowed to be or seem by poets who are fighters for ideas.

WILLIAM NICHOLSON (1782-1849) [1]

WILLIAM NICHOLSON was the son of a Galloway carrier, and he turned pedlar, and had many ups and downs, until, under the advice of Hogg and other good friends, he printed his own poems and took them about in his pack. He went to fairs as singer and piper; then took to drink, and a new gospel, which he wanted to preach to the king; but, coming back unsatisfied, became a drover.

Three editions have appeared of his 'Tales in Verse and Miscellaneous Poems'; the first with a preface of his own, the two others with memoirs. There is a rough swing in his verses, and some hearty matter for the rhymes of them. He can turn a phrase sometimes as neatly as this: —

> 'Ilk is in its season sweet;
> So love is, in its noon.'

ANN TAYLOR (1782-1866), AND JANE TAYLOR (1783-1824) [2]

THESE sisters both wrote poems of great charm and simplicity for 'infant minds,' which have absorbed and not yet let go such treasures of song as 'Twinkle, Twinkle, Little Star,' the most eminent and irresistible of them. Their simple elegance and friendly feeling for the young gave them a more enviable

---

[1] *Tales in Verse and Miscellaneous Poems, descriptive of Rural Life and Manners*, 1814, 1828, 1878.

[2] Jane Taylor wrote *Essays in Rhyme*, 1816; and *Contributions of Q. Q.*, 2 vols. in prose and verse, 1824. Ann Taylor, *The Wedding among the Flowers*, 1808. Their other books were written together, namely: (1) *Original Poems for Infant Minds by Several Young Persons*, 1804. (2) *Rhymes for the Nursery*, 1806. (3) *Poetical Works*, 1807. (4) *Limed Twigs to catch Young Birds*, 1808. (5) *Hymns for Infant Minds*, 1810. (6) *Signor Topsy-Turvey's Wonderful Magic Lantern*, 1810. (7) *Original Hymns for Sunday Schools*, 1812.

place than that of most of their more florid and famous feminine contemporaries. The talents of Jane were more considerable than those of Ann. She is something what Longfellow would like to have been; but her art is far above his. Look at 'The Squire's Pew,' with its imaginative touches, as where the carven sons and daughters on a tomb kneel devoutly —

> 'As though they did intend
> For past omissions to atone
> By saying endless prayers in stone.'

What esprit and good sense and telling rhythm in the poem on 'Accomplishment,' with its fine ending: —

> 'Then Science distorted, and torn into bits,
> Art tortur'd, and frighten'd half out of her wits,
> In portions and patches, some light and some shady,
> Are stitch'd up together, and make a young lady.'

And what technique, what ironical tenderness, in the sketch of the little town, with its gaieties and sorrows, ending with the query, May we not see those faces now? and the answer: —

> 'Then hither turn — yon waving grass
> And mould'ring stones will show;
> For these transactions came to pass
> A hundred years ago.'

Is it not Wordsworth who is rebuked in these lines: —

> 'Now, let the *light of nature*-boasting man,
> "Do so with his enchantments" if he can! —
> Nay, let him slumber in luxurious ease,
> Beneath the umbrage of his idol trees,
> Pluck a wild daisy, moralise on that,
> And drop a tear for an expiring gnat,
> Watch the light clouds o'er distant hills that pass,
> Or write a sonnet to a blade of grass.'

And what neatness in the turn of such a couplet as this! —

> 'And 't is but here and there you may descry
> The camel passing through the needle's eye.'

REGINALD HEBER, LORD BISHOP OF CALCUTTA
(1783–1826) [1]

IT is difficult to see why Bishop Heber had, in his day, a certain reputation. He had a real sense of parody, and some of his rhymes in 'Blue Beard'—

> 'Was your father a wolf? was your nurse an opossum,
> That your heart does not melt her distresses to view?'

anticipate Mr. Gilbert and the 'Bab Ballads.' He wrote doggerel verses in several languages, and translated, in rather an episcopal way, some poems from Eastern sources and six of the odes of Pindar. 'Southey and Pindar,' he said, 'might seem to have drunk at the same source.' He left fragments of various calm attempts at romantic work, and of a 'World before the Flood,' with other biblical narratives, which he completed, in the manner of the time. He also wrote a number of hymns, not nearly as good as Montgomery's, though some of them have remained popular in all the churches. 'From Greenland's Icy Mountains' is not the best, but it is the best known, and can hardly have been forgotten by any one who had heard it sung repeatedly in his youth. I cannot see that there is any resemblance to poetry even in the famous:—

> 'Though every prospect pleases
> And only man is vile,'

which would have pleased Cowper. Personally I prefer the ballad-like effect of 'God is gone up with a merry noise,' though the remainder is less profane than might be conjectured from the commencement. But I do not see that any of the hymns pass from the condition of hymn to that of poem.

[1] (1) *Palestine*, 1807. (2) *Poems*, 1812. (3) *Poetical Works*, 1841.

JAMES SHERIDAN KNOWLES (1784–1862) [1]

JAMES SHERIDAN KNOWLES had some of the Irish qualities for writing for the stage, and was, besides, himself an actor. All the 'ebullition of an Irish heart,' as the prologue to one of his plays called it, did not prevent him from writing much dull work of the romantic kind, in which the Elizabethan domestic drama, as we see it in such plays as 'A Woman Killed with Kindness,' is imitated in a merely exterior way, without any of the natural pathos and instinctive poetry of that minor growth of a great period. Where he is at his best is in a comedy like 'The Love-Chase,' which does over again, with vitality and lightness, some of the characteristic comic work of the eighteenth century. The verse is adequate to material so slight and effective, and the two women, the hoyden Constance and the Widow Green, are good studies in almost serious farce. Elsewhere in plays that try to represent romance in modern life, the form and material never come together, and the colloquial verse of the speech is apt to take refuge in the worse than prose of such inversions as: 'Where bought you it?' The romance is of a purely stage kind, and the touches of nature that come into it are hardly at home there. It seems to be trying to fill a gap between the stage and literature. In all the verse, among much clever writing, and some good sense and piquancy in what it has to render, there is never anything one can properly call poetry. It is quite easy to see that such work must have been popular in its time.

---

[1] (1) *The Welsh Harper*, 1796. (2) *Fugitive Pieces*, 1810. (3) *Brian Boroihme*, 1811. (4) *Caius Gracchus*, 1815. (5) *Virginius*, 1820. (6) *William Tell*, 1825. (7) *Alfred the Great*, 1831. (8) *A Masque on the Death of Sir Walter Scott*, 1832. (9) *The Hunchback*, 1832. (10) *The Wife*, 1833. (11) *The Beggar of Bethnal Green*, 1834. (12) *The Daughter*, 1837. (13) *The Love-Chase*, 1837. (14) *The Bridal*, 1837. (15) *Woman's Wit*, 1838. (16) *The Maid of Mariendorpt*, 1838. (17) *Love*, 1839. (18) *John of Procida*, 1840. (19) *Old Maids*, 1841. (20) *The Rose of Aragon*, 1842. (21) *The Secretary*, 1843. (22) *True unto Death*, 1863.

BERNARD BARTON (1784–1849) [1]

THE Quaker poet, Bernard Barton, is remembered only because he was a friend of Lamb. We gather a pleasant sense of him as a man from Lamb's letters and from the memorial sketch by Edward FitzGerald, printed as an introduction to the last collection of his poems. FitzGerald admits that 'he was not fastidious himself about exactness of thought or of harmony of numbers, and he could scarce comprehend why the public should be less easily satisfied.' Lamb said that one poem in memory of Bloomfield was 'sweet with Doric delicacy,' and here and there we may find a sort of pious epigram not wholly without merit, to those at least who do not require pleasant versification to be poetry. Gentle and ineffectual, he is without affectation, and it is easy to see what Lamb, who was lenient to his friends, found to like in verses that are hardly likely to be read any longer.

WILLIAM TENNANT (1784–1848) [2]

TENNANT's 'Anster Fair,' published in 1814, is a partly burlesque and partly realistic poem, written in the ottava rima, 'shut with the Alexandrine of Spenser, that its close may be

[1] (1) *Metrical Effusions*, 1812. (2) *The Convict's Appeal*, 1818. (3) *Poems by an Amateur*, 1818. (4) *Poems*, 1820. (5) *Napoleon and other Poems*, 1822. (6) *Verses on the Death of P. B. Shelley*, 1822. (7) *Devotional Verses*, 1826. (8) *A Missionary's Memoir*, 1826. (9) *A Widow's Tale*, 1827. (10) *A New Year's Eve*, 1828. (11) *The Reliquary* (with his daughter), 1836. (12) *Household Verse*, 1845. (13) *Seaweeds*, 1846. (14) *Birthday Verses at Eighty-four*, 1846. (15) *A Memorial of J. J. Gurney*, 1847. (16) *A Brief Memorial of Major E. M. Wood*, 1848. (17) *On the Signs of the Times*, 1848. (18) *Ichabod*, 1848. (19) *Poems and Letters*, 1849.

[2] (1) *Anster Fair*, 1814. (2) *Elegy on Trottin' Nanny*, 1814. (3) *Dominie's Disaster*, 1816. (4)*The Thane of Fife*, 1822. (5) *Cardinal Beaton*, 1823. (6) *John Balliol*, 1825. (7) *Papistry Storm'd*, 1827. (8) *Hebrew Dramas*, 1845.

more full and sounding.' The metrical ignorance shown in this disfigurement of a fine metre, wholly adequate within its own limits, is further shown by the attempt to get burlesque rhymes out of such combinations as 'Hercules' and 'a most confounded yerk, alas.' 'Ancient and modern manners are mixed and jumbled together,' as the writer truthfully admits, 'to heighten the humour or variegate the description.' Local colour there is, but of a truly jumbled kind; and the humour, part pleasant, part fairy, is unconvincing. The writer's prayer was no doubt answered: —

> 'O that my noddle were a seething kettle,
> Frothing with bombast o'er the Muses' fire!'

'The Thane of Fife,' written seven years afterwards in the same metre, tries to be more serious, and introduces imagery of this kind: —

> 'Now, in the very navel of the sky,
> Rolled in the vestment of her own fair light,
> The gentle moon was walking upon high.'

It ends in the middle of a stanza, and the author (though, he says, 'I have never allowed the writing of verses to interfere either with my professional duties or my more solid and nutritive studies') promises, in return for approval, a continuation, which never seems to have been required.

JAMES HENRY LEIGH HUNT (1784–1859) [1]

THE poetry of Leigh Hunt has more importance historically than actually. Historically, it has its place in the romantic

[1] (1) *Juvenilia*, 1801. (2) *The Feast of the Poets*, 1814. (3) *The Descent of Liberty*, 1815. (4) *The Story of Rimini*, 1816. (5) *Foliage*, 1818. (6) *Poetical Works*, 1819. (7) *Hero and Leander*, 1819. (8) *Amyntas*, 1820. (9) *Ultra-Crepidarius*, 1823. (10) *Bacchus in Tuscany, from Francesco Redi*, 1825. (11) *Captain Sword and Captain Pen*, 1835. (12) *Blue Stocking Revels*, undated. (13) *The Legend of Florence*, 1840. (14) *The Palfrey*, 1842. (15) *Stories in Verse*, 1855. (16) *Poetical Works*, incomplete, 1860.

movement, where Leigh Hunt is seen fighting, though under alien colours, by the side of Wordsworth. His chief aim was to bring about an emancipation of the speech and metre of poetry, and he had his share in doing so. The early style of Keats owes much of its looseness and lusciousness to an almost deliberate modelling himself upon the practice and teaching of Hunt. 'I have something in common with Hunt,' Keats admitted, in a letter written in 1818; and the 'Quarterly,' in its review of 'Endymion,' defined Keats as a 'simple neophyte of the writer of "The Story of Rimini."' That poem had been published only two years, but had already made a small revolutionary fame of its own.

For its actual qualities, this poetry, which seems now to have so slight an existence by the side of the still almost popular prose-writings, is not so easily valued. Infinite tiny sparks flicker throughout, but are rarely alight long enough to set a steady fire burning. One lyric, a few sonnets, an anecdote or two, a few passages of description or of dialogue, — can we reckon up more than these in a final estimate of the value of this poetry as a whole? Yet are not these few successful things, each rare of its kind, themselves sufficient to make the reputation of one who was content to be remembered in whatever 'humble category of poet, or in what humblest corner of the category,' it remained for 'another and wholly dispassionate generation' to place him?

'The Story of Rimini' as it was published in 1816 is a very different thing from the revised version of 1832, with its 'rejection of superfluities,' its correction of 'mistakes of all kinds.' It may be quite true, as the author protested, that the first edition contained weak lines, together with 'certain conventionalities of structure, originating in his having had his studies too early directed towards the artificial instead of the natural poets.' Yet, in fact, the second version is much more artificial than the first, and what was young, spontaneous, really new at the time, has given way to a firmer but less felicitous style of speech and versification. Such puerilities, of the kind which Hunt very nearly taught to Keats, as, —

> 'What need I tell of lovely lips, and eyes,
> A clipsome waist, and bosom's balmy rise?'

are indeed partly, though not wholly obliterated, and for the better; and the terrible line, revealing all Hunt's vulgarities at a stroke, —

> 'She had stout notions on the marrying score,'

disappears into the discreet —

> 'She had a sense of marriage, just and free.'

Yet what goes, and is ill supplied, is such frank bright speech as, —

> 'A moment's hush succeeds; and from the walls,
> Firm and at once, a silver answer calls,' —

which turns into the droning, —

> 'The crowd are mute; and from the southern wall,
> A lordly blast gives welcome to the call.'

The simple country landscape is changed, because the author has seen Italy, to the due citrons and pine-trees; but such evocations of the fancy cannot be done twice over, and the freshness goes as the 'local colour' comes on. Even more inexcusable are the moral interpositions, such as the tears and explanations of Francesca at the fatal moment, by which Dante and the picture are spoiled. 'The mode of treatment still remains rather material than spiritual,' Hunt admits, without fully realising how much he is losing in material beauty, and how incapable he is of replacing it by any kind of spiritual beauty.

Byron, to whom 'The Story of Rimini' is dedicated, said of it in a letter: 'Leigh Hunt's poem is a devilish good one — quaint here and there, but with the substratum of originality, and with poetry about it that will stand the test.' It has not stood the test, and is now quoted nowhere but in the footnotes to Keats; but it is full of those suggestions which lesser men are often at the pains of making for the benefit of their betters. All its 'leafy' and rejoicing quality, its woodlands and painted 'luxuries,' were to have their influence, direct or reflected, on much of the romantic poetry of the century.

Before writing 'The Story of Rimini,' Hunt had published a satire in verse, called 'The Feast of the Poets,' which he was to rewrite and republish at intervals during his life. It was the first of what was to be a series of bookish poems, in which he expressed the most personal part of himself, but that part which was best fitted perhaps for poetry. Few men have loved literature more passionately and more humbly than Leigh Hunt, or with a generosity more disinterested. Books were nearer to him than men, though he sought in books chiefly their human or pleasing qualities. But his poetry about books never passes from criticism to creation, as when Drayton writes his letter to H. Reynolds, and Shelley his letter to Maria Gisborne. We shall find no 'brave translunary things' and no 'hooded eagle among blinking owls.' He tells us that what the public approved of in 'The Feast of the Poets' was a 'mixture of fancy and familiarity'; but the savour has wholly gone out of it. The criticism in the twenty-five pages of the poem is superficial and obvious, and the verse jingles like the bells on a fool's bauble. The criticism in the one hundred and twenty-five pages of the notes has still interest for us, if not value. There is always in Leigh Hunt's criticism something of haste and temporariness, and it is generally revised in every new edition. Here, the recognition, on second thoughts, that Wordsworth is the chief poet of the age, together with the good-natured, superior, and impertinent advice which he gives him for the bettering of his poetry, has something more than curiosity as coming from Leigh Hunt, and in 1814. The scorn of Southey, who 'naturally borrows his language from those who have thought for him,' remains good criticism, and there are phrases in a somewhat unjust estimate of Scott which are not without relevance; as when we are told that 'he talks the language of no times and of no feelings, for his style is too flowing to be ancient, too antique to be modern, and too artificial in every respect to be the result of his own first impressions.' He is reasonably fair to Crabbe, though with evident effort, and sees through Rogers without effort. But the accidental qualities of his taste betray themselves in the sympathetic praise of Moore, in the preference for 'Gertrude of Wyoming' as 'the finest narrative poem that has been produced in the present day,' in the contemptuous reference to Landor as 'a very worthy person,' and to 'Gebir' as 'an epic piece of gossiping,' and in the uncertainty and apparent distaste of what is meant to be said not unfavourably of Coleridge. In the final edition, nearly fifty years later, Coleridge, 'whose poetry's poetry's self,' is promoted to the place of Wordsworth.

Hunt's miscellaneous mind was active, sympathetic, foraging; he made discoveries by some ready instinct which had none of the certainty of the divining rod; he was a freebooter, who captured various tracts of the enemy, but could not guard or retain them. He was among the first to help in breaking down the eighteenth-century formalism in verse, in letting loose a free and natural speech; but his influence was not always a safe one. In 1829 Shelley writes to him, in sending the manuscript of 'Julian and Maddalo': 'You will find the little piece, I think, in some degree consistent with your own ideas of the manner in which poetry ought to be written. I have employed a certain familiar style of language to express the actual way in which people talk with each other, whom education and a certain refinement of sentiment have placed above the use of vulgar idioms.'

It was just that proviso that Leigh Hunt neglected. What he really brings into poetry is a tone of chatty colloquialism, meant to give ease, from which, however, the vulgar idioms are not excluded. He introduces a new manner, smooth, free, and easy, a melting cadence, which he may have thought he found in Spenser, whom he chooses among poets 'for luxury.' The least lofty of English poets, he went to the loftiest among them only for his sensitiveness to physical delight. His own verse is always feminine, luscious, with a luxury which is Creole, and was perhaps in his blood. He would go back to such dainty Elizabethans as Lodge, but his languid pleasures have no edge of rapture; the lines trot and amble, never fly.

Hunt mastered many separate tricks and even felicities in verse, and acquired a certain lightness and deftness which is occasionally almost wholly successful, as in an actual masterpiece of the trifling, like 'Jenny kissed me.' But he did not realise that lightness cannot be employed in dealing with tragic material, unless it is sharpened to so deadly a point as Byron and Heine could give to it. It is difficult to realise that it is the same hand which writes the line that delighted Keats, —

> 'Places of nestling green for poets made,' —

and, not far off, these dreadful lines, —

> 'The two divinest things the world has got,
> A lovely woman in a rural spot.'

The ignoble quality of jauntiness mars almost the whole of Hunt's work, in which liberty cannot withhold itself from license. The man who can wish a beloved woman

> 'To haunt his eye, like taste personified,'

cannot be aware of what taste really is; and, with a power of rendering sensation, external delicacies of sight and hearing, which is to be envied and outdone by Keats, he is never quite certain in his choice between beauty and prettiness, sentiment and sentimentality.

In his later works Hunt learned something of restraint, and

when he came to attempt the drama, though he tried to be at the same time realistic and romantic, was more able to suit his manner to his material. The 'Legend of Florence' has his ripest feeling and his most chastened style, and more than anything else he did in verse reflects him to us as, in Shelley's phrase, 'one of those happy souls

"Which are the salt of the earth."'

The gentle Elizabethan manner is caught up and revived for a moment, and there is a human tenderness which may well remind us of such more masterly work as 'A Woman Killed with Kindness.'

Hunt was convinced that 'we are more likely to get at a real poetical taste through the Italian than through the French school,' and he names together Spenser, Milton, and Ariosto, thinking that these in common would 'teach us to vary our music and to address ourselves more directly to nature.' Naming his favourite poets, he begins with 'Pulci, for spirits and a fine free way.' To acquaint English taste with Italian models he did many brilliant translations, Dante being less perfectly within his means than Ariosto or Tasso. He was best and most at his ease in rendering the irregular lines of Redi, whose 'Bacchus in Tuscany' he translated in full. In this, and in the version from the Latin of Walter de Mapes, there is a blithe skill which few translators have attained. It was through his fancy for Italian burlesque that Hunt came to do a number of his characteristic and least English things, like the laughing and lilting verses which sometimes, as in 'The Fairy Concert,' attain a kind of glittering gaiety, hardly mere paste, though with no hardness of the diamond. There is some relationship between this verse and what we call *vers de société;* but it is more critical, and has something of the epigram set to a jig. So far as it is meant for political satire, it is only necessary to compare even so brilliant a squib as the 'Coronation Soliloquy of George IV' with Coleridge's 'Fire, Famine, and Slaughter,' to realise how what in Hunt remains buffoonery and perhaps argument can be carried to a point of imagination at which it becomes poetry.

Hunt has a special talent, connected with his feeling for whatever approached the form of the epigram, for the writing of brief narrative poems. Can it be denied that so masterly an anecdote as 'Abou ben Adhem' has in it some of the qualities, as it seems to have some of the results, of poetry? Read the same story in the French prose of the original: nothing is changed, nothing added; only the form of the verse, barely existent as it is, has given a certain point and finish to the prose matter. Here and in the two or three other stories there is a very precise and ingenious grasp on story-telling, worthy of Maupassant; and there is a kernel of just, at times of profound, thought, which suggests something of the quality of an Eastern apologue. Was it the more than half prose talent of Hunt that gave him, when he concentrated so tightly his generally diffuse and wandering verse, this particular, unusual kind of success? When, as in blank verse pieces such as 'Paganini,' he tried to get a purely emotional effect, not by narrative but in the form of confession, his failure was complete; all is restlessness and perturbation. But, once at least, in a little piece called 'Ariadne Walking,' there is something of the same happy concentration, the same clean outlines; and the poem may be paralleled with a lovely poem of Alfred de Vigny. The technique, as in almost, or, perhaps, everything of Hunt, is not perfect; and there are words of mere prose, like 'the feel of sleep.' How was it that a man, really poetically minded, and with so much knowledge of all the forms of verse, was never quite safe when he wrote in metre?

A stanza in a poem on poppies may be compared, almost in detail, with a corresponding sentence in prose, which occurs in a rambling essay. They both say the same thing, but the verse says, —

> 'We are slumberous poppies,
> Lords of Lethe downs,
> Some awake and some asleep,
> Sleeping in our crowns.
> What perchance our dreams may know,
> Let our serious beauty show.'

And the prose says, 'They look as if they held a mystery at their hearts, like sleeping kings of Lethe,' and comes nearer to poetry.

From the epigram to the sonnet there is but one step, and Leigh Hunt's finest and most famous line, —

> 'The laughing queen that caught the world's great hands,' —

is found in a sonnet on the Nile, written impromptu in rivalry with Keats and Shelley, and more successful, within its limits, than its competitors. And the sonnet, written against Keats, on the subject of 'The Grasshopper and the Cricket,' would be good as well as characteristic if it were not flawed by words like 'feel' and 'class' and 'nick,' used to give the pleasant charm of talk, but resulting only in a degradation of refined and dignified speech. Three sonnets called 'The Fish, the Man, and the Spirit,' which might easily have been no more than one of Hunt's clever burlesques, seem to me for once to touch and seize and communicate a strange, cold, inhuman imagination, as if the very element of water entered into chill communion with the mind. Lamb might have shared the feeling, the epithets are like the best comic Greek compounds; the poetry, which begins with a strange familiarity, ends with a strangeness wholly of elemental wonder: —

> 'Man's life is warm, glad, sad, 'twixt love and graves,
> Boundless in hope, honoured with pangs austere,
> Heaven-gazing; and his angel-wings he craves:
> The fish is swift, small-needing, vague yet clear,
> A cold, sweet, silver life, wrapped round in waves,
> Quickened with touches of transporting fear.'

There, at least, Leigh Hunt speaks the language of poetry, and with a personal accent.

ALLAN CUNNINGHAM (1784–1842) [1]

ALLAN CUNNINGHAM has been praised, with and without discrimination, by many more famous persons, from Scott, who christened him 'honest Allan,' to Southey, who called him 'Allan, true child of Scotland'; but he has never been better characterised than by a Mr. McDiarmid, at a banquet given in his honour at Dumfries: 'As a poet he leans to the ballad style of composition, and many of his lyrics are eminently sweet, graceful, and touching.' So much may be said in his favour, though it is difficult to be very precise in dealing with one who had so little sense of the difference between what was his and what came from others. He began by inventing a series of Scotch 'remains' for the inveterate Cromek, who rewarded him with 'a bound copy' of a book not even published under his name. There is generally in his verse, which is equally telling in a Scotch ballad in the manner of Burns, such as 'My Nannie O,' or an English sea-ballad in the manner of Dibdin, such as 'A wet sheet and a flowing sea,' some sort of imitation, something not wholly individual, and at his best he does not go beyond a pleasant spontaneity in which there is no really lasting quality. His kindest critic, Scott, who called him a man of genius, noted in his diary that he 'required the tact of knowing when and where to stop'; and in a letter to him he said candidly: 'Here and there I would pluck a flower from your posy to give what remains an effect of greater simplicity.' The same luxuriance renders his prose vague, as his facts are, in the 'Lives of British Painters,' meant to be instructive, and in their way really sympathetic. He had many lively and attractive qualities, as a man and as a writer; and received at least his due measure of fame during his lifetime.

[1] (1) *Songs, Chiefly in the Rural Dialect of Scotland*, 1813. (2) *Remains of Nithsdale and Galloway Song*, 1820. (3) *Sir Marmaduke Maxwell*, 1822. (4) *The Songs of Scotland, Ancient and Modern*, 1825. (5) *The Maid of Elvar*, 1833.

REV. CHARLES STRONG (1785–1864) [1]

CHARLES STRONG is remembered only by two sonnets, his best, which are to be seen in anthologies, the one beginning 'Time, I rejoice, amid the ruin wide,' and another beginning 'My window's open to the evening sky.' The greater number of the other sonnets in his single book of original verse are worked up a little consciously towards a final effect in the last line, and are somewhat obvious in the meditations over foreign sites which make up much of their substance. Occasionally we meet with a good separate line or two, such as: —

'On the blue waste a pyramid of sails';

or as this: —

'And, on the true vine grafted, there remain
A living branch, until the vintage bears.'

A more carefully cultivated sonority distinguishes the translated verse in the 'Specimens of Sonnets from the Most Celebrated Italian Poets,' a chill and literal rendering of Italian sonnets from Dante to Metastasio. They take no new growth in English soil, but retain that formal eloquence which in so much of Italian verse takes the place of poetry. Could Fracastoro have desired a translator more after his heart than the writer who follows him, slow-pacing, with: —

'Whether it be Achilles' high disdain
Or wise Ulysses' toilsome pilgrimage'?

HENRY KIRKE WHITE (1785–1806) [2]

THE discovery of Kirke White was one of the unlucky discoveries of Southey, who tells us that, but for him, 'his papers

[1] (1) *Specimens of Sonnets from the Most Celebrated Italian Poets; with Translations*, 1827. (2) *Sonnets*, 1835.

[2] (1) *Clifton Grove*, 1804. (2) *Life and Remains*, edited by Southey 2 vols., 1810.

would probably have remained in oblivion, and his name, in a few years, have been forgotten.' 'Unhappy White,' as Byron called him in a passage which has been remembered for its imagery, died in his twenty-second year, and his papers were handed over to Southey, who tells us 'Mr. Coleridge was present when I opened them, and was, as well as myself, equally affected and astonished at the proofs of industry which they displayed.' He adds: 'I have inspected all the existing manuscripts of Chatterton, and they excited less wonder than these.' 'He surely ranks next to Chatterton,' said Byron, when Southey published the 'Remains' with a memoir and some five and thirty pages of memorial verses by various hands. Kirke White had published a small volume at the age of eighteen, and a judicious critic in the 'Monthly Review' had said of the writer: 'We commend his exertions, and his laudable endeavours to excel; but we cannot compliment him with having learned the difficult art of writing good poetry.' This opinion, which seemed to Southey a 'cruelty,' a 'wicked injustice,' requires no revision.

'It is not possible,' says Southey, 'to conceive a human being more amiable in all the relations of life,' and he assumes that the reader 'will take some interest in all those remains because they are his; he who shall feel none must have a blind heart, and therefore a blind understanding.' There is, indeed, no other reason for interest in these generally unaffected but always conventional verses than because they are the expression, tinged with reluctant resignation, of one who is, as he says, about to 'compose his decent head, and breathe his last.' What Byron called his 'bigotry' is a genuine but not very individual sense of piety, and all his verse is an amiable echo of such literature as most appealed to one who found 'a nervous strength of diction and a wild freedom of versification, combined with an euphonious melody and consonant cadence, unequalled in the English language' in the sonnets of Bowles, and said of Milton's sonnets that 'those to the Nightingale and to Mr. Lawrence are, I think, alone entitled to the praise of mediocrity.' Nothing can be more inoffensive than the mild fancies and plaintive pieties of a young writer who has often been wrongly characterised as immature. The crop was ripe enough, but it was a thin crop. They are alone, I think, entitled to the praise of mediocrity.

THOMAS LOVE PEACOCK (1785–1866) [1]

PEACOCK'S novels are unique in English, and are among the most scholarly, original, and entertaining prose writings of the century.

> 'A strain too learned for a shallow age,
> Too wise for selfish bigots,'

Shelley defined it, and added prophetically:—

> 'let his page
> Which charms the chosen spirits of the time
> Fold itself up for the serener clime
> Of years to come, and find its recompense
> In that just expectation.'

His learned wit, his satire upon the vulgarity of progress, are more continuously present in his prose than in his verse; but the novels are filled with cheerful scraps of rhyming, wine-songs, love-songs, songs of mockery, and nonsense jingles, some of which are no more than the scholar's idle diversions, but others of a singular excellence. They are like no other verse; they are startling, grotesque, full of hearty extravagances, at times thrilling with unexpected beauty. The masterpiece, perhaps, of the comically heroic section of these poems is 'The War-Song of Dinas Vawr,' which is, as the author says in due commendation of it, 'the quintessence of all war-songs that ever were written, and the sum and sub-

---

[1] (1) *Palmyra*, 1806. (2) *The Genius of the Thames*, 1810. (3) *Rhododaphne*, 1818. (4) *Paper Money Lyrics*, privately printed, 1825.

stance of all the appetencies, tendencies, and consequences of military.' Is there any casual reader who has ever been able to put out of his head the divinely droll first lines: —

> 'The mountain sheep are sweeter,
> But the valley sheep are fatter;
> We therefore deemed it meeter
> To carry off the latter.'

Was comic verse ever more august? And of wine-songs is there any, outside Burns (and with how great a difference!), in which a poetic decorum dignifies revel more effectually than in the refrain: —

> 'And our ballast is old wine,
> And your ballast is old wine'?

There is another after-dinner ballad, 'In life three ghostly friars were we,' and a 'Hail to the Headlong,' mere cataract of sound, as 'The Three Little Men' and the chorus of 'Our balances, our balances' are afterwards to be, in the later parodies of politics: all these have their place among Peacock's cleverest ingenuities. When he is serious and lengthy, as in the 'Rhododaphne,' which Shelley thought worth liking, every poetical quality deserts him except a faint and ineffectual eloquence. But there are two lyrics of a delicate tenderness, 'In the Days of Old' and 'Love and Age,' in which he is content to remember the past and to sing from memory out of a lover's experience.

JOHN WILSON (1785–1841) [1]

WILSON left minor poems in which he tries to be a 'Lake-poet,' even writing lines on an ass, though on an Ass in a Dutch picture. Much of the verse is almost as prettified as

[1] (1) *The Isle of Palms*, 1812. (2) *The City of the Plague*, 1816. (3) *Works*, 1855–58.

that of Thomas Moore, though the sentiment of it is better. None of the reflections on the subjects of the day, ruined abbeys, the banks of Windermere, moonlight at sea, midnight on Helm Crag, the voice of departed friendship, can now be read with any attention. The continual faint fancy of these and of the long poem, 'The Isle of Palms,' which is too thin a cobweb for a spider to hang by, wearies the reader who asks for imagination. The longest poem of all, 'The City of the Plague,' a rhapsody divided into acts and scenes, is one of the weakest and most lavish pieces of sensational extravagance in our language, much fiercer and feebler than anything in the Elizabethan tragedy of blood. Beddoes might have made something, within a brief space, of this nightmare subject, but there is none of his mastery of the grotesque in this long eloquent raving, these 'horrid demons in a dream.' 'The Convict,' which is shorter, and aims at a kind of realism, though it is nearly as horrible, has some of the merit of melodrama. But whether we are served, as in the minor poems, with sighs, or, in these lengthy compositions, with yells, there is an equal failure to make any articulate form of art out of either. Everything that is superficial and second-rate in the 'Noctes Ambrosianae,' their haste and heat, are here; but no more than a glimpse of the qualities to which Christopher North owes a name better known than his own.

SIR AUBREY DE VERE (1786-1846)[1]

WORDSWORTH said of the sonnets of Sir Aubrey de Vere that they were 'among the most perfect of our age'; and the author, in dedicating them to him, hoped 'to be named hereafter as one among the friends of Wordsworth.' Not always perfect as sonnets, they have often both intellectual symmetry and moral distinction; many of them are 'trophies,' resonant

[1] (1) *Julian the Apostate*, 1822. (2) *The Duke of Mercia*, 1823. (3) *The Song of Faith*, 1842. (4) *Mary Tudor*, 1847.

with the clarions of Crusaders, and with homages and condemnations of kings. There is in some of them, not least in such religious ones as that on 'Universal Prayer,' a noble Wordsworthian quality, worthy of Wordsworth's praise.

CAROLINE ANNE BOWLES SOUTHEY (1786-1854) [1]

THE poems of Mrs. Southey, now as forgotten as her husband's, are of a far finer quality. They show the continual influence of Wordsworth, but at its best the influence passes almost into personal creation. She is full of gentle meditation over passing things, flowers and animals, above all, dogs, and there is a genuinely womanly quality in her poems, full of tenderness and quiet observation. Often a phrase has fine precision, as in: —

> 'Finding thine own distress
> With accurate greediness.'

The lyrics, though they tend to become monotonous, are more than facile; they have often a distinction of a personal kind. There is no strong emotion in them, but delicate insight, natural simplicity, a choiceness of phrase and cadence. A long poem in blank verse, which has almost a suggestion of Jane Austen in its slightly formal detail, is written in a style of easy colloquialism which seems midway between the verse of 'The Prelude' and that of 'Aurora Leigh.' Lines like these might almost have been found in 'Bishop Blougram': —

> 'True, they seem starving; but 't is also true
> The parish sees to all those vulgar wants;
> And when it does not, doubtless there must be —
> Alas! too common in this wicked world —
> Some artful imposition in the case.'

Caroline Southey was an artist, and has been undeservedly forgotten.

[1] (1) *Ellen Fitzarthur*, 1820. (2) *The Widow's Tale*, 1822. (3) *Tales of the Factories*, 1823. (4) *Solitary Hours*, prose and verse, 1826. (5) *The Birthday*, 1836.

GEORGE BEATTIE (1786–1823) [1]

GEORGE BEATTIE was a crofter's son, who, having fallen in love with a woman who had encouraged him until she came into some money, 'died of despair,' his strange biographer, a Mr. Mt. Cyrus, tells us. The last confession which he wrote before going out to shoot himself ('a dying man may surely be allowed to state what he believed or rather knew to be the fact') is a document of value in the study of human nature. We see, in the incoherent assurances, the wild, scarcely sane excitement of a man brooding over 'the deep and indelible wrongs' done to him. Most of his poems are personal, and delineate bad dreams, or shipwreck, or the scene of murder; but there are one or two lyrics, like the 'Fragment' with the refrain 'Igo and ago,' which have a lilt of their own. His best work was the ballad of 'John O'Arnha,' done under the influence of Burns; there is a wild hurrying fancy in it, tossed about by weird demons, 'grisly ghaists,' and 'whinnering goblins'; 'a waesome, wan, wanliesum sight!' The verse gallops like a witch on her broomstick, riding against the wind.

MARY RUSSELL MITFORD (1787–1855) [2]

MISS MITFORD tells us that the need of making money 'made it a duty to turn away from the lofty steep of Tragic Poetry to the every-day path of Village Stories.' We may have gained, in getting 'Our Village,' but there is a nearer approach to both poetry and drama in the plays, now completely for-

---

[1] *George Beattie, of Montrose, a Poet, a Humourist, and a Man of Genius*, by A. S. Mt. Cyrus, M. A., no date [1863?].

[2] (1) *Poems*, 1810. (2) *Christina*, 1811. (3) *Blanche of Castile*, 1812. (4) *Watlington Hill*, 1812. (5) *Narrative Poems on Female Characters*, 1813. (6) *Julian*, 1823. (7) *Foscari*, 1826. (8) *Rienzi*, 1828. (9) *Charles I*, 1834. (10) *Sadak and Kalasrade*, 1836. (11) *Dramatic Works*, 2 vols., 1854.

gotten, than most people are likely to imagine. The most serious of them is 'Charles I,' which George Colman, then Censor, would not allow to be acted. There was no danger to the state in it, and it has some fine characterisation, together with dignified and pathetic speech. In several of the other plays the action is allowed to run quite wild, and preposterous horrors traverse the stage in an almost artless profusion. What is curious is, that even in scenes of chaotic impossibility, there is a certain kind of human feeling which comes through a thin and uncertain verse, which can pass unconsciously from such dreadful dissonances as: —

> 'That on a point of time so brief, that scarce
> The sand wags in the hour-glass, hangs man's all,'

to so assured a cadence as: —

> 'The mind of man
> When fashioning the myriad sounds that lend
> A winged life to thought, ne'er framed a name
> For the slayer of his children.'

The people are for the most part martyrs, fanatics, parricides, always headstrong, often light-hearted in the midst of disasters partly of their causing; and the action turns generally about a tangle of unlikely crimes. These unnatural deeds, which were meant to create a vivid drama, defeat the nature in the words of characters whose speech is often so probable. It is all a woman's world, a kind of soft and touching, sometimes thrilling melodrama. The people, in the midst of confusions and catastrophes, are intensely alert, and their frenzies are often touched by a kind of irrelevant and not quite achieved beauty. You feel behind them a capable, enthusiastic woman, writing too loosely, with too feminine a sense of romance, but not without a natural impulse, a ready and human eloquence.

BRYAN WALLER PROCTER: BARRY CORNWALL
(1787–1874) [1]

WHEN Leigh Hunt reviewed the 'Lamia' volume of Keats in the 'Examiner,' in the summer of 1820, he did not think it necessary to tell the story of 'Isabella,' as the public had 'lately been familiarized with it in the "Sicilian Story" of Mr. Barry Cornwall.' How lately, we know from a letter of Keats to Reynolds, at the end of February, 1820, in which he says that Barry Cornwall has sent him not only his 'Sicilian Story,' but his 'Dramatic Scenes.' 'I confess they tease me,' he says; 'they are composed of amiability, the Seasons, the Leaves, the Moon, etc., upon which he rings (according to Hunt's expression) triple bob majors. However that is nothing — I think he likes poetry for its own sake, not his.' The 'Sicilian Story' is a faint, pretty telling, rather in the manner of Leigh Hunt, of the story out of Boccaccio which Keats had been telling in his own way. The difference between them may be sufficiently indicated by Barry Cornwall's note: 'I have ventured to substitute the heart for the head of the lover. The latter appeared to me to be a ghastly object to preserve.' In the same volume is an equally faint, but not even pretty, Spanish tale done after Byron in ottava rima. Of this poem Shelley wrote to Peacock: 'The man whose critical gall is not stirred up by such ottava rima as Barry Cornwall's, may safely be conjectured to possess no gall at all. The world is pale with the sickness of such stuff.' 'Marcian Colonna,' which preceded 'A Sicilian Story,' is indistinguishable from it in manner; both are the kind of work which follows closely upon good originals, and often gets the earliest credit; for Byron is in the story, and Leigh Hunt and Keats are both in

---

[1] (1) *Dramatic Scenes*, 1819. (2) *A Sicilian Story*, 1820. (3) *Marcian Colonna*, 1820. (4) *Mirandola*, 1821. (5) *Poetical Works*, 3 vols., 1822. (6) *The Flood in Thessaly*, 1823. (7) *English Songs*, 1832.

the style. In the same volume there is a curious fragment in modern drama, called 'Ametra Wentworth,' which in its attempt at a kind of plaintive realism may have filled some intermediate gap between the romantic group and Tennyson. 'Mirandola' followed, and was acted, and had its success, as everything of Barry Cornwall had, for its moment. The particular dim echo which he contrived to get from the Elizabethan drama, which Lamb had not so long ago revealed to the poets of that time, seemed to give out a real music, and the tune was easy to follow. When that tune turned to the borrowed but easier jig of the 'English Songs,' Barry Cornwall seemed to have found his place among English poets.

'Taken altogether,' said Lamb, of the 'English Songs,' ''t is too Lovey'; but he immediately qualifies this good criticism by adding: 'But what delicacies!' And he names his favourites, of which one is 'glorious 'bove all.' If we read the particular songs which Lamb liked we shall see perhaps a kind of novelty, or what was a novelty in 1832, and must remember that it is not always easy to appreciate such things immediately at their true value. The songs are indeed 'too Lovey'; they are also as much too diluted in sentiment as they are too carelessly improvised in form. Such music as is in them is rarely more than a child's forefinger could pick out on a piano. It has been let out by candid friends that they have no personal sincerity; but this is a secondary matter, for such a song as 'The sea! the sea! the open sea!' is not more worthless as a poem because the author was only once on the sea, and was then seasick. Sincerity to his art is what was not in Barry Cornwall; he liked it, as Keats said, for its own sake, but his liking was far too platonic ever to become creative.

Few writers were more loved in their own day, or more quickly forgotten, than Barry Cornwall. Praised by Landor, who said: —

> 'No other in these later times
> Has bound me in so potent rhymes,'

and by Mr. Swinburne in a lovely elegy, there is scarcely one of his contemporaries who did not know and like him, and few who did not confuse that personal liking with literary esteem. When the last of his friends is gone, will any one have a good word to say for him? In the course of a long life he went through many schools and periods of poetry; all left their influence on him, and some sympathetic, attaching quality in him caught up the hints from one which he seems to have passed on to another. He accompanies the general movement, and it is instructive to see one who began with pale romantic elegances falling at last into the clash and colloquialism of Browning. He speaks with affection of 'Landor's verse and Browning's rhyme,' and he imitated the very tricks of both: Browning badly and with almost an anticipation of Robert Buchanan; Landor, in perhaps his best piece of verse, an 'Inscription for a Fountain,' to better effect. It is not at all certain that there are not suggestions in his work which may have affected later and greater men, as what is worthless in itself has a way of doing. I should be surprised if the opening lines of a poem of Browning, published in 1845: —

'I've a friend over the sea,
I like him but he loves me,'

did not come into his head, consciously or unconsciously, as an echo of some doggerel of Barry Cornwall, published in 1832, which begins —

'I've a friend who loveth me,
And sendeth me Ale of Trinitie.'

And it is not less possible that some of the crudest of Mr. Swinburne's 'Poems and Ballads' owed, for all their magnificence, a certain impulse to the showy attempts to be dramatically and passionately lyrical which we find in some of Barry Cornwall's later work. Anticipation or imitation, it matters little to us now; but if Barry Cornwall really did throw out hints to others, incapable as he was of realising them himself, the fact may explain some of the pleasant things which were said about him.

GEORGE GORDON, LORD BYRON (1788–1824)[1]

THE life of Byron was a masque in action, to which his poetry is but the moralising accompaniment of words. 'One whose dust was once all fire' (words which Byron used of Rousseau, and which may still more truthfully be used of himself), Byron still lives for us with such incomparable vividness because he was a man first and a poet afterwards. He became a poet for that reason, and that reason explains the imperfection of his poetry. Most of his life he was a personality looking out for its own formula, and his experiments upon that search were of precisely the kind to thrill the world. What poet ever had so splendid a legend in his lifetime? His whole life was lived in the eyes of men, and Byron had enough of the actor in him to delight in that version of 'all the world's a stage.' His beauty and his deformity, his 'tenderness, roughness, delicacy, coarseness, sentiment, sensuality, soaring and grovelling, dirt and deity, all mixed up in that one compound of inspired clay' (it is his own summary of Burns), worked together with circumstances to move every heart to admiration and pity. He was a poet, and he did what others only wrote;

[1] (1) *Poems on Various Occasions*, 1807. (2) *Hours of Idleness*, 1807. (3) *English Bards and Scottish Reviewers*, 1809. (4) *Childe Harold*, a Romaunt, 1812. (5) *The Curse of Minerva*, 1812. (6) *The Waltz*, 1813. (7) *The Giaour*, 1813. (8) *The Bride of Abydos*, 1813. (9) *The Corsair*, 1814. (10) *Ode to Napoleon*, 1814. (11) *Lara*, with Rogers' *Jacqueline*, 1814. (12) *Hebrew Melodies*, 1815. (13) *The Siege of Corinth*, 1816. (14) *Parisina*, 1816. (15) *Poems*, 1816. (16) *The Prisoner of Chillon*, 1816. (17) *Childe Harold's Pilgrimage*, Canto III, 1816. (18) *Monody on the Death of Sheridan*, 1816. (19) *Manfred*, 1817. (20) *The Lament of Tasso*, 1817. (21) *Childe Harold's Pilgrimage*, Canto IV, 1818. (22) *Beppo*, a Venetian Story, 1818. (23) *Mazeppa*, 1819. (24) *Marino Faliero*, 1820. (25) *The Prophecy of Dante*, 1821. (26) *Sardanapalus, The Two Foscari, Cain*, 1821. (27) *Werner*, 1822. (28) *The Age of Bronze*, 1823. (29) *The Island*, 1823. (30) *The Deformed Transformed*, 1824. (31) *Don Juan*, Cantos I, II, 1819; Cantos III, IV, V, 1821; Cantos VI, VII, VIII, 1823; Cantos IX, X, XI, 1823; Cantos XII, XIII, XIV, 1823; Cantos XV, XVI, 1824.

he seemed to write what others dared not think. It was a romantic time, 'gigantic and exaggerated,' as he said, the age of the French Revolution, the age of Napoleon; Trafalgar and Waterloo were contemporary moments. The East was the new playground of the imagination: Byron, and Byron alone of the Orientalising poets, had been there. He was a peer and a republican, at twenty-four the most famous poet of the day, the idol of one London season and cast out with horror by the next, an exile from his country, equally condemned and admired, credited with abnormal genius and abnormal wickedness, confessing himself defiantly to the world, making a public show of a very genuine misery, living with ostentatious wildness in Venice, reclaimed to a kind of irregular domesticity, giving up everything, life itself, in the cause of liberty and for a nation with a tradition of heroes, a hero in death; and he was one whom Scott could sum up, as if speaking for England, at the news of that death, as 'that mighty genius, which walked amongst us as something superior to ordinary mortality, and whose powers were beheld with wonder, and something approaching to terror, as if we knew not whether they were of good or evil.'

Circumstances made Byron a poet; he became the poet of circumstance. But with Byron, remember, a circumstance was an emotion; the idealist of real things, and an imperfect idealist, never without a certain suspicion of his ideal, he turned life, as it came to him, into an impossible kind of romance, invented by one who was romantic somewhat in the sense that a man becomes romantic when he loves. Such an experience does not change his nature; it does not give him sincerity in romance. Byron's sincerity underlies his romance, does not transmute it. This is partly because the style is the man; and Byron had not style, through which alone emotion can prove its own sincerity. 'All convulsions end with me in rhyme,' he writes; and all through his letters we see the fit working itself out. 'I wish I could settle to reading again,' he notes in his journal; 'my life is monotonous, and yet desultory. I take up my books and fling them down again. I began a comedy, and burnt it because the scene ran into reality: a novel for the same reason. In rhyme I can keep more away from facts; but the thought always runs through . . . yes, yes, through.' Convinced that 'the great object of life is sensation — to feel that we exist, even though in pain,' Byron was constantly satisfying himself of the latter part of his conviction. Rhyme was at once the relief and the expression; and, in his verse, we see the confusion of that double motive. 'To withdraw *myself* from *myself* — oh, that cursed selfishness — has ever been my sole, my entire, my sincere motive in scribbling at all.' Now this conflict between the fact which insists on coming with the emotion, and the alien kind of fact which presents itself as an escape from the emotion, does much to render Byron's earlier poetry formless, apparently insincere. Byron wrote with a contempt for writing; 'managing his pen,' in Scott's phrase which has become famous, 'with the careless and negligent ease of a man of quality.' 'God help him!' he writes of a gentleman who has published a book of verses; 'no one should be a rhymer who could be anything better.' And again, more deliberately: 'I by no means rank poetry or poets high in the scale of intellect. This may look like affectation, but it is my real opinion. It is the lava of the imagination, whose eruption prevents an earthquake. . . . I prefer the talents of action.'

'The lava of the imagination, whose eruption prevents an earthquake,' is indeed precisely what poetry was to Byron; and it is characteristic of him that he cannot look beyond himself even for the sake of a generalisation. If we would define yet more precisely his ideal we must turn to a certain stanza in 'Childe Harold' : —

> 'Could I embody and unbosom now
> That which is most within me, — could I wreak
> My thoughts upon expression, and thus throw

Soul — heart — mind — passions — feelings — strong or weak —
All that I would have sought, and all I seek,
Bear — know — feel — and yet breathe — into one word,
And that one word were Lightning, I would speak';

and so, indeed, at his best, he did speak, condensing the indignation of his soul or the wrath of Europe into one word, and that word lightning. But the word flashes out intermittently from among the dreariest clouds, and he is not even sure whether his lightning has flashed or not, waiting to know whether it has been seen before he has any positive opinion of his own. Sending the manuscript of 'Manfred' to Murray, he writes: 'I have not an idea if it is good or bad. . . . You may put it into the fire if you like, and Gifford don't like.' He sends the first part of 'Heaven and Earth,' saying: 'I wish the first part to be published before the second, because if it don't succeed it is better to stop there than to go on in a fruitless experiment.' Such indifference, partly but not wholly pose though it may be, such dependence on outside judgements and the mere whim of the public, on 'success,' shows us, with singular clearness, Byron's lack of conviction, of reverence, of serious feeling for art. It brings out the strain of commonness which we find in the greatest of those to whom action was more than thought, the external world more real than the inner world; the commonness which seems to be part of a very masculine genius, to which contemplation has not brought the female complement of energy; the commonness which made Napoleon, at that very epoch, fall just so far short of greatness.

Byron's fame, which was never, like that of every other English poet, in his lifetime, a merely English reputation, has been kept alive in other countries, more persistently than in our own, and comes back to us now from abroad with at times almost the shock of a new discovery. It is never possible to convince a foreigner that Byron is often not even correct as a writer of verse. His lines, so full of a kind of echoing substance, ring true to the ear which has not naturalised itself in English poetry; and, hearing them march so directly and with such obvious clangour, the foreigner is at a loss to understand why one should bring what seems to him a petty charge against them. The magic of words, in which Byron is lacking, the poverty of rhythm, for which he is so conspicuous, do not tell with any certainty through the veil of another idiom. How many Englishmen know quite how bad, as verse, is the verse of the French Byron, as he has been called, Alfred de Musset, and quite why it is bad? And as Byron's best verse, even more than Musset's, is worldly verse, it is still more difficult to detect a failure in accent, in that finer part of what Byron calls 'the poetry of speech'; so delicate a difference separating what may be almost the greatest thing in poetry, a line of Dante, from something, like too much of Byron, which is commoner than the commonest prose.

Byron's theory of poetry and his practice were two very different things, both faulty, and telling against one another. His theory was that the finest English poetry is to be found in Pope: 'what I firmly believe in as the Christianity of English poetry, the poetry of Pope.' Admitting frankly that he had not followed so correct a master with any sort of attention, he apologised on the ground that 'it is easier to perceive the wrong than to pursue the right.' 'But I have lived in far countries abroad,' he tells us, 'or in the agitating world at home, which was not favourable to study or reflection, so that almost all I have written has been mere passion — passion, it is true, of different kinds, but always passion.' And he adds: 'But then I did other things besides write.'

'We are all wrong, except Rogers, Crabbe, and Campbell,' he laments, going on his own way, all the same, for good and evil. And his own way, until he accustomed himself frankly to 'wandering with pedestrian Muses,' as he tells us in 'Don Juan,' and thus adding to the ground a splendour which he could not capture from the skies, was a very uneven way with many turnings. 'My qualities,' he tells us of his school-days at Harrow, 'were much more oratorical than poetical, and Dr. Drury, my grand patron, had a great notion that I should turn out an orator, from my fluency, my turbulence, my voice, my copiousness of declamation, and my action.' The criticism justified itself; Byron's qualities in verse are indeed 'much more oratorical than poetical'; and, in all his earlier work, theory accentuated this natural tendency so fatally that we have to scrape off a great deal of false glitter if we are to find the good metal which is often enough to be found, even in the metrical romances, with their pseudo-romance, founded on direct observation, their pseudo-passion, doing injustice to a really passionate nature, their impossible heroes, not without certain touches of just self-portraiture, their impossible heroines, betraying after all a certain first-hand acquaintance with the 'dreadful heart of woman.' In narrative verse Byron finally made for himself a form of his own which exactly suited him, but in lyrical verse he never learnt to do much that he could not already do in the 'Hours of Idleness.' His 'last lines' are firmer in measure, graver in substance, but they are written on exactly the same principle as the 'Well! thou art happy' of 1808. There is the same strained simplicity of feeling, in which a really moved directness comes through the traditional rhetoric of the form. Every stanza says something, and it says exactly what he means it to say, without any of the exquisite evasions of a more purely poetic style; without, too, any of the qualifying interruptions of a more subtle temperament. Byron's mind was without subtlety; whatever he felt he felt without reservations, or the least thinking about feeling: hence his immediate hold upon the average man or woman, who does not need to come to his verse, as the verse of most other poets must be approached, with a mind already prepared for that communion. There is force, clearness, but no atmosphere; everything is seen detached, a little bare, very distinct, in a strong light without shadows.

In studying Byron one is always face to face with the question: Can intention, in art, ever excuse performance? Can (one is tempted to say) the sum of a number of noughts arrive at an appreciable figure? Wordsworth wearies us by commonplace of thought and feeling, by nervelessness of rhythm, by a deliberate triviality; Coleridge offers us metaphysics for poetry; Browning offers us busy thinking about life for meditation; there is not a scene in Shakespeare which is perfect as a scene of Sophocles is perfect; but with Byron the failure is not exceptional, it is constant; it is like the speech of a man whose tongue is too large for his mouth. There are indeed individual good lines in Byron, a great number of quite splendid lines, though none indeed of the very finest order of poetry; but there is not a single poem, not a single passage of the length of 'Kubla Khan,' perhaps not a single stanza, which can be compared as poetry with a poem or passage or stanza of Keats or Shelley, such as any one will find by merely turning over the pages of those poets for five minutes at random. What is not there is precisely the magic which seems to make poetry its finer self, the perfume of the flower, that by which the flower is remembered, after its petals have dropped or withered. Even Browning abandons himself at times to the dream which floats, musically or in soft colour, through the senses of his mind. But Byron, when he meditates, meditates with fixed attention; if he dreams, he dreams with open eyes, to which the darkness is aglow with tumultuous action; he is at the mercy of none of those wandering sounds, delicate spirits of the air, which come entreating their liberty from the indefinite, in the releasing bondage of song. He has certain things to say, he has certain impulses to embody; he has, first, a certain type of character, then a view of the world which is more obviously the prose than the poetic view of the world, but certainly a wide view, to express; and it remains for him, in this rejection or lack of all the lesser graces, to be either Michael Angelo or Benjamin Haydon.

Or, at least, so it would seem; and yet, so it does not seem to be. Byron is not Michael Angelo, not merely because his conceptions were not as great as Michael Angelo's, but because he had not the same power of achieving his conceptions, because he had not the same technical skill. When Michael Angelo left great naked vestiges of the rock still clinging about the emerging bodies of his later sculpture, it was not because he could not finish them with the same ivory smoothness as the 'Pietà' in St. Peter's; it was because he had found out all the art of man's visible body, and had apprehended that deeper breathing of the spirit of life, which is in the body, yet which is not the body; and was caught in the agony of the last conflict with the last mystery. To leave an appealing or terrifying or lamentable incompleteness, where before there had been the clear joy of what is finished and finite: there, precisely, was the triumph of his technique. But Byron is not Haydon, because he is not a small man struggling to be a great man, painting large merely because he cannot paint small, and creating chaos on the canvas out of ambition rather than irresistible impulse. He is fundamentally sincere, which is the root of greatness; he has a firm hold on himself and on the world; he speaks to humanity in its own voice, heightened to a pitch which carries across Europe. No poet had ever seemed to speak to men so directly, and it was through this directness of his vision of the world, and of his speech about it, that he became a poet, that he made a new thing of poetry.

Look, for instance, at his epithets and at his statements, and you will find, whenever he is at his best, an unparalleled justness of expression, a perfect hitting of the mark, which will sometimes seem rather the vigour of prose than the more celestial energy of poetry, but not always. When, in the 'Vision of Judgment,' George III is brought pompously to the gate of Heaven and is seen to be nothing but

'An old man
With an old soul, and both extremely blind';

when, in 'Childe Harold,' Napoleon is seen

> 'With a deaf heart that never seemed to be
> A listener to itself';

when

> 'France gets drunk with blood to vomit crime';

when Cromwell

> 'Hewed the throne down to a block';

when history is defined as 'the Devil's scripture,' Rome as 'the Niobe of nations,' ivy as 'the garland of eternity'; when Castlereagh's speeches are summed up: —

> 'Nor even a sprightly blunder's spark can blaze
> From that Ixion grindstone's ceaseless toil,
> That turns and turns to give the world a notion
> Of endless torment and perpetual motion';

there is at least, in all these vivid and unforgettable phrases, a heat of truth which has kindled speech into a really imaginative fervour. Seen in the form which perhaps more immediately impressed the world, as being liker to the world's notion of poetry —

> 'Admire — exult — despise — laugh — weep — for here
> There is such matter for all feeling: Man!'

it is sheer rhetoric, and, for all its measure of personal sincerity, becomes false through over-emphasis. The closer Byron's writing seems to come to prose the nearer it really comes to poetry, because it comes nearer to humanity and to the world, his subject-matter, which appears to take him for its voice, rather than to be chosen by him with any conscious selection.

Byron loved the world for its own sake and for good and evil. His quality of humanity was genius to him, and stood to him in the place of imagination. Whatever is best in his work is full of this kind of raw or naked humanity. It is the solid part of his rhetoric, and is what holds us still in the apparently somewhat theatrical addresses to the Dying Gladiator and the like. Speaking straight, in 'Don Juan' and 'The Vision of Judgment,' it creates almost a new kind of poetry, the poetry of the world, written rebelliously, but on its own level, by a man to whom the world was the one reality. Only Byron, and not Shelley, could lead the revolt against custom and convention, against the insular spirit of England, because to Byron custom and convention and the insular spirit were so much more actual things. Rage first made him a poet: the first lines of verse he ever wrote were written at the age of nine, against an old lady whom he disliked; and when the weak and insincere sentimentalities of the 'Hours of Idleness' had been scourged by Brougham in the 'Edinburgh,' it was a most human desire for revenge which stirred him instantly into a vigorous satirist. His very idealism was a challenge and a recoil. He went about Europe like a man with a hazel wand in his hand, and wherever the forked branch dipped, living water rose to him out of the earth. Every line he wrote is a reminiscence, the reminiscence of a place or a passion. His mind was a cracked mirror, in which everything reflected itself directly, but as if scarred. His mind was never to him a kingdom, but always part of the tossing democracy of humankind. And so, having no inner peace, no interior vision, he was never for long together the master or the obedient vassal of his imagination; and he has left us tumultuous fragments, in which beauty comes and goes fitfully, under pained disguises, or like a bird with impatient wings, tethered at short range to the ground.

Byron was at once the victim and the master of the world. Two enemies, always in fierce grapple with one another, yet neither of them ever thrown, Byron and the world seem to touch at all points, and to maintain a kind of equilibrium by the equality of their strength. To Byron life itself was imaginative, not the mere raw stuff out of which imagination could shape something quite different, something far more beautiful, but itself, its common hours, the places he passed on the way, a kind of poem in action. All his verse is an attempt to make his own poetry out of fragments of this great poem of life, as it came to him on his heedful way through the midst of it. All Byron's poetry is emphasis, and he obtains his tremendous emphasis by a really impersonal interest in the circumstances of the drama which he knew himself to be acting. Building entirely on his personal, his directly personal emotion, he never allows that emotion to overpower him. He makes the most of it, even with what may easily pass for a lack of sincerity, but is only an astonishing way of recovering himself after an abandonment to feeling. Imagination comes to him as self-control. Himself in actual life the least controlled of men, or controlled only with a violence itself excessive, a great emergency always found him quietly ready for it, from that first voyage when he wrapped himself in his cloak and went to sleep on the deck of a Turkish vessel in danger of shipwreck, to the day when the Greek mutineers broke into the room where he lay dying, and found him more than their master. This manly quality was his imagination; the quality of restraint in extremity, which he has praised in some of his most famous lines, on the statue of the Dying Gladiator. It may seem to be the quality of a man rather than of a poet, and is indeed one of the reasons why without Byron the man no one would have cared for Byron the poet. But it is more than this; it becomes in him a poetic quality, the actual imaginative force by which he dramatises himself, not as if it were his own little naked human soul, shiveringly alone with God, but as a great personage, filling the world, like Napoleon, and seen always against a background of all the actual pomps of the world.

And it was as a Napoleon, 'the grand Napoleon of the realms of rhyme,' that he filled Europe, as no other poet in the history of literature has filled Europe. Famous men do not always choose the form in which fame shall come to them, but the greatest men always choose their own fame. It was through no mere accident that Byron built up his own romance. It was the particular quality of his mind acting upon the helpless helpfulness of event; his genius, turning life into art after his own fashion. Fame meant so much to Byron because fame is a personal, active thing, concerned with one's self while one lives, bringing one into the sight of other people so vividly. He could never have gone on writing as Shelley went on writing, obscurely, loved by a few, not even publicly enough hated. To Shelley, with his secluded interior life, fame meant very little, except for an almost wholly disinterested enthusiasm for ideas, which he would gladly have served with more immediate effect, as a more famous poet. But Byron exacted fame from the world as he exacted deference to his rank from strangers. His conception of himself would not have been complete without it. If one bases success, ever so little, upon action, that is, upon something external, a private or a deferred triumph must mean very little. Napoleon, a prisoner at Elba without the interval between Elba and St. Helena: would that have been the same Napoleon?

And so it was no vulgarity of mind, as some have fancied, nor even a necessarily very morbid condition, that made Byron so eager for applause, so conscious of notoriety. All that, so pleasing and so unessential to the student or the studious artist, was to Byron an actual part of his art. It was the canvas itself, upon which he had to weave his coloured patterns. It was necessary to him; for, with Byron's amplitude of self-dramatisation, there was but that one traditional step from the sublime to the ridiculous. An obscure person on his travels, taking the world into his confidence with so lofty a naïveté, might have written the most beautiful poetry; but, without an audience, how ludicrous would have been the spectacle! 'What is a man beside a mount?' writes Browning, mocking Byron; but precisely what Byron did was to show the insignificance of the mountains in the presence of man. He could write of the Alps, and fill the imagination of Europe with the mere fact of his presence there; adding history to Waterloo,

because 'his tread was on an empire's dust,' when the history of that field had only just written itself. In a letter to his mother, written at the age of twenty-three, on his first visit to Athens, Byron declared sententiously:—
'I am so convinced of the advantages of looking at mankind instead of reading about them, and the bitter effects of staying at home with all the narrow prejudices of an islander, that I think there should be a law among us, to set our young men abroad for a term, among the few allies our wars have left us.'

Eight years later he wrote to Murray: 'I am sure my bones would not rest in an English grave or my clay mix with the earth of that country.' Byron was so English, English even in that, in its lofty petulance; and he had the characteristically English love of travel, the quality of Burton, of Borrow, of his own grandfather, the sea-wanderer, but which it remained for Byron to turn into a really thrilling poetic quality. He travelled because the adventure pleased him, because, as he said, it 'awakened the gipsy in him,' and he was drawn by the mere adventurous search after new sensations to the East, to Greece, to Italy, to the countries which other people were writing about without seeing them, and which he visited, certainly with no conscious intention of writing about them. Poetry came to him by a happy and inevitable accident; it was his way of recording the sensations. In the preface to 'Childe Harold' he speaks of 'the beauties of nature and the stimulus of travel (except ambition, the most powerful of all excitements)'; and it was a mere statement of a fact when he wrote:

'Where rose the mountains, there to him were friends;
Where rolled the ocean, thereon was his home;
Where the blue sky, and glowing clime extends,
He had the passion and the power to roam;
The desert, forest, cavern, breaker's foam,
Were unto him companionship; they spake
A mutual language.'

'A world to roam through' is the first of his two wishes in his 'Epistle to Augusta'; and that simple love of wandering, which no other great poet has ever had in anything like the same degree, but which is the most vivid quality of many of the most vivid people in the world, discoverers, travelling students, or gipsies, was at the root of all his nature-worship, as it has been called, and all his eloquent writing about landscapes and places. It was a part of his tendency towards action, of his human rather than literary quality. Taste in landscape has changed; we no longer admire the Alps, or, if we do, scarce dare admit it; we have almost forgotten that there is anything in nature but fine shades, and the materials for a picture, in which nature shall be trimmed to the pattern of frugal souls. Byron liked nature in vast movement:—

> 'Sky — mountains — river — woods — lake — lightnings! ye!
> With night, and clouds, and thunder — and a soul
> To make these felt and feeling.'

His storms at sea and his storms among the Alps are touched with a quality of rapture, because he really was 'a sharer' in that 'fierce and far delight'; and, here as elsewhere in his work, truth lies at the root of rhetoric, giving it life, lifting it into a kind of powerful, naked, and undeniable poetic existence.

And then, beyond this raw personal quality, the fact of feeling it intensely whenever he had 'made him friends of mountains,' 'and on Parnassus seen the eagles fly,' there was a quality of feeling still more deeply personal, a psychological note, the landscape being a 'state of soul,' perhaps not quite as Amiel meant it. Together with an astonishing sense of the beauty of the natural world, and especially of its power, splendour, the overwhelming energy of water, the 'beautifying' and consuming energy of time, the unlimited bounds of space, the 'swimming shadows and enormous shapes' of night and storm, he had the unvarying consciousness of his own presence there, so insignificant and so absorbing. 'Childe Harold' has been called a kind of diorama; but the picture is seen always flowing through a single passionate, sorrowful, and sensitive soul, and coloured by its passage there. The secret seems to be suddenly let out, when, seated by the tomb of Cecilia Metella on the Appian Way and dreaming of 'a little bark of hope,' he begins to wonder whither he should steer his little bark if he had it, and can but answer: —

'There woos no home, no hope, nor life, save what is here.'

Here, the present moment, best enjoyed in some active form of exile, among great memories, the memories of empires, of what is most liberating in history, or with nature at some height of ecstasy, in the peril of the sea, of snow, of the hills: that is left to him, and may be enjoyed with what forgetting exultation and melancholy pleasure he can bring to it.

Byron has power without wisdom, power which is sanity, and human at heart, but without that vision which is wisdom. His passion is without joy, the resurrection, or that sorrow deeper than any known unhappiness, which is the death by which we attain life. He has never known what it is to be at peace, with himself or with outward things. There is a certain haste in his temper, which does not allow him to wait patiently upon any of the spiritual guests who only come unbidden, and to those who await them. His mind is always full of busy little activities, with which a more disinterested thinker would not be concerned. Himself the centre, he sees the world revolving about him, seemingly as conscious of him as he of it. It is not only that he never forgets himself, but he never forgets that he is a lord, and that one of his feet is not perfect.

In his letters, with their brilliant common sense, their wit, their clear and defiant intellect, their intolerant sincerity, as in his poems, it is not what we call the poet who speaks, it is what we call the natural man. Byron is the supreme incarnation of the natural man. When he gets nearest to philosophical thought it is in an amazingly frank statement of the puzzle of the natural man before the facts of the universe, a puzzle which, like him, he laughs off: —

'And that which after all my spirit vexes,
Is, that I find no spot where man can rest eye on,
Without confusion of the sorts and sexes,
Of beings, stars, and this unriddled wonder,
The world, which at the worst's a glorious blunder.'

His feeling for the arts is on the same level, with the same earnest, uneducated quickness of feeling, when once the feeling is stirred. 'At Florence,' he writes in a letter, 'I remained but a day, having to hurry for Rome. However, I went to the two galleries, from which one returns drunk with beauty; but there are sculpture and painting which, for the first time, gave me an idea of what people mean by their *cant* about those two most artificial of the arts.' 'You must recollect, however,' he says in another letter (after some beautiful and passionate sentences on a portrait of 'some learned lady centuries old'), 'that I know nothing of painting, and that I detest it, unless it reminds me of something I have seen, or think it possible to see.' The portrait of the learned lady is 'the kind of face to go mad for, because it cannot walk out of its frame'; its 'beauty and sweetness and wisdom' are its human attributes, not the attributes of its art; here, as always, it is for life that Byron cries out, the naked contact of humanity, as the only warmth in the world.

And so, not so very long before it was too late, he discovered how he was meant to write in verse, 'with common words in their common places,' as Jeffrey defined it; and then, for the first time, his verse became as good as his prose, and a stanza of his rhyme could be matched as mere writing against a paragraph from one of his letters. Neither Keats nor Shelley, not even Wordsworth, much less Coleridge, was content with our language as we have it; all, on theory or against theory, used inversions, and wrote otherwise than they would speak; it was Byron, with his boisterous contempt for rules, his headlong way of getting to the journey's end, who discovered that poetry, which is speech as well as song, and speech not least when it is most song, can be written not only with the words

GEORGE GORDON, LORD BYRON

we use in talking, but in exactly the same order and construction. And, besides realising this truth for other people who were to come later and make a different use of the discovery, he realised for himself that he could make poetry entirely conversational, thus getting closer to that world which was 'too much with him.' Who in English poetry before Byron has ever talked in verse? Taking a hint from Frere, who had nothing to say, and did but show how things might be said, Byron gave up oratory and came nearer than he had yet come to poetry by merely talking. 'I have broken down the poetry as nearly as I could to common language,' he says in a letter, referring to 'Sardanapalus'; but in such attempts to be 'as simple and severe as Alfieri,' the lamentable attempts of the dramas, there is only too thorough a 'breaking down' of poetry to a level which is not even that of good prose. In 'Beppo,' in the 'Vision of Judgment,' and in 'Don Juan,' words, style, language, subject, are at one; the colloquial manner is used for what is really talk, extraordinarily brilliant talk, and at the same time, as Goethe saw, a 'classically elegant comic style'; the natural man is at last wholly himself, all of himself, himself not even exaggerated for effect.

Never, in English verse, has a man been seen who was so much a man and so much an Englishman. It is not man in the elemental sense, so much as the man of the world, whom we find reflected, in a magnificent way, in this poet for whom (like the novelists, and unlike all other poets) society exists as well as human nature. No man of the world would feel ashamed of himself for writing poetry like 'Don Juan,' if he could write it; and not only because the poet himself seems conscious of all there is ridiculous in the mere fact of writing in rhyme, when everything can be so well said in prose. It is the poetry of middle age (premature with Byron, '*ennuyé* at nineteen,' as he assures us), and it condenses all the temporary wisdom, old enough to be a little sour and not old enough to have recovered sweetness, of perhaps the least profitable period of life. It is sad and cynical with experience, and is at the stage between storm and peace; it doubts everything, as everything must be doubted before it can be understood rightly and rightly apprehended; it regrets youth, which lies behind it, and hates the thought of age, which lies before it, with a kind of passionate self-pity; it has knowledge rather than wisdom, and is a little mirror of the world, turned away from the sky, so that only the earth is visible in it. Shakespeare has put all the world's motley into his picture; but is not the world, to Shakespeare, that 'insubstantial pageant' which is always about to fade, and which fades into nothingness whenever Hamlet gets alone with his soul, or Macbeth with his conscience, or even Othello with his honour? Byron's thought, which embraced Europe as another man's thought might have embraced the village from which he had risen, was too conscious of politics, nations, events, Napoleon, George III, and other trifles in eternity, to be quite free to overlook the edge of the globe, and bring back news, or at least a significant silence, from that ultimate inspection. He taught poetry to be vividly interested in all earthly things, and for their own sake; and if any one had reminded him with Calderon that 'Life's a dream, and dreams themselves are a dream,' he would have replied that, at all events, the dream is a real thing, and the only reality, to the dreamer, and that he was not yet through with his sleep.

What came to give him his measure of distinction, his dark background, whatever he has of depth, was, characteristically, a personal accident, as it might seem, a fiery melancholy, for which he held the nature of things, no less than his own nature, responsible. Conscience, some inexplicable self-torture, a gloomy belief that the sun

> 'shall not beam on one
> To whom the gifts of life and warmth have been
> Of a more fatal nature';

these, with almost an admitted pride in their potency, and a strenuous and reiterated pride in dominating them, were given to Byron lest the world should have satisfied him, which is failure in life. One of the spirits in 'Manfred' says to the other: —

> 'This is to be a mortal,
> And seek the things beyond mortality';

and the other answers: —

> 'Yet, see, he mastereth himself, and makes
> His torture tributary to his will.
> Had he been one of us, he would have made
> An awful spirit.'

It was good for Byron that he was unhappy, that memories and apprehensions came to rescue him harshly out of the present, in which he might so easily have taken too unthinking a pleasure. The triviality which was one side of his manliness, the scorn of vague speculation, which was in danger of drifting into an indifference towards ideas, the excess of his mental tendency towards action, were all lying in wait for him, and, in the absence of some overshadowing and overpowering idea, would have found him at their mercy. Byron was not a thinker, but he was afraid of hell, and his courage throughout life was the genuine courage of one to whom death was really terrifying. 'The worst of it is that I *do* believe,' he said; and his belief was that he was predestined to fall endlessly into the power of evil. It is his own portrait, as he conceived it, that he draws in 'Manfred' : —

> 'This should have been a noble creature: he
> Hath all the energy which should have made
> A goodly frame of glorious elements,
> Had they been wisely mingled; as it is,
> It is an awful chaos — light and darkness —
> And mind and dust — and passions and pure thoughts,
> Mixed, and contending without end or order,
> All dormant and destructive.'

What other, more human memories, regrets, unavailing repentances mingled with this fatalistic sense of condemnation, we cannot tell; but certainly Byron's half-proud and half-desperate sense of sin was no pose, but almost the deepest part of his inner life.

> 'Our life is a false nature — 't is not in
> The harmony of things, — this hard decree,
> This uneradicable taint of sin,
> This boundless Upas, this all-blasting tree,
> Whose root is Earth':

such an outcry, in 'Childe Harold,' means at least all that it says. If Byron's fixed unhappiness were but the weariness of one to whom pleasure had been too kind, or a mere scowl for effect, like the 'unhappy' expression which he assumed when sitting for his bust to Thorwaldsen, then his personality, the one thing which has profoundly interested the world in him, was but a playing at hide-and-seek with emotion. Not to have been sincere (sincere at root, beneath all the rhetoric) would have been, for Byron, to have lost all hold on our sympathy, all command of our admiration.

Byron's ennui, what he meant when he called himself 'the earth's tired denizen,' was made up of many elements, but it was partly of that most incurable kind which comes from emptiness rather than over-fulness; the ennui of one to whom thought was not satisfying, without sustenance in itself, but itself a cause of restlessness, like a heady wine drunk in solitude. 'The blight of life, the demon thought,' he called it, so early as the first canto of 'Childe Harold'; and a motto to the third canto, seven years later, is a quotation from a letter of Frederick the Great to D'Alembert, endeavouring to console him for the loss of Mlle. de Lespinasse, and advising 'quelque problème bien difficile à résoudre,' 'afin que cette application vous forçât à penser à autre chose. Il n'y a en vérité de remède que celui-là et le temps.' To think of something else! the mockery of a remedy, and yet the only one. Byron clamoured for all the good things of life, as a child clamours, passionately, amidst storms of tears, when one of them is denied him.

Seeming to others to have got more than his share, he was discontented if he did not get all he wanted; and no one, in this world, gets quite all he wants when he wants so many things as Byron. It has seemed strange to some that Byron should have been so sensitive to dispraise, so restive under any check. But it was part of his nature; it was but another manifestation of that 'straining after the unlimited' which Goethe saw to be one of his main characteristics.

And then Byron suffered, we can hardly doubt, from that too vivid sense of humanity which is like a disease, that obsession to which every face is a challenge and every look an acceptance or a rebuff. How is content in life possible to those condemned to go about like magnets, attracting or repelling every animate thing, and tormented by the restlessness which their mere presence communicates to the air about them? This magnetic nature is not given to man for his happiness. Condemning him to 'plunge into the crowd,' it leaves him at the crowd's mercy, as he sensitively feels the shock of every disturbance which he causes there. Driving him into solitude for an escape, it will not let him even there escape the thought of what in himself is so much an epitome of humanity, for 'quiet to quick bosoms is a hell.' Nature becomes painfully human to him, and seems a sort of external memory, recorded in symbols. A note in Byron's Swiss Journal, afterwards brought almost word for word into 'Manfred,' shows us this effect of nature: 'Passed whole woods of withered pines, all withered; trunks stripped and barkless, branches lifeless, done by a single winter; their appearance reminded me of me and my family.' We find him declaring, with unaccustomed solemnity, that 'neither the music of the shepherd, the crashing of the avalanche, nor the torrent, the mountain, the glacier, the forest, nor the cloud, have for one moment lightened the weight upon my heart nor enabled me to lose my own wretched identity in the majesty, and the power, and the glory, around, above, and beneath me.' Byron's thought about the universe, even when it came nearest to abstract thinking, was always conditioned, and for the most part quite frankly, by his personal circumstances. He wrote 'Manfred' because of 'the Steinbach, and the Jungfrau, and something else, much more than Faustus.' He filled 'Cain' with exactly the same arguments that he used in his conversations with Dr. Kennedy. 'Don Juan' speaks in almost the same words as his familiar letters.

The melancholy of Childe Harold, of Byron himself, which has been so often associated with the deeper and more thoughtful melancholy of René, of Obermann, is that discontent with the world which comes from too great love of the world, and not properly an intellectual dissatisfaction at all. It gave birth to a whole literature of pessimism, in which what had been in Byron an acute personal ache became an imagined travailing of the whole world in a vast disgust at its own existence. Where Byron, as he admitted, 'deviated into the gloomy vanity of "drawing from self,"' less energetic and more contemplative writers spoke for humanity, as they conceived it, and found everything grey with their own old age of soul, which had never been young. It was only Byron who could say, after a visit to the opera, on which he comments with the most cheerful malice: 'How I do delight in observing life as it really is!' And it is just here that he distinguishes himself from his followers, in his right to say, as he said: —

> 'But I have lived, and have not lived in vain.'

Byron is a moralist, and a moralist of great simplicity. He had

> 'That just habitual scorn, which could contemn
> Men and their thoughts,'

at the same time that he was conscious of his own most human weaknesses; and, in a fragment not included in 'Don Juan,' he cries very sincerely: —

> 'I would to heaven that I were so much clay,
> As I am blood, bone, marrow, passion, feeling.'

He speaks his impressive epitaph over human greatness and the wrecks of great cities, because it is the natural impulse of the natural man; and his moralisings, always so personal, are generally what would seem to most people the obvious thought under the circumstances. When he is most moved, by some indignation, which in verse and prose always made him write best, he seems to resign himself to what was noblest in him; the passion for liberty (a passion strong enough to die for, as he proved), the passion against injustice, the passion of the will to live and the will to know, fretting against the limits of death and ignorance. It was then that 'thoughts which should call down thunder' came to him, calling down thunder indeed, on the wrongs and hypocrisies of his time and country, as a moralist more intellectually disinterested, further aloof from the consequences of his words, could not have done.

Byron had no philosophy; he saw no remedy or alternative for any evil, least of all in his own mind, itself more tossed than the world without him. He had flaming doubts, stormy denials; he had the idealism of revolt, and fought instead of dreaming. His idolatry of good is shown by his remorseful consciousness of evil, morbid, as it has seemed to those who have not realised that every form of spiritual energy has something of the divine in it, and is on its way to become divine. 'Cain' is a long, restless, proud, and helpless questioning of the powers of good and evil, by one who can say: —

'I will have nought to do with happiness
Which humbles me and mine,'

with a pride equal to Lucifer's; and can say also, in all the humility of admitted defeat: —

'Were I quiet earth,
That were no evil.'

'Obstinate questionings,' resolving themselves into nothing except that pride and that humility of despair, form the whole drama in which Byron has come nearest to abstract thinking, in his 'gay metaphysical style,' as he called it. 'Think and endure' is Lucifer's last counsel to Cain. 'Why art thou wretched?' he has already asked him; and been answered: 'Why do I exist?' Cain's arraignment of God, which has nothing startling to us, who have read Nietzsche, raised all England in a kind of panic; religion itself seemed to be tottering. But Byron went no further in that direction; his greater strength lay elsewhere. Dropping heroics, he concludes, at the time that he is writing 'Don Juan,' that man 'has always been and always will be an unlucky rascal,' with a tragic acquiescence in that summary settlement of the enigma, laughingly. Humour was given us that we might disguise from ourselves the consciousness of our common misery. Humour turned by thought into irony, which is humour thinking about itself, is the world's substitute for philosophy, perhaps the only weapon that can be turned against it with success. Byron used the world's irony to condemn the world. He had conquered its attention by the vast clamour of his revolt; he had lulled it asleep by an apparent acceptance of its terms; now, like a treacherous friend, treacherous with the sublime treachery of the intellect, he drove the nail into its sleeping forehead.

And so we see Byron ending, after all the 'daring, dash, and grandiosity' (to use Goethe's words, as they are rendered by Matthew Arnold) of his earlier work, a tired and melancholy jester, still fierce at heart. Byron gives us, in an overwhelming way, the desire of life, the enjoyment of life, and the sense of life's deceit, as it vanishes from between our hands, and slips from under our feet, and is a voice and no more. In his own way he preaches 'vanity of vanities,' and not less cogently because he has been drunk with life, like Solomon himself, and has not yet lost the sense of what is intoxicating in it. He has given up the declamation of despair, as after all an effect, however sincere, of rhetoric; his jesting is more sorrowful than his outcries, for it shows him to have surrendered.

'We live and die,
But which is best, you know no more than I.'

All his wisdom (experience, love of nature, passion, tenderness, pride, the thirst for knowledge) comes to that in the end, not even a negation.

RICHARD HARRIS BARHAM (1788–1845) [1]

THE Rev. Richard Harris Barham was a great creator of nonsense, and he had a prodigious faculty for versifying. He wrote entirely for his own amusement; or, as a friend said of him: 'The same relaxation which some men seek in music, pictures, cards, or newspapers, he sought in verse.' Most of his rhymes were written down at odd moments, often after midnight, and with a facility, his son tells us, 'which not only surprised himself, but which he actually viewed with distrust; and he would not unfrequently lay down his pen, from an apprehension that what was so fluent must of necessity be feeble.' In all this helter-skelter of 'mirth and marvels,' begun for Bentley's 'Miscellany' in 1837, when he was nearly fifty years of age, there is nothing feeble in all the fluency. No verse that has been written in English goes so fast or turns so many somersaults on the way. He said once, of a poem which he did not care for,'that the only chance to make it effective was to strike out something newish in the stanza, to make people stare.' If that was ever his aim, he attained it, and not in his rhymes only. The rhymes are marvellous, and if they are not the strictest, have the most spontaneous sound of any in English. The clatter of 'atmosphere' and ' that must fear,' the gabble of —

'And so like a dragon he
Looked in his agony,'

with even the more elaborately manufactured —

[1] (1) *Ingoldsby Legends*, first series, 1840; second series, 1843; third series, 1847. (2) *Lyrics*, 1881.

> 'twisting dom-
> estic and foreign necks all over Christendom,'

have so easy a jingle as they go galloping over the page, that we are hardly conscious how artificial they really are. With the rhymes go rhythms, so bold, swift, and irreverent, and with pauses so alarming that one is never able, if one has read them as a child, to get out of one's head the solemn thrill of —

> 'Open lock
> To the Deadman's knock!'

or the ghastly gaiety in the sound of —

> 'Hairy-faced Dick at once lets fly,
> And knocks off the head of young Hamilton Tighe.'

Under all the extravagance, like a light through a lantern, there is meaning, let wildly loose, but with something macabre, grim, ghastly, above all haunted, in it. Barham's material came to him partly out of old books, which he read to catch from them a harsh Protestant laughter against Catholics; but for the better part from legends which he found in his own neighbourhood. A scholar revels throughout these unclerical rhymes, drawing wicked and harmless imps out of book and bottle as he pores, past midnight, over his black-letter folios and his port. And so we find, in these poems made up of fear, fun, and suspense, a kind of burlesque which is not quite like any other, so jolly is it as it fumbles with death, murder, tortures, and terrors of the mind. Here is burlesque of that excessive kind which foreigners see in the tragic laughing white clown in the arena, with his touch of mortal colour in the cheeks. And it is full of queer ornament, as in this interior of Bluebeard's castle, furnished as if by Beardsley: —

> 'It boasts not stool, table, or chair,
>   Bloudie Jacke!
> But one Cabinet, costly and grand,
>   Which has little gold figures
>   Of little gold niggers,
> With fishing-rods stuck in each hand;
>   It's japanned,
> And it's placed on a splendid buhl stand.'

REV. HENRY HART MILMAN 265

Was there ever a gayer and ghastlier farce than in this very poem, 'Bloudie Jacke of Shrewsberrie,' which goes to the jingling of bells, in a metre invented as if to fit into an interval between Poe and Browning? To be so successfully vulgar in 'Misadventures at Margate' is to challenge the lesser feats of Hood, and the prose of a narrative like 'The Leech of Folkestone' (part of what the writer called 'prose material to serve as sewing-silk and buckram') is, for all its oddity, almost as chilling to the blood as Sheridan Lefanu's in his book of vampires, 'In a Glass Darkly.' But where Barham is most himself, and wonderful in his way, is in the cascading of cadences rhymed after this fashion: —

> 'There's Setebos, storming because Mephistopheles
> Gave him the lie,
> Said he'd "blacken his eye,"
> And dashed in his face a whole cup of hot coffee-lees.'

Not Butler nor Byron nor Browning, the three best makers of comic rhyme, has ever shown so supreme an inventiveness in the art.

REV. HENRY HART MILMAN (1791-1868)[1]

OF Milman's plays three are Biblical and lifeless; one, 'Fazio,' is moving, for all its childishness of construction, its scenes of a few lines, the naïveté with which the speeches follow one another with too carefully irregular a logic of the passions. There is a quaint, unnatural neatness in these small scenes, with their brief statement, not action, written after the Elizabethan manner by one who has often a firm vigour in

[1] (1) *The Apollo Belvidere*, 1810. (2) *Fazio*, 1815. (3) *Samor*, 1818. (4) *The Fall of Jerusalem*, 1820. (5) *The Belvidere Apollo*, 1821. (6) *The Martyr of Antioch*, 1822. (7) *Belshazzar*, 1822. (8) *Anne Boleyn*, 1826. (9) *Mahābhārata* (translated from the Sanscrit), 1835. (10) *Poetical Works*, 3 vols., 1839. (11) *Agamemnon* (translation), 1865. (12) *Bacchae* (translation), 1865.

speech, a diction sometimes really poetical, but no mastery of drama, either as life or as form. In lines like these,—

> 'If that ye cast us to the winds, the winds
> Will give us their unruly restless nature;
> We whirl and whirl; and where we settle, Fazio,
> But he that ruleth the mad winds can know,'

there is a suggestion never fully realised, of sensitive dramatic speech.

The three Biblical plays, 'The Fall of Jerusalem,' 'The Martyr of Antioch,' and 'Belshazzar,' are almost equally pompous, lifeless, and artificial. Frigid blank verse, sometimes strained and gaudy, sometimes dragging with it heavy loads of false sentiment, alternates with rhymed verse, brought in for no sufficient reason, and producing no effect even of relief. The author assures us, but needlessly, that his plays were not intended for the stage. They were read and admired in their day for what was supposed to be a kind of 'classical' merit. The 'Quarterly Review,' reviewing 'The Fall of Jerusalem', in 1820, and rebuking Shelley for having, in 'The Cenci,' 'expected to afford mankind delight by a facsimile of unmingled wickedness and horror,' goes on to say that the clerical author had produced a poem, 'to which, without extravagant encomium, it is not unsafe to promise whatever immortality the English language can bestow.' To-day all three lie bound like mummies, warning us against the death of reputations.

REV. CHARLES WOLFE (1791-1823) [1]

WOLFE is remembered by one poem, 'The Burial of Sir John Moore,' in which he competes with Campbell, and goes beyond

[1] *Remains of the late Rev. Charles Wolfe, A. B., Curate of Bomoughmore, Diocese of Armagh; with a brief Memoir of his Life*, by the Rev. John A. Russell, M. A., Archdeacon of Clogher, 1825.

at all events the poem which he chiefly admired, 'Hohenlinden.' He did nothing really good besides this poem, but it was the outcome of a nature in which poetry germinated. Everything we are told about his short and attractive life shows us a sensitive temperament, very much under the influence of music, and a mind of intense but strictly limited concentration, capable of momentary absorption, but no more. He was, within his limits, a careful artist; and even when he seems to imitate Moore or other bad models he is for the most part working on a genuine, though faint and transitory, impulse, like those lines, whose pathos is taken straight from the natural pathos of an Irish air, which 'he had sung over and over till he burst into tears, in which mood he composed the words.' Thus the one poem in which he is perfectly successful is no happy and inexplicable accident, but the culmination of all his qualities as an artist. He distrusted his own impulse, and only once met with a subject which so completely possessed him that it gave substance to his material and gravity to his style. There is in this poem, which is one of the most simple and direct poems of the kind in any language, a touch which links it with the characteristic Irish lyric, the line: —

'And we far away on the billow.'

The epithets, 'distant and random,' 'sullenly,' are precise and unusual; and from beginning to end there is what poems of the sort usually lack, atmosphere. It has a masculine tenderness which no doubt was largely what made Byron divine in it, as it floated anonymously about the country, a thing 'little inferior to the best which the present prolific age has brought forth.'

PERCY BYSSHE SHELLEY (1792-1822)[1]

I

'I HAVE the vanity to write only for poetical minds,' Shelley said to Trelawny, 'and must be satisfied with few readers.' 'I am, and I desire to be, nothing,' he wrote to Leigh Hunt, while urging him to 'assume a station in modern literature which the universal voice of my contemporaries forbids me either to stoop or to aspire to.' Yet he said also, 'Nothing is more difficult and unwelcome than to write without a confidence of finding readers'; and, 'It is impossible to compose except under the strong excitement of an assurance of finding sympathy in what you write.' Of the books which he published during his lifetime, some were published without his name, some were suppressed at the very moment of publication. Only 'The Cenci' went into a second edition. Without readers, he was without due recognition from the poets of his time. Byron was jealous, if we may believe Trelawny, but neither Keats nor Wordsworth nor Leigh Hunt nor Southey nor Landor seems ever to have considered him seriously as a rival. We must go to the enthusiastic unimportant Wilson, to find an adequate word of praise; for to Wilson 'Mr. Shelley was a poet, almost in the very highest sense of that mysterious word.'

[1] (1) *Original Poetry by Victor and Cazire*, 1810. (2) *Posthumous Fragments of Margaret Nicholson*, 1810. (3) *The Devil's Walk*, a broadside, 1812. (4) *Queen Mab*, 1813, 1821. (5) *Alastor*, 1816. (6) *Laon and Cythna*, 1818. (7) *The Revolt of Islam*, 1818. (8) *Rosalind and Helen*, 1819. (9) *The Cenci*, 1819. (10) *Prometheus Unbound*, 1820. (11) *Œdipus Tyrannus; or, Swellfoot the Tyrant*, 1820. (12) *Adonais*, 1820. (13) *Epipsychidion*, 1821. (14) *Hellas*, 1822. (15) *Poetical Pieces*, 1823. (16) *Posthumous Poems*, 1824. (17) *The Masque of Anarchy*, 1832. (18) *The Shelley Papers*, prose and verse, 1833. (19) *Poetical Works*, edited by Mrs. Shelley, 1839. (20) *Relics of Shelley*, edited by Dr. Garnett, 1862. (21) *The Dæmon of the World*, edited by H. B. Forman, 1876. (22) *Poetical Works*, edited by H. B. Forman, 8 vols., 1876-80.

The general public hated him without reading him, and even his death did not raise him from oblivion. But Time has been on his side, and to-day the general reader, if you mention the word poet to him, thinks of Shelley.

It is only by reading contemporary writings and opinions in published letters of the time, — such as Southey's when he writes to Shelley, that the manner in which his powers for poetry 'have been employed is such as to prevent me from feeling any desire to see more of productions so monstrous in their kind, and pernicious in their tendency,' — that we can, with a great effort, realise the aspect under which Shelley appeared to the people of his time. What seems to us abnormal in its innocence was to them abnormal in guilt; they imagined a revolution behind every invocation to liberty, and saw Godwin charioted in the clouds of 'Prometheus Unbound.' They saw nothing else there, and Shelley himself had moments when he thought that his mission was a prophet's rather than a poet's. All this, which would mean so little to-day, kept Shelley at that time from ever having an audience as a poet. England still feared thought, and still looked upon poetry as worth fearing.

No poet has defined his intentions in poetry more carefully than Shelley. 'It is the business of the poet,' he said, in the preface to 'The Revolt of Islam,' 'to communicate to others the pleasure and the enthusiasm arising out of those images and feelings in the vivid presence of which, within his own mind, consists at once his inspiration and his reward.' But, he says further, 'I would only awaken the feelings, so that the reader should see the beauty of true virtue, and be incited to those enquiries which have led to my moral and political creed, and that of some of the subtlest intellects in the world.' In the preface to 'Prometheus Unbound' he says, 'Didactic poetry is my abhorrence; nothing can be equally well expressed in prose that is not tedious and supererogatory in vein. My purpose has hitherto been simply to familiarise the highly refined imagination of the more select classes of poetical readers with beautiful idealisms of moral excellence.' Writing to Godwin, he says acutely, 'My power consists in sympathy, and that part of the imagination which relates to sentiment and contemplation. ... I am formed ... to apprehend minute and remote distinctions of feeling, whether relative to external nature or the living beings which surround us, and to communicate the conceptions which result from considering either the moral or the material universe as a whole.' And we are told by Mrs. Shelley that 'he said that he deliberated at one time whether he should dedicate himself to poetry or metaphysics.'

Shelley was born to be a poet, and his 'passion for reforming the world,' as well as what he fancied to be his turn for metaphysics, were both part of a temperament and intelligence perhaps more perfectly fitted for the actual production of poetry than those of any other poet. All his life Shelley was a dreamer; never a visionary. We imagine him, like his Asia on the pinnacle, saying, —

'my brain
Grows dizzy: see'st thou shapes within the mist?'

The mist, to Shelley, was part of what he saw; he never saw anything, in life or art, except through a mist. Blake lived in a continual state of vision, Shelley in a continual state of hallucination. What Blake saw was what Shelley wanted to see; Blake never dreamed, but Shelley never wakened out of that shadow of a dream which was his life.

His poetry is indeed made out of his life; but what was his life to Shelley? The least visible part of his dreams. As the Fourth Spirit sings in 'Prometheus Unbound,' —

'Nor seeks nor finds he mortal blisses,
But feeds on the aërial kisses
Of shapes that haunt thought's wildernesses.'

He lived with ardour among ideas, aspirations, and passions in which there was something at once irresponsible and abstract. He followed every impulse, without choice or restraint, with the abandonment of a leaf in the wind. 'O lift me as a wave, a leaf, a cloud!' was his prayer to the west wind and to every influence. Circumstances meant so little to him that he was unconscious of the cruelty of change to sentiment, and thus of the extent of his cruelty to women. He aimed at moral perfection, but was really of a perfect æsthetic selfishness. He was full of pity and generosity, and desired the liberation and uplifting of humanity; but humanity was less real to him than his own witch of Atlas. He only touched human action and passion closely in a single one of his works; and he said of 'The Cenci,' 'I don't think much of it. My object was to see how I could succeed in describing passions I have never felt.'

To Shelley the word love meant sympathy, and that word, in that sense, contains his whole life and creed. Is this not why he could say, —

'True love in this differs from gold and clay,
That to divide is not to take away'?

It is a love which is almost sexless, the love of an enthusiastic youth, or of his own hermaphrodite. He was so much of a sentimentalist that he could conceive of incest without repugnance, and be so innocently attracted by so many things which, to one more normally sexual, would have indicated perversity. Shelley is not perverse, but he is fascinated by every problem of evil, which draws him to contemplate it with a child's enquiring wonder of horror. No poet ever handled foulness and horror with such clean hands or so continually. The early novels are filled with tortures, the early poems profess to be the ravings of a hanged madwoman; 'Alastor' dwells lingeringly on death, 'Queen Mab' and 'The Revolt of Islam' on blood and martyrdom; madness is the centre of 'Julian and Maddalo,' and a dungeon of 'Rosalind and Helen'; the first act of 'Prometheus' celebrates an unearthly agony, and 'The Cenci' is a mart and slaughter-house of souls and bodies; while a comic satire is made up wholly out of the im-

agery of the swine-trough. Shelley could touch pitch and be
undefiled; he writes nobly of every horror; but what is curious
is that he should so persistently seek his beauty in such black-
ness. That a law or tradition existed was enough for him to
question it. He does so in the name of abstract liberty, but
curiosity was part of his impulse. A new Adam in Eden, the
serpent would have tempted him before Eve. He wanted to
'root out the infamy' of every prohibition, and would have
tasted the forbidden fruit without hunger.

And Shelley was the same from the beginning. In the notes
to 'Queen Mab' he lays down with immense seriousness the
rules on which his life was really to be founded. 'Constancy
has nothing virtuous in itself,' he tells us, 'independently
of the pleasure it confers, and partakes of the temporising
spirit of vice in proportion as it endures tamely moral defects
of magnitude in the object of its indiscreet choice.' Again:
'The connection of the sexes is so long sacred as it contributes
to the comfort of both parties, and is naturally dissolved when
its evils are greater than its benefits.' This doctrine of 'the
comfort of both parties' was what Shelley always intended
to carry out, and he probably supposed that it was always
the fault of the 'other party' when he failed to do so. Grave
charges have been brought against him for his cruelty to
women, and in particular to Harriet; and it is impossible to
forgive him, as a reasonable man, for his abandonment of
Harriet. But he was never at any time a reasonable man, and
there was never a time when he was not under one form or
another of hallucination. It was not that he was carried away
irresistibly by a gross passion, it was that he had abandoned
himself like a medium to a spiritual influence. A certain selfishness is the inevitable result of every absorption; and Shelley,
in every new rapture, was dizzy with it, whether he listened
to the skylark in the sky or to the voice of Mary calling to him
from the next room. In life, as in poetry, he was the slave of
every impulse, but a slave so faultlessly obedient that he mas-

tered every impulse in achieving it, so that his life, which seems casual, was really what he chose to make it, and followed the logic of his being.

Shelley had intuition rather than instinct, and was moved by a sympathy of the affections rather than by passion. His way of falling into and out of love is a sign that his emotions were rapid and on the surface, not that they were deep or permanent. The scent or music of love came to him like a flower's or bird's speech; it went to his head, it did not seize on the heart in his body. It must have filled him with astonishment when Harriet drowned herself, and he could never have really understood that it was his fault. He lived the life of one of those unattached plants which float in water; he had no roots in the earth, and he did not see why any one should take root there. His love for women seems never to have been sensuous, or at least to have been mostly a matter of sympathies and affinities; if other things followed, it seemed to him natural that they should, and he encouraged them with a kind of unconsciousness. Emilia Viviani, for whom he wrote the sacred love-song of the 'Epipsychidion,' would have embarrassed him, I doubt not, if she had answered his invocation practically. He would have done his best for her, and, at the same time, for Mary.

'Epipsychidion' celebrates love with an icy ecstasy which is the very life-blood of Shelley's soul; there are moments, at the beginning and end, when its sympathy with love passes into the actual possession. But for the most part it is a declaration, not an affirmation; its love is sisterly, and can be divided; it says for once, exultingly and luxuriously and purely, the deepest thing that Shelley had to say, lets out the secret of his feminine or twy-fold soul, and is the epitaph of that Antigone with whom 'some of us have in a prior existence been in love.' Its only passion is for that intellectual beauty to which it is his greater hymn, and, with Emilia Viviani, he confessed to have been the Ixion of a cloud. 'I think,' he said in a letter, 'one is always in love with something or other; the error, and I confess it is not easy for spirits cased in flesh and blood to avoid it, consists in seeking in a mortal image the likeness of what is, perhaps, eternal.' In the poem he has done more than he meant to do, for it is the eternal beauty that it images for us, and no mortal lineaments. Just because it is without personal passion, because it is the worship of a shadow for a shadow, it has come to be this thing fearfully and wonderfully made, into which the mystical passion of Crashaw and the passionate casuistry of Donne seem to have passed as into a crucible: —

> 'Thou art the wine whose drunkenness is all
> We can desire, O Love!'

and the draught is an elixir for all lovers.

That part of himself which Shelley did not put into 'Epipsychidion' he put into 'Adonais.' In that pageantry of sorrow, in which all temporal things mourn for the poet, and accept the consolation of eternity, there is more of personal confession, more of personal foreboding, than of grief for Keats, who is no less a cloud to him than Emilia Viviani, and whom indeed we know he did not in any sense properly appreciate, at his actual value. The subtlest beauty comes into it when he speaks of himself, 'a pardlike spirit beautiful and swift,' with that curious self-sympathy which remains not less abstract than his splendid and consoling Pantheism, which shows by figures a real faith in the truth and permanence of beauty. Shelley says of it and justly, 'it is a highly wrought piece of art, and perhaps better, in point of composition, than anything I have written.' The art is conscious, and recreates 'Lycidas' with entire originality; but the vessel of ancient form carries a freshly lighted flame.

Shelley, when he died, left unfinished a splendid fragment, 'The Triumph of Life,' which, inspired by Petrarch, as 'Adonais' was inspired by Milton, shows the deeper influence of Dante. It ends with an interrogation, that interrogation which he had always asked of life and was about to ask of death. He had wanted to die, that he might 'solve the great mystery.' His last poem comes to us with no solution, but breaks off as if he died before he could finish telling the secret which he was in the act of apprehending.

II

There are two kinds of imagination, that which embodies and that which disembodies. Shelley's is that which disembodies, filling mortal things with unearthly essences or veiling them with unearthly raiment. Wordsworth's imagination embodies, concentrating spirit into man, and nature into a wild flower. Shelley is never more himself than in the fantasy of 'The Witch of Atlas,' which he wrote in three days, and which is a song in seventy-eight stanzas. It is a glittering cobweb, hung on the horns of the moon's crescent, and left to swing in the wind there. What Fletcher would have shown and withdrawn in a single glimpse of magic, Shelley calls up in a vast wizard landscape which he sets steadily before us. He is the enchanter, but he never mistakes the images which he calls up for realities. They are images to him, and there is always between him and them the thin circle of the ring. In 'Prometheus Unbound,' where he has made a mythology of his own by working on the stable foundation of a great myth of antiquity, his drama is a cloudy procession of phantoms, seen in a divine hallucination by a poet whose mind hovered always in that world —

> 'where do inhabit
> The shadows of all forms that think and live
> Till death unite them, and they part no more;
> Dreams and the light imaginings of men,
> And all that faith creates or love desires,
> Terrible, strange, sublime, and beauteous shapes.'

The shapes hover, pause, and pass on unflagging wings. They are not symbols, they are not embodiments of powers and passions; they are shining or shadowy images of life and death, time and eternity; they are much more immaterial than judgment or mercy, than love or liberty; they are phantoms, 'wrapped in sweet sounds as in bright veils,' who pass, murmuring 'intelligible words and music wild'; but their music comes from somewhere across the moon or under the sea, and their words are without human passion. The liberty which comes to Prometheus is a liberty to dream forever with Asia in a cave; the love which sets free the earth is, like the music, extra-lunar; this new paradise is a heaven made only for one who is, like Shelley, —

'the Spirit of wind
With lightning eyes, and eager breath, and feet
Disturbing not the drifted snow.'

The imagination which built this splendid palace out of clouds, of sunset and sunrise, out of air, water, and fire, has unbodied the human likeness in every element, and made the spirit of the earth itself only a melodious voice, 'the delicate spirit' of an eternal cloud, 'guiding the earth through heaven.' When the 'universal sound like wings' is heard, and Demogorgon affirms the final triumph of good, it is to an earth dying like a drop of dew and to a moon shaken like a leaf. And we are left 'dizzy as with delight,' to rise, like Panthea, —

'as from a bath of sparkling water,
A bath of azure light, among dark rocks,
Out of the stream of sound.'

It was among these forms of imagination, —

'Desires and adorations,
Winged Persuasions and veiled Destinies,
Splendours, and Glooms, and glimmering Incarnations
Of hopes and fears, and twilight Phantasies,—'

as he sees them in 'Adonais,' that Shelley most loved to walk; but when we come to what Browning calls 'the unrivalled "Cenci,"' we are in another atmosphere, and in this atmosphere, not his own, he walks with equal certainty. In the preface to 'The Cenci' Shelley defines in a perfect image the quality of dramatic imagination. 'Imagination,' he says, 'is as the immortal God which should assume flesh for the redemption of mortal passion.' And, in the dedication, he distinguishes it from his earlier works, 'visions which impersonate my own apprehensions of the beautiful and the just.' 'The Cenci' is the greatest play written in English since 'The Duchess of Malfy,' but, in the work of Shelley, it is an episode, an aside, or, as he puts it in his curious phrase, 'a work of art.' 'Julian and Maddalo' is not less a work of art, and, for Shelley, an exception. In 'Julian and Maddalo' and in the 'Letter to Maria Gisborne' he has solved the problem of the poem which shall be conventional speech and yet pure poetry. It is astonishing to think that 'Julian and Maddalo' was written within a year of 'Rosalind and Helen.' The one is Byron and water, but the other is Byron and fire. It has set the pattern of the modern poem, and it was probably more difficult for him to do than to write 'Prometheus Unbound.' He went straight on from the one to the other, and was probably unconscious quite how much he had done. Was it that a subject, within his personal interests and yet of deep significance, came to him from his visit to Byron at Venice, his study of Byron's mind there, which, as we know, possessed, seemed to overweigh him? Shelley required no impetus, but he required weight. Just as the subject of 'Prometheus Unbound,' an existing myth into which he could read the symbol of his own faith, gave him that definite unshifting substance which he required, and could not invent, so, no doubt, this actual substance in 'Julian and Maddalo' and the haunting historic substance of 'The Cenci' possessed him, drawing him down out of the air, and imprisoning him among human fortunes. There is no doctrine and no fantasy in either, but imagination speaking human speech.

And yet, as Browning has pointed out, though 'Prometheus,' 'Epipsychidion,' and the lyrics are 'the less organised matter,' the 'radiant elemental foam and solution' of Shelley's genius, it is precisely in these, and not in any of the more human works, that we must look for the real Shelley. In them it is he himself who is speaking, in that 'voice which is contagion to the world.' The others he made, supremely well; but these he was.

What he made he made so well because he was so complete a man of letters, in a sense in which no other of his contemporaries was. Wordsworth, when he turned aside from his path, wandered helplessly astray. Byron was so helplessly himself that when he wrote plays he wrote them precisely in the manner which Shelley rightly protested that he himself had not: 'under a thin veil converting names and actions into cold impersonations of his own mind.' But Shelley could make no such mistake in form. It may be doubted whether the drama of real life would ever have become his natural medium; but, having set himself to write such a drama, he accepted the laws or limitations of the form to the extent of saying, 'I have avoided with great care, in writing this play, the introduction of what is commonly called mere poetry.' In so doing he produced a masterpiece, but knew himself too well to repeat it.

And he does not less adequately whatever he touches. Shelley had no genius for fun or caricature, but in 'Swellfoot the Tyrant,' in 'Peter Bell the Third,' he develops a satirical joke with exquisite literary skill. Their main value is to show how well he could do the things for which he had no aptitude. 'The Mask of Anarchy' is scarcely more important as a whole, though more poignant in detail. It was done for an occasion, and remains, not as an utterance, but for its temper of poetic eloquence. Even 'Hellas,' which he called 'a mere improvise,' and which was written out of a sudden political enthusiasm, is remembered, not for its 'figures of indistinct and visionary delineation,' but for its 'flowery and starry' choruses. Yet not one of the four was written for the sake of writing a piece of literature; each contains a condemnation, a dogma, or a doctrine.

To Shelley doctrine was a part of poetry; but then, to him doctrine was itself the voice of ecstasy. He was in love not only with love, but with wisdom; and as he wished every one to be good and happy, he was full of magics and panaceas, Demogorgons or Godwins, which would rejuvenate or redeem the world. There was always something either spiritual or moral in his idea of beauty; he never conceived of æsthetics as a thing apart from ethics; and even in his descriptions he is so anxious to give us the feeling before the details, that the details are as likely as not to go out in a rosy mist.

There are pictures in Shelley which remind us of Turner's. Pure light breaks into all its colours and floods the world, which may be earth or sea or sky, but is, above all, rapture of colour. He has few twilights but many dawns; and he loves autumn for its wild breath and broken colours. Fire he plays with, but air and water are his elements; thoughts of drowning are in all his work, always with a sense of strange luxury. He has, more than any poet, Turner's atmosphere; yet seems rarely, like Turner, to paint for atmosphere. It is part of his habitual hallucination; it comes to him with his vision or message, clothing it.

He loved liberty and justice with an impersonal passion, and would have been a martyr for many ideals which were no more to him than the substance itself of enthusiasm. He went about the world, desiring universal sympathy, to suffer delicious and poignant thrills of the soul, and to be at once sad and happy. In his feeling for nature he has the same vague affection and indistinguishing embrace as in his feeling for humanity; the daisy, which was the eye of day to Chaucer, is not visible as a speck in Shelley's wide landscapes; and though in one of his subtlest poems he has noticed 'the slow soft toads out of damp corners creep,' he is not minutely observant of whatever is not in some way strange or unusual. Even his significant phrase about 'the worm beneath the sod' is only meant as a figure of the brain. His chief nature poem, 'The Skylark,' loses the bird in the air, and only realises a voice, an 'unbodied joy'; and 'The Sensitive Plant' is a fairy, and the radiant illustration of 'a modest creed.'

III

In a minute study of the details of Shelley's philosophy, Mr. Yeats has reminded us, 'In ancient times, it seems to me that Blake, who for all his protest was glad to be alive, and ever spoke of his gladness, would have worshipped in some chapel of the Sun, and that Keats, who accepted life gladly, though "with a delicious, diligent indolence," would have worshipped in some chapel of the Moon, but that Shelley, who hated life because he sought "more in life than any understood," would have wandered, lost in a ceaseless reverie, in some chapel of the Star of infinite desire.' Is not Shelley's whole philosophy contained in that one line, 'the desire of the moth for the star'? He desired impossible things, and his whole theory of a reorganization of the world, in which anarchy was to be a spiritual deliverer, was a dream of that golden age which all mythologies put in the past. It was not the Christian's dream of heaven, nor the Buddhist's of Nirvana, but a poetical conception of a perfected world, in which innocence was lawless, and liberty selfless and love boundless, and in which all was order and beauty, as in a lovely song or stanza, or the musical answering of line and line in drama. He wrote himself down an atheist, and Browning thinks that in heart he was always really a Christian, so unlimited were his ideals, so imaginary his paradises. When Shelley thought he was planning the reform of the world, he was making literature; and this is shown partly by the fact that no theory or outcry or enthusiasm is ever strong enough to break through the form which carries it like a light in a crystal.

The spirit of Shelley will indeed always be a light to every seeker after the things that are outside the world. He found nothing, he did not even name a new star. There is little actual wisdom in his pages, and his beauty is not always a very vital kind of truth. He is a bird on the sea, a sea-bird, a winged diver, swift and exquisite in flight, an inhabitant of land, water, and sky; and to watch him is to be filled with joy, to forget all mean and trivial things, to share a rapture. Shelley teaches us nothing, leads us nowhere, but cries and flies round us like a sea-bird.

Shelley is the only poet who is really vague, and he gets some of his music out of that quality of the air. Poetry, to him, was an instinctive utterance of delight, and it recorded his lightest or deepest mood with equal sensitiveness. He is an unconscious creator of joy, and the mood most frequent with him is the joy of sadness. His poetry, more than that of any poet, is the poetry of the soul, and nothing in his poetry reminds us that he had a body at all, except as a nerve sensitive to light, colour, music, and perfume. His happiness is —

'To nurse the image of unfelt caresses
Till dim imagination just possesses
The half-created shadow,'

and to come no nearer to reality. Poetry was his atmosphere, he drew his breath in it as in his native element. Because he is the one perfect illustration of the poetic nature, as that nature is generally conceived, he has sometimes been wrongly taken to be the greatest of poets. His greatness may be questioned, not his authenticity.

Shelley could not write unpoetically. Wordsworth, who is not more possessed than Shelley with ideas of instruction, moral reformation, and the like, drops constantly out of poetry into prose; Shelley never does. Not only verse but poetry came to him so naturally that he could not keep it out, and the least fragment he wrote has poetry in it. Compare him, not only with Wordsworth, but with Keats, Coleridge, Byron, Landor, with every poet of his period, and you will find that while others may excel him in almost every separate poetical quality, none comes near him in this constant level of general poetical excellence.

Is it an excellence or an acquirement? No doubt it was partly technique, the technique of the born executant. It is too often forgotten that technique, like talent, must be born, not made, if it is to do great work. Shelley could not help writing well, whatever he wrote; he was born to write. He was the one perfectly equipped man of letters of his circle, and he added that accomplishment to his genius as a poet. There was nothing he could not do with verse as a form, and his translations from Greek, from Spanish, or from German, are not less sensitive to the forms which he adapted. He had a sound and wide literary culture, and, with curious lack of knowledge, a generalised appreciation of art. He wrote a 'Defence of Poetry' which goes far beyond Sidney's and is the most just and noble eulogy of poetry that exists. His letters have grace and facility, and when Matthew Arnold made his foolish joke about his prose being better than his verse (which is as untrue as to say that Milton's prose was better than his verse), he was no doubt rightly conscious that Shelley might have expressed in prose much of the actual contents of his poetry. What would have been lost is the rarest part of it, in its creation of imaginative beauty. It is that rare part, that atmosphere which belongs to a region beyond technique, which, more certainly than even his technique, was what never left him, what made it impossible for him to write unpoetically.

No poetry is more sincere than Shelley's, because his style is a radiant drapery clinging closely to the body which it covers. What he has to express may have little value or coherence, but it is the very breath of his being, or, it may be, the smoke of that breath. He says rightly, in one of his earliest prefaces, that he has imitated no one, 'designing that even if what I have produced be worthless, it should still be properly my own.' There is no poet, ancient or modern, whom he did not study; but, after the first boyish bewitchment by what was odd in Southey's 'Thalaba,' and a casual influence here and there, soon shaken off, whatever came to him was transformed by his inner energy, and became his own. Every poem, whatever else it is, is a personal expression of feeling. There is no egoism of the passionate sort, Catullus's or Villon's; his own passions are almost impersonal to him, they turn to a poem in the mere act of giving voice to themselves. It is his sincerity that so often makes him superficial. Shelley is youth. Great ideas or deep emotions did not come to him, but warm ideas and eager emotions, and he put them straight into verse. You cannot imagine him elaborating a mood, carving it, as Keats does, on the marble flanks of his Grecian urn.

Shelley is the most spontaneous of poets, and one of the most careless among those who, unlike Byron, are artists. He sings naturally, without hesitation, liquidly, not always flawlessly. There is something in him above and below literature, something aside from it, a divine personal accident. His technique, in lyrics, is not to be compared with Coleridge's, but where Keats speaks he sings.

The blank verse of Shelley, at its best in 'Prometheus Unbound,' has none of the sweetly broken music of Shakespeare or of the organ harmonies of Milton. It is a music of aërial eloquence, as if sounded by —

'The small, clear, silver lute of the young spirit
That sits i' the morning star.'

There is in it a thrilling music, rarer in liquid sound than that of any other poet, and chastened by all the severity that can clothe a spirit of fire and air, an Ariel loosed from Prospero. Can syllables turn to more delicate sound and perfume than in such lines as these: —

'When swift from the white Scythian wilderness
A wind swept forth wrinkling the Earth with frost:
I looked and all the blossoms were blown down'?

If words can breathe, can they breathe a purer breath than in these strange and simple lines in which every consonant and every vowel have obeyed some learned spell unconscious of its witchcraft? Horror puts on all the daintiness of beauty, losing none of its own essence, as when we read how —

> 'foodless toads
> Within voluptuous chambers panting crawled.'

And out of this 'music of lyres and flutes' there rises a symphony of many instruments, a choral symphony, after which no other music sounds for a time musical. Nor is it only for its music —

> 'Clear, silver, icy, keen, awakening tones
> Which pierce the sense and live within the soul—'

that this blank verse has its power over us. It has an illumined gravity, a shining crystal clearness, a luminous motion, with, in its ample tide, an 'ocean-like enchantment of strong sound,' and a measure and order as of the paces of the boundless and cadenced sea.

But it is, after all, for his lyrics that Shelley is best remembered, and it is perhaps in them that he is at his best. He wrote no good lyrical verse, except a few stanzas, before the age of twenty-three, when he wrote the song beginning, 'The cold earth slept below,' in which we find, but for a certain concentration, all the poetic and artistic qualities of 'A widow bird sat mourning for her love,' which belongs to the last year of his life. In the summer of the year 1816 he wrote the 'Hymn to Intellectual Beauty,' and had nothing more to learn. In a letter to Keats he said, 'In poetry I have sought to avoid system and mannerism,' and in the lyrical work written during the six remaining years of his life there will be found a greater variety, a more easily and continually inventive genius, than in the lyrical work of any other English poet. This faculty which came to him without warning, like an awakening, never flags, and it is only for personal, not for artistic reasons, that it ever exercises itself without a continual enchantment. There are, among these supreme lyrics, which no one but Shelley could have either conceived or written, others, here and there, in which the sentimentalist which was in Shelley the man improvises in verse as Thomas Moore would have improvised if he could. He could not; but to compare with his best lyrics a lyric of Shelley's such as, 'The keen stars were twinkling,' is to realise how narrow, as well as how impassable, is the gulf between what is not, and what just is, poetry. In the clamorous splendour of the odes there is sometimes rhetoric as well as poetry, but is it more than the tumult and overflow of that poetry? For spiritual energy the 'Ode to the West Wind,' for untamable choric rapture the 'Hymn to Pan,' for soft brilliance of colour and radiant light the 'Lines written among the Euganean Hills,' are not less incomparable than the rarest of the songs (such songs as 'The golden gates of sleep unbar,' or 'When the lamp is shattered,' or 'Swiftly walk over the western wave'), in which the spirit of Fletcher seems returned to earth with a new magic from beyond the moon. And all this work, achieved by a craftsman as if for its own sake, will be found, if read chronologically, with its many fragments, to be in reality a sort of occasional diary. If ever a poet expressed himself fully in his verse, it was Shelley. There is nothing in his life which you will not find written somewhere in it, if only as 'the ghost of a forgotten form of sleep.' In this diary of lyrics he has noted down whatever most moved him, in a vivid record of the trace of every thrill or excitement, on nerves, or sense, or soul. From the stanzas, 'To Constantia singing,' to the stanzas, 'With a guitar, to Jane,' every woman who moved him will have her place in it; and everything that has moved him when, as he said in the preface to 'The Revolt of Islam,' 'I have sailed down mighty rivers, and seen the sun rise and set, and the stars come forth whilst I have sailed night and day down a rapid stream among mountains.' This, no doubt, is his way of referring to the first and second travels abroad with Mary, and to the summer when he sailed up the Thames to its source, — the time of his awakening. And in all this, made day by day out of the very substance of its hours, there will not be a single poem in which the occasion will disturb or overpower the poetical impulse, in which the lyrical cry will be personal at the expense of the music. Or, if there is one such poem, it is that most intimate one which begins: 'The serpent is shut out of Paradise.' Is there, in this faultless capacity, this inevitable transposition of feeling into form, something lacking, some absent savour? Is there, in this evocation of the ghost of every thrill, the essence of life itself?

REV. JOHN KEBLE (1792–1866) [1]

DEAN STANLEY, wishing to praise Keble, tells us that it was Southey, more than all, who 'kindled his flame and coloured his diction.' The influence of that bad model is indeed visible in much that is rhetorical in Keble. There is something in his best poems which has a neatness of epithet, a personal way of putting piety into verse, by which he may for a moment seem to become a poet. But his piety was no burning flame of a Crashaw, his Anglican mind was tied down from any of the higher flights of religious ecstasy. He can be read, not without respect, sometimes with pleasure, never with satisfied delight.

DR. WILLIAM MAGINN (1793–1842) [2]

'BRIGHT, broken Maginn' was in his time a notorious writer of satirical prose and verse; he is remembered now chiefly

[1] (1) *The Christian Year*, 2 vols., 1827. (2) *The Psalter, or Psalms of David in English Verse*, 1839. (3) *Lyra Innocentium*, 1846. (4) *Miscellaneous Poems*, posthumous, 1869.

[2] (1) *Homeric Ballads*, 1850. (2) *Miscellanies*, 5 vols., New York, 1855–57. (3) *Miscellanies: Prose and Verse*, 2 vols., London, 1885.

DR. WILLIAM MAGINN

because Lockhart, in his epitaph, perpetuated a passing name on the barb of a kindly jest. He was a scholar and a wit, a disorderly, untrustworthy person; his facility was apt to pass into vulgarity, and he has left nothing of really permanent value. But there was hardly anything that he could not do. He invented a ballad metre for the translation of Homer, which no one has quite known whether to take seriously or not; and set Lucian's dialogues, with better skill, into comedies in English blank verse. A few of his short stories are striking: 'The Man in the Bell' is almost like another version of 'The Pit and the Pendulum,' though not so intense in its horror; 'Bob Burke's Duel with Ensign Brady' is a masterpiece of Irish humour. Prose bursts into verse on every page, and his easy, careless, inaccurate mastery of comic metre is marvellous of its kind, and delights us by the mere rollicking sound of it. 'Captain Godolphin was a very odd and stingy man' might be taken for the original of some of the puns and processes of metre in the 'Bab Ballads,' while not even in 'Alice in Wonderland' is there a finer invention of nonsense names than in this refrain: —

> 'Oh! the Powldoodies of Burran,
> The green green Powldoodies of Burran,
> The green Powldoodies, the clean Powldoodies,
> The gaping Powldoodies of Burran!'

Maginn parodied all his contemporaries; and while some, like the venomous onslaught on 'Adonais' and the vulgar travesty of 'Christabel,' are indefensibly brutal, others, without the malice or dullness of these, have a fine humour and insight of their own. He wrote them in English, Latin, and Greek, and his version of 'Chevy Chase' is a piece of delicious dog-Latin. I must give Lockhart's epitaph, which is more adequate than any criticism: —

> 'Here, early to bed, lies kind William Maginn,
> Who with genius, wit, learning, life's trophies to win,
> Had neither great lord, nor rich cit of his kin,
> Nor discretion to set himself up as to tin:

So, his portion soon spent, like the poor heir of Lynn,
He turn'd author while yet was no beard on his chin;
And whoever was out, or whoever was in,
For your Tories his fine Irish brains he would spin,
Who received prose and rhyme with a promising grin —
"Go ahead, you queer fish, and more power to your fin!"
But to save from starvation stirr'd never a pin.
Light for long was his heart, though his breeches were thin,
Else his acting for certain was equal to Quin:
But at last he was beat, and sought help from the bin
(All the same to the Doctor, from claret to gin),
Which led swiftly to gaol, with consumption therein;
It was much, when the bones rattled loose in his skin,
He got leave to die here, out of Babylon's din.
Barring drink and the girls, I ne'er heard of a sin:
Many worse, better few, than bright, broken Maginn.'

JOHN CLARE (1793–1864) [1]

WE are told in the introduction to a volume of poems by John Clare, published in 1820, 'They are the genuine productions of a young peasant, a day-labourer in husbandry, who has had no advantages of education beyond others of his class; and though poets in this country have seldom been fortunate men, yet he is, perhaps, the least favoured by circumstances, and the most destitute of friends, of any that ever existed.' If the writer of the introduction had been able to look to the end of the career on whose outset he commented, he would have omitted the 'perhaps.' The son of a pauper farm labourer, John Clare wrote his earlier poems in the intervals of hard manual labour in the fields, and his later poems in lucid intervals in a madhouse, to which ill-health, overwork, and drink had brought him. In a poem written before he was seventeen he had asked that he might

'Find one hope true — to die at home at last,'

[1] (1) *Poems descriptive of Rural Life and Scenery*, 1820. (2) *The Village Minstrel*, 2 vols., 1821. (3) *The Shepherd's Calendar*, 1827. (4) *The Rural Muse*, 1835. (5) The 'Asylum Poems' are contained in the *Life and Remains of John Clare*, by J. E. Cherry, 1873.

and his last words, when he died in the madhouse, were, 'I want to go home.' In another early poem he had prayed, seeing a tree in autumn, that, when his time came, the trunk might die with the leaves. Even so reasonable a prayer was not answered.

In Clare's early work, which is more definitely the work of the peasant than perhaps any other peasant poetry, there is more reality than poetry.

'I found the poems in the fields,
And only wrote them down,'

as he says with truth, and it was with an acute sense of the precise thing he was saying, that Lamb complimented him in 1822 on the 'quantity' of his observation.

No one before him had given such a sense of the village, for Bloomfield does not count, not being really a poet; and no one has done it so well since, until a greater poet, Warner, brought more poetry with him. His danger was to be too deliberate, unconscious that there can be choice in descriptive poetry, or that anything which runs naturally into metre may not be the best material for a particular poem. His words are for the most part chosen only to be exact, and he does not know when he is obvious or original in his epithets. The epithets, as he goes on, strengthen and sharpen; in his earliest period he would not have thought of speaking of 'bright glib ice' or of the almanac's 'wisdom gossiped from the stars.' He educated himself with rapidity, and I am inclined to doubt the stories of the illiterate condition of even his early manuscripts. His handwriting, as early as the time of his first published book, is clear, fluent, and energetic. In 1821 Taylor saw in his cupboard copies of Burns, Cowper, Wordsworth, Coleridge, Keats, and Crabbe. And in a printed letter of 1826, addressed to Montgomery, Clare says that he has 'long had a fondness for the poetry of the time of Elizabeth,' which he knows from Ellis's 'Specimens of Early English Poets' and Ritson's 'English Songs.' It was doubtless in Ellis that he found some of the metres in which we may well be surprised to find him writing as early as 1821; Villon's ballad metre, for instance, which he uses in a poem in 'The Village Minstrel,' and which he might have found in poems of Henryson and other Scottish poets quoted in Ellis. Later on, among some poems which he wrote in deliberate imitation of Elizabethan poets, we shall find one in a Wyatt metre, which reads like an anticipation of Bridges.

Thus it cannot be said that in Clare's very earliest work we have an utterance which literary influences have not modified. The impulse and the subject-matter are alike his own, and are taken directly from what was about him. There is no closer attention to nature than in Clare's poems; but the observation begins by being literal; nature a part of his home, rather than his home a part of nature. The things about him are the whole of his material, he does not choose them by preference out of others equally available; all his poems are made out of the incidents and feelings of humble life and the actual fields and flowers of his particular part of England. He does not make pictures, which would imply aloofness and selection; he enumerates, which means a friendly knowledge. It is enough for him, enough for his success in his own kind of poetry, to say them over, saying, 'Such they were, and I loved them because I had always seen them so.'

Yet his nerves were not the nerves of a peasant. Everything that touched him was a delight or an agony, and we hear continually of his bursting into tears. He was restless and loved wandering, but he came back always to the point from which he had started. He could not endure that anything he had once known should be changed. He writes to tell his publisher that the landlord is going to cut down two elm-trees at the back of his hut, and he says: 'I have been several mornings to bid them farewell.' He kept his reason as long as he was left to starve and suffer in that hut, and when he was taken from it, though to a better dwelling, he lost all hold on himself. He was torn up by the roots, and the flower of his mind withered. What this transplanting did for him is enough to show how native to him was his own soil, and how his songs grew out of it.

In the last book published before he entered the asylum, 'The Rural Muse,' he repeated all his familiar notes with a fluency which long practice had given him, and what he gains in ease he loses in directness. All that remains to us of his subsequent work is contained in the 'Asylum Poems,' first printed in 1873; and it is to be regretted that the too scrupulous editor, Mr. Cherry, did not print them as they stood. 'Scarcely one poem,' he tells us, 'was found in a state in which it could be submitted to the public without more or less of revision and correction.' It is in these poems that, for the first time, Clare's lyrical quality gets free. Strangely enough, a new joy comes into the verse, as if at last he is at rest. It is only rarely, in this new contentment, this solitude even from himself, that recollection returns. Then he remembers —

'I am a sad lonely hind:
Trees tell me so, day after day,
As slowly they wave in the wind.'

He seems to accept nature now more easily, because his mind is in a kind of oblivion of everything else; madness being, as it were, his security. He writes love songs that have an airy fancy, a liquid and thrilling note of song. They are mostly exultations of memory, which goes from Mary to Patty, and thence to a gipsy girl and to vague Isabellas and Scotch maids. A new feeling for children comes in, sometimes in songs of childish humour, like 'Little Trotty Wagtail' or 'Clock-a-Clay,' made out of bright, laughing sound; and once in a lovely poem, one of the most nearly perfect he ever wrote, called 'The Dying Child,' which reminds one of beautiful things that have been done since, but of nothing done earlier. As we have them (and so subtle an essence could scarcely be extracted by any editor) there is no insanity; they have only dropped nearly all of the prose. A gentle hallucination comes in from time to time, and, no doubt, helps to make the poetry better.

It must not be assumed that because Clare is a peasant, his poetry is in every sense typically peasant poetry. He was gifted for poetry by those very qualities which made him ineffectual as a peasant. The common error about him is repeated by Mr. Lucas in his life of Lamb: 'He was to have been another Burns, but succeeded only in being a better Bloomfield.' The difference between Clare and Bloomfield is the difference between what is poetry and what is not, and neither is nearer to or farther from being a poet because he was also a peasant. The difference between Burns and Clare is the difference between two kinds and qualities of poetry. Burns was a great poet, filled with ideas, passions, and every sort of intoxication; but he had no such minute local love as Clare, nor, indeed, so deep a love of the earth. He could create by naming, while Clare, who lived on the memory of his heart, had to enumerate, not leaving out one detail, because he loved every detail. Burns or Hogg, however, we can very well imagine at any period following the plough with skill or keeping cattle with care. But Clare was never a good labourer; he pottered in the fields feebly, he tried fruitless way after way of making his living. What was strangely sensitive in him might well have been hereditary if the wild and unproved story told by his biographer Martin is true: that his father was the illegitimate son of a nameless wanderer, who came to the village with his fiddle, saying he was a Scotchman or an Irishman, and taught in the village school, and disappeared one day as suddenly as he had come. The story is at least symbolic, if not true. That wandering and strange instinct was in his blood, and it spoiled the peasant in him and made the poet.

FELICIA DOROTHEA HEMANS (1793–1835)[1]

It was said at the time of Mrs. Hemans' death that she had 'founded a school of imitators in England, and a yet larger one in America.' 'So general has been the attention,' it was said in America, 'to those of her pieces adapted to the purposes of a newspaper, we hardly fear to assert that throughout a great part of this country there is not a family of the middling class in which some of them have not been read.' And the same writer assures us that 'the voice of America, deciding on the literature of England, resembles the voice of posterity more nearly than anything else that is contemporaneous can do.' Has the voice of posterity, in this instance, corroborated the voice of America?

Out of the seven volumes of her collected works, not seven poems are still remembered, and these chiefly because they were taught, and probably still are, to children. There are 'Casabianca,' 'The Graves of a Household,' 'The Homes of England,' 'The Fall of d'Assas,' with a few others; these are not fundamentally different from the hundreds of poems which have been forgotten, or which seem to us now little more than the liltings of a kind of female Moore. But they have the merit of being not only very sincere and very straightforward, but of concentrating into themselves a more definite parcel of the floating sensibility of a woman who was tremulously awake

[1] (1) *Poems*, 1808. (2) *England and Spain*, 1808. (3) *Domestic Affections*, 1812. (4) *Translations from Camoens, and other Poets*, 1818. (5) *Tales and Historic Scenes*, 1819. (6) *The Meeting of Bruce and Wallace*, 1820. (7) *The Sceptic*, 1820. (8) *Superstition and Error*, 1820. (9) *Welsh Melodies*, 1822. (10) *The Vespers of Palermo*, 1823. (11) *The Siege of Valencia*, 1823. (12) *De Chantillon*, 1823. (13) *Lays of Many Lands*, 1825. (14) *The Forest Sanctuary*, 1825. (15) *Records of Women*, 1828. (16) *Songs of the Affections*, 1830. (17) *Hymns on the Wake of Nature*, 1833. (18) *Hymns for Childhood*, 1834. (19) *National Lyrics and Songs for Music*, 1834. (20) *Scenes and Hymns of Life*, 1834. (21) *Collected Poems*, 7 vols., 1839; 1 vol., 1849.

to every appeal of beauty or nobility. 'The highest degree of beauty in art,' she wrote, 'certainly always excites, if not tears, at least the inward feeling of tears.' She has 'a pure passion for flowers,' and suffers from the intense delight of music, without which she feels that she would die; the sight and society of Scott or Wordsworth fill her with an ecstasy hardly to be borne; she discovers Carlyle writing anonymously on Burns in the 'Edinburgh Review' and she notes: 'I wonder who the writer is; he certainly gives us a great deal of what Boswell, I think, calls bark and steel for the mind.' She had all the feminine accomplishments of her time, and they meant to her, especially her harp, some form of personal expression. She wrote from genuine feeling and with easy spontaneity, and it may still be said of her verse, as Lord Jeffrey said of it: 'It may not be the best imaginable poetry, and may not indicate the highest or most commanding genius, but it embraces a great deal of that which gives the very best poetry its chief power of pleasing.'

Its chief power, that is, of pleasing the majority. In spite of an origin partly Irish, partly German, blended with an Italian strain, there was no rarity in her nature, or if it was there, it found no expression in her poems. She said of Irish tunes that there was in them 'something unconquerable yet sorrowful'; but that something, though she compared herself to an Irish tune, she never got. Living much of her life in Wales, and caring greatly for its ancient literature, she loses, in the improvisations of the 'Welsh Melodies,' whatever is finest and most elemental in her Celtic originals. It is sufficient criticism to set side by side the first stanza of 'The Hall of Cynddylan' and the opening of the poem of Llwarch Hen. Mrs. Hemans says, lightly: —

> 'The Hall of Cynddylan is gloomy to-night;
> I weep, for the grave has extinguished its light;
> The beam of the lamp from its summit is o'er,
> The blaze of its hearth shall give welcome no more.'

But what Llwarch Hen has said is this: 'The Hall of Cynddylan is gloomy this night, without fire, without bed: I must weep awhile, and then be silent.'
That is poetry, but the other is a kind of prattle. It is difficult to say of Mrs. Hemans that her poems are not womanly, and yet it would be more natural to say that they are feminine. The art of verse to her was like her harp and her sketch-book, not an accomplishment indeed, but an instrument on which to improvise. One of her disciples, Letitia Landon, imagined that she was only speaking in her favour when she said: 'One single emotion is never the original subject' of her poems. 'Some graceful or touching anecdote or situation catches her attention, and its poetry is developed in a strain of mourning melody and a vein of gentle moralising.' Her poems are for the most part touching anecdotes; they are never without some gentle moralising. If poetry were really what the average person thinks it to be, an idealisation of the feelings, at those moments when the mind is open to every passing impression, ready to catch at similitudes and call up associations, but not in the grip of a strong thought or vital passion, then the verse of Felicia Hemans would be, as people once thought it was, the ideal poetry. It would, however, be necessary to go on from that conclusion to another, which indeed we find in the surprising American Professor, who, 'after reading such works as she had written,' could not but perceive, on turning over 'the volumes of a collection of English poetry, like that of Chalmers,' that 'the greater part of it appears more worthless and distasteful than before.'

JOHN GIBSON LOCKHART (1794–1854)[1]

JOHN GIBSON LOCKHART, the biographer of Scott, a fierce critic, a brilliant prose-writer, the writer of a remarkable

[1] *Ancient Spanish Ballads*, 1823.

novel, 'Adam Blair,' is best remembered for his achievement as a translator of ancient Spanish ballads and songs. 'That old Spanish minstrelsy,' as he calls it, 'which has been preserved in the different *Cancioneros* and *Romanceros* of the sixteenth century,' was unknown in England before Lockhart, in 1823, published his vivid and glowing versions, which will always have their place among the romantic work of the period. He revealed a whole new world, in which chivalry was lofty, with the proud dignity, sombre simplicity, strange barbarity and stranger gentleness of the Spaniard, with, through it all, an Oriental undercurrent, the incalculable mystery of the Moor. What a sense, in these old ballads, which at times wail with the lamenting voice that one can still hear at night on any country road in Spain, of the dramatic moment, the situation, the crisis! The Spanish, as he says, 'is, like the sister Italian, music in itself, though music of a bolder character.' This music Lockhart rendered for the most part in that galloping measure which so easily delights men's ears, and which is a living and moving thing, no less when it turns to the childlike humour of 'My ear-rings! my ear-rings! they've dropt into the well' or to the witty delicacy of some of the Moorish songs. There is one song, 'The Wandering Knight's Song,' which I must give in full, for it anticipates, by nearly three centuries, a masterpiece of Keats, 'La Belle Dame sans Merci': —

> 'My ornaments are arms,
> My pastime is in war,
> My bed is cold upon the wold,
> My lamp yon star.
>
> 'My journeyings are long,
> My slumbers short and broken;
> From hill to hill I wander still,
> Kissing thy token.
>
> 'I ride from land to land,
> I sail from sea to sea;
> Some day more kind I fate may find,
> Some night kiss thee.'

After that nothing that Lockhart wrote in his own person, not even the song written to comfort Carlyle in bereavement, though that has a rare twist of the mind,

> 'Be constant to the dead,
> The dead cannot deceive';

not that even rises to the wild and patient ecstasy of the Spanish Song. And there is one other ballad, of his own writing, with its fine refrain of 'For we ne'er shall see the like of Captain Paton no mo'e!' which, in its shedding of 'punch and tears' for this 'prince of good deal fellows,' is splendid, and not since excelled in its kind.

THOMAS CARLYLE (1795-1881)

CARLYLE was a poet in prose, as Ruskin, marvellously eloquent, never was. Thus when Ruskin wrote verse, it was lamentable, not because it was uncouth, like Carlyle's few uneasy fragments, but because there was no poet at work in it Carlyle has said supreme things about a few great poets whom he cared for most; he has shown a sense of what poetry really was, under a cynic's cloak of ragged contempt. Has anything more fundamental been said of drama than this, in a letter to Barry Cornwall: 'What I object to in our damnable dramatists is: that they have in them no *thing*, no event or character, that looks musical and glorious to them'? Many things looked so to Carlyle, but he had no skill beyond his prose. His ear could not discriminate between the good line and the bad, and in his few attempts at verse he has chosen the bad tune because he could not help it. Some of the best sayings in them seem as if translated laboriously from the German, as in this stanza: —

> 'What is Man? A foolish baby,
> Vainly strives, and fights, and frets;
> Demanding all, deserving nothing;
> One small grave is all he gets.'

He tries to call back for his use the old ballad form, with its repetitions, and is then at his best, particularly in the sententious little song of the wind's way: —

> 'The wind blows east, the wind blows west,
> And the frost falls and the rain;
> A weary heart went thankful to rest,
> And must rise to toil again, 'gain,
> And must rise to toil again.'

How that stumbles, unable to say what it wants, like the epigram on the beetle: —

> 'What Debrett's peer surpasseth thee?
> Thy ancestor was in Noah's Ark.'

It is Dr. Garnett, who, in one of his characteristic images, has said the final thing: 'The demand for poetical form is to Carlyle what the vase is to the imprisoned Genie, abolish it and the mighty figure overshadows land and sea.'

JOHN KEATS (1795–1821)[1]

KEATS had the courage of the intellect and the cowardice of the nerves. That 'terrier-like resoluteness' which a schoolfellow observed in him as a boy was still strong when the first certainty of his death came to him. 'Difficulties nerve the spirit of a man,' he wrote, with a full sense of the truth to himself of what he was saying; and there is genuine intellectual courage in the quaint summing-up: 'I never quite despair, and I read Shakespeare.' When the 'Quarterly' and 'Blackwood' attacked him, he wrote: 'Praise or blame has but

[1] (1) *Poems*, 1817. (2) *Endymion*. A Romance, 1818. (3) *Lamia, Isabella, The Eve of St. Agnes, and other Poems*, 1820. (4) *Poetical Works*, published by Smith, 1840 and 1841. (5) *Poetical Works*, Moxon, 1846-1851. (6) *Life, Letters, and Literary Remains*, edited by Richard Monckton Milnes, 2 vols., 1848. (7) *Poetical Works*, Aldine Edition, 1876. (8) *Poetical and other Writings now first brought together*, edited by H. Buxton Forman, 4 vols., 1883.

a momentary effect on the man whose love of beauty in the abstract makes him a severe critic on his own works.' But, at the age of seventeen, he could write, with an equally keen self-knowledge: 'Truth is, I have a horrid morbidity of temperament, which has shown itself at intervals; it is, I have no doubt, the greatest stumbling-block I have to fear; I may surer say, it is likely to be the cause of my disappointment.' 'I carry all matters to an extreme,' he says elsewhere, 'so that, when I have any little vexation, it grows, in five minutes, into a theme for Sophocles.' To the man who has nerves like this, calmness under emotion is impossible.; all that can be asked of him is that he shall realise his own condition, and, as far as may be, make allowances for it. This, until perhaps the very end, when, on his death-bed, he put aside unopened the letters that he dared not read, Keats had always the intellectual strength to do; after the event, if not before it, and generally at the very moment of the event. When he writes most frantically to Fanny Brawne, he confesses, in every other sentence, that he does not really mean what he is saying, at the same time that he cannot help saying it. And are not such letters written, after all, with so touching a confidence in their being understood, seen through, by the woman to whom they were written, really a kind of thinking aloud? A letter, when it is the expression of emotion, is as momentary as a mood, which may come and go indeed while one is in the act of writing it down; so that a letter of two pages may begin with the bitterest reproaches, and end, just as sincerely, and with no sense of contradiction, in a flood of tenderness. One is loth to believe that Fanny Brawne ever complained of what the critics have been so ready to complain of on her behalf. She may have understood Keats very little as a poet, and the fact that he tells her nothing of his work seems to show that he was aware of it, and probably more than half indifferent to it; but if she did not understand him as a man, as a lover, if she would have had him change one of his reproaches into a compliment, or wipe out one of the insults of his agony, then she had less of a woman's 'intelligence in love' than it is possible to imagine in a woman beloved by Keats.

That man must have loved very calmly and very contentedly, with a strange excess of either materialism or spirituality, who has not felt much of what Keats expressed with so intense and faithful a truth to nature. Keats was not a celestial lover, nor a sentimentalist, nor a cynic. He was earthly in his love, as in the very essence of his imagination; passion was not less a disease to him than the disease of which he died, or than the act of writing verse. Stirred to the very depths of his soul, it was after all through the senses, and with all the aching vividness to which he had trained those senses, that memory came to him. And he was no less critical of love than of everything else in the world; he had no blind beliefs, and there were moments when even poetry seemed to him 'a mere Jack o' Lanthorn to amuse whoever may chance to be struck with its brilliance.' Doubting himself so much, he doubted others, of whose intentions he was less certain; and, in love, doubt is part of that torture without which few persons of imagination would fling themselves quite heartily into the pursuit. Had he been stronger in body, he would have luxuriated in just those lacerating pains which seemed, as it was, to be bringing him daily nearer to the grave. It was always vision that disturbed him, the too keen sense of a physical life going on, perhaps so calmly, so near him, and yet as much beyond his control as if he were at the end of the earth.

Have you ever thought of the frightful thing it is to shift one's centre? That is what it is to love a woman. One's nature no longer radiates freely, from its own centre; the centre itself is shifted, is put outside one's self. Up to then, one may have been unhappy, one may have failed, many things may seem to have gone wrong. But at least there was this security: that one's enemies were all outside the gate. With the woman whom one loves one admits all one's enemies. Think: all one's happiness to depend upon the will of another, on that other's fragility, faith, mutability; on the way life comes to the heart, soul, conscience, nerves of some one else, no longer the quite sufficient difficulties of a personal heart, soul, conscience, and nerves. It is to call in a passing stranger and to say: Guard all my treasures while I sleep. For there is no certainty in the world, beyond the certainty that I am I, and that what is not I can never draw one breath for me, though I were dying for lack of it.

That, or something like it, may well have been Keats' consciousness of the irreparable loss and gain which came to him with his love. He was no idealist, able to create a world of his own, and to live there, breathing its own sharp and trying air of the upper clouds; he wanted the actual green world in which we live, men and women as they move about us, only more continuously perfect; themselves, but without a flaw. He wanted the year to be always at the height of summer, and there is no insect or gross animal, a butterfly or a pig, whom he does not somewhere envy for its power of annihilating every consciousness but that of sensuous delight in the moment. Conscious always that his day was to have so few to-morrows, he clung to every inch of daylight which he could capture before night-time. And there was none of to-morrow's aloofness in his apprehension of human qualities; in his feeling for women, for instance. He demanded of a woman instant and continuous responsiveness to his mood, with a kind of profound nervous selfishness, not entirely under his physical control.

'I am certain [he wrote in a letter] I have no right feeling towards women — at this moment I am striving to be just to them, but I cannot. Is it because they fall so far beneath my boyish imagination? . . . I have no right to expect more than their reality. . . . Is it not extraordinary? — When among men I have no evil thoughts, no malice, no spleen; I feel free to speak or to be silent; I can listen, and from every one I can learn; my hands are in my pockets, I am free from all suspicion, and comfortable. When I am among women, I have evil thoughts, malice, spleen; I cannot speak or be silent; I am full of suspicion, and therefore listen to nothing; I am in a hurry to be gone. . . . I must absolutely get over this — but how?'

In all this there is properly no idealism, but rather a very exacting kind of materialism. His goddess must become flesh and blood, and at once put off and retain godhead. To the idealist, living in a world of imagination, which may indeed easily be a truer world, a world more nearly corresponding to unseen realities, there is no shock at finding earth solid under one's feet, and dust in the earth. He lives with a life so wholly of the spirit that, to him, only the spirit matters. But to Keats every moment mattered, and the warm actual life of every moment. His imagination was a faculty which made the experience of actual things more intense, more subtle, more sensitive to pain and pleasure, but it was concerned always with actual things. He had none of that abstract quality of mind which can take refuge from realities, when they become too pressing and too painful, in an idea. Ideas, with him, were always the servants, never the masters, of sensation.

What he most desired, all his life, was strength 'to bear unhurt the shock of extreme thought and sensation.' And he cries: 'O for a life of sensations rather than thoughts!' On his death-bed he confessed that 'the intensest pleasure he had received in life was in watching the growth of flowers.' 'I feel the flowers growing over me,' he said at the last, with a last touch of luxuriousness in his apprehension of the earth. 'Talking of luxuriousness,' he writes in a letter, 'this moment I was writing with one hand, and with the other holding to my mouth a nectarine. Good Lord, how fine! It went down soft and pulpy, slushy, oozy — all its delicious *embonpoint* melted down my throat like a large beatified strawberry.' And, in a much earlier letter, he writes with a not less keen sense of the luxury which lies in discomfort, if only it be apprehended poignantly enough, to the point at which pain becomes a pleasure: 'I lay awake last night listening to the rain, with a sense of being drowned and rotted like a grain of wheat.' In this sensual ecstasy there is something at once childlike and morbid. It is like a direct draught from the earth, taken with violence. And it is part of his unquenchable thirst for beauty. 'On my word,' he writes, 'I think so little, I have not one opinion upon anything except in matters of taste. I can never feel certain of any truth, but from a clear perception of its beauty.' But Keats, remember, was not the friend of beauty, he was her very human lover, sighing after her feverishly. With him beauty was always a part of feeling, always a thing to quicken his pulses, and send the blood to his forehead; he could no more be calm in the presence of beauty than he could be calm in the presence of the woman he loved. With Shelley beauty was an ideal thing, not to be touched by human hands; his was 'the desire of the moth for the star,' while Keats', if you like, was sometimes that fatal desire of the moth for the candle-flame. It is characteristic that Shelley writes his confession of faith in a 'Hymn to Intellectual Beauty'; Keats, in an 'Ode on a Grecian Urn.'

The poetry of Keats is an aspiration towards happiness, towards the deliciousness of life, towards the restfulness of beauty, towards the delightful sharpness of sensations not too sharp to be painful. He accepted life in the spirit of art, asking only for the simple pleasures, which he seemed to be among the few who could not share, of physical health, the capacity to enjoy sensation without being overcome by it. He was not troubled about his soul, the meaning of the universe, or any other metaphysical questions, to which he shows a happy indifference, or rather, a placid unconsciousness. 'I scarcely remember counting upon any happiness,' he notes. 'I look not for it if it be not in the present hour. Nothing startles me beyond the moment. The setting sun will always set me to rights, or if a sparrow were before my window, I take part in its existence, and pick about the gravel.' It is here, perhaps, that he is what people choose to call pagan; though it would be both simpler and truer to say that he is the natural animal, to whom the sense of sin has never whispered itself. Only a cloud makes him uneasy in the sunshine. 'Happy days, or else to die,' he asks for, not aware of any reason why he should not easily be happy under flawless weather. He knows that —

> 'All charms fly
> At the mere touch of cold philosophy,'

and he is not cursed with that spirit of analysis which tears our pleasures to pieces, as in a child's hands, to find out, what can never be found out, the secret of their making. In a profound passage on Shakespeare he notes how 'several things dovetailed in my mind, and at once it struck me what quality went to form a man of achievement, especially in literature, and which Shakespeare possessed so enormously — I mean *Negative Capability*, that is, when a man is capable of being in uncertainties, mysteries, doubts, without any irritable reaching after fact and reason. Coleridge, for instance, would let go a fine isolated verisimilitude, caught from the Penetralium of mystery, from being incapable of remaining content with half-knowledge.' And so he is willing to linger among imaginative happinesses, satisfyingly, rather than to wander in uneasy search after perhaps troubling certainties. He had a nature to which happiness was natural, until nerves and disease came to disturb it. And so his poetry has only a sort of accidental sadness, reflected back upon it from our consciousness of the shortness of the time he himself had had to enjoy delight.

> 'And they shall be accounted poet-kings
> Who simply tell the most heart-easing things,'

he says in 'Sleep and Poetry'; and, while he notes with admiration that Milton 'devoted himself rather to the ardours than the pleasures of song, solacing himself at intervals with cups of old wine,' he adds that 'those are, with some exceptions, the finest parts of the poem.' To him, poetry was always those 'cups of old wine,' a rest in some 'leafy luxury' by the way.

That joy, which is fundamental in Keats, is a quality coming to him straight from nature. But, superadded to this, there is another quality, made up out of unhealthy nerves and something feminine and twisted in the mind, which is almost precisely what it is now the fashion to call decadent. Keats was more than a decadent, but he was a decadent, and such a line as —

'One faint eternal eventide of gems,'

might have been written, in jewelled French, by Mallarmé. He luxuriates, almost like Baudelaire, in the details of physical discomfort, in all their grotesque horror, as where, in sleeplessness, —

'We put our eyes into a pillowy cleft,
And see the spangly gloom froth up and boil.'

He is neo-Latin, again like Baudelaire, in his insistence on the physical symptoms of his lovers, the bodily translations of emotion. In Venus, leaning over Adonis, he notes —

'When her lips and eyes
Were closed in sullen moisture, and quick sighs
Came vexed and panting through her nostrils small';

and, in a line afterwards revised, he writes at first : —

'By the moist languor of thy breathing face.'

Lycius, in 'Lamia,' —

' Sick to lose
The amorous promise of her lone complain,
Swooned, murmuring of love, and pale with pain';

and all that swooning and trembling of his lovers, which English critics have found so unmanly, would at all events be very much at home in modern French poetry, where love is again, as it was to Catullus and to Propertius, a sickness, a poisoning, or an exhausting madness. To find anything like the same frank subtlety of expression, we must, in English poetry, go back to the Elizabethan age, to which Keats so often comes as a kind of echo; we may also look forward, and, as Mr. Bridges notes, find it once more in Rossetti and his followers.

Keats, at a time when the phrase had not yet been invented, practised the theory of art for art's sake. He is the type not of the poet, but of the artist. He was not a great personality; his work comes to us as a greater thing than his personality. When we read his verse, we think of the verse, not of John Keats. When we read the verse of Byron, of Shelley, of Wordsworth, we are conscious, in different degrees, of the work being a personal utterance, and it obtains much of its power over us by our consciousness of that fact. But when we read the verse of Keats, we are conscious only of an enchantment which seems to have invented itself. If we think of the writer, we think of him as of a flattering mirror, in which the face of beauty becomes more beautiful; not as of the creator of beauty. We cannot distinguish him from that which he reflects.

And Keats was aware of the fact, and has elaborated it, with a not unnatural application to poets in general, in one of his letters.

'A poet [he writes] is the most unpoetical of anything in existence, because he has no identity; he is continually in for, and filling, some other body. The sun, the moon, the sea, and men and women, who are creatures of impulse, are poetical, and have about them an unchangeable attribute, the poet has none, no identity. . . . It is a wretched thing to confess, but it is a very fact, that not one word I ever utter can be taken for granted as an opinion growing out of my identical nature. How can it, when I have no nature? . . . The faint conceptions I have of poems to come bring the blood frequently into my forehead. All I hope is, that I may not lose all interest in human affairs — that the solitary indifference I feel for applause, even from the finest spirits, will not blunt any acuteness of vision I may have. I do not think it will. I feel assured I should write from the mere yearning and fondness I have for the beautiful, even if my night's labours should be burnt every morning, and no eye ever shine upon them. But even now I am perhaps not speaking from myself but from some character in whose soul I now live.'

There, subtly defined, is the temperament of the artist, to whom art is more than life, and who, if he realises that 'Beauty is Truth, Truth Beauty,' loves truth for being beautiful and not beauty for its innermost soul of spiritual truth. Very coolly the master of himself when he sat down to write, Keats realised that the finest part of his writing must always be that part which he was least conscious of, as he wrote it down. To have 'no identity'; to be a voice, a vision; to pass on a message, translating it, flawlessly, into another, more easily apprehended, tongue: that was the poet's business amid the cloudy splendours of natural things. His own personality seemed to him to matter hardly more than the strings of the lyre; without which, indeed, there would be no music audible, but which changed no single note of the music already existing, in an expectant silence. And it is through that humility, in his relations with beauty, that Keats has come nearer than most others to a final expression of whatever he has chosen, or been chosen, to express. Byron has himself to talk about, Coleridge the metaphysics of the universe, Shelley, Wordsworth, each a message of his own which he searches for in natural things, rather than elicits from them; but Keats is the one quite perfect lover, offering and asking nothing, all blind devotion, and with an inexhaustible memory for delight.

In his most famous line he has said, once for all: —

' A thing of beauty is a joy for ever.'

Well, his own poetry has much of this joy, only a little pensive, as a human reflection steals in upon it now and again, of beautiful, changeless things, new every season, or every morning, or every minute, but returning, with inevitable patience, as long as time goes on. He is watching —

'How tip-toe Night holds back her dark-grey hood,'

and seems but to give choice words to the sight; seeming even to come more minutely close to the exact form and sound of things, —

'As when heard anew
Old ocean rolls a lengthened wave to the shore,
Down whose green back the short-lived foam, all hoar,
Bursts gradual, with a wayward indolence.'

He has that power, which he rightly attributes to Milton, of 'stationing': 'he is not content with simple description, he must station.' He cannot name daffodils without seeing 'the green world they live in.' Distance, or the time of day, must be measured visibly: —

'There she stood
About a young bird's flutter from a wood,'

he tells us of Lamia waiting for Lycius; and when Lycius comes to meet her, it is

'On the moth-time of that evening dim.'

As Venus, in 'Endymion,' descends from heaven to find Adonis, the silent wheels of her car, —

'Fresh wet from clouds of morn,
Spun off a drizzling dew, which falling chill
On soft Adonis' shoulders, made him still
Nestle and turn uneasily about';

and the doves, as they come near the ground, are seen with 'silken traces lightened in descent.' And, with Keats, abstract things become not less visibly apportioned to their corner of the universe than the things which we call actual.

'Obstinate silence came heavily again,
Feeling about for its old couch of space
And airy cradle.'

But his truth to nature, as we call it, to his own apprehension of things seen and felt, is always a beautiful truth, differing in this from some of those poets who have tried to come closest to realities. There are moments, rare enough, when he forgets his own wise care in this matter, and writes of one who

'Bent his soul fiercely like a spiritual bow,
And twanged it inwardly.'

But, even earlier than this, which we find in 'Endymion,' he has learnt the secret of precision in beauty, and, at twenty-two, can evoke for us the myrtle that —

'Lifts its sweet head into the air, and feeds
A silent space with ever-sprouting green.'

He tells us, but always in beautiful words, because in words born of that 'lust of the eyes' which in him was inseparable from sight, of 'the tiger-moth's deep-damasked wings,' of 'the lidless-eyed train of planets,' of the 'chuckling' linnet, the 'low creeping' strawberries, the 'freckled' wings of the butterflies. He realised at every moment that —

'The poetry of Earth is never dead,'

and it seemed to him a simple thing to transplant that poetry into his pages, as one transplants a root from the woods into one's own garden. All the tenderness of his nature seemed to go out to the green things which grow in the soil, to trees and plants and flowers, the whole 'leafy world'; as all his feeling for the spiritual part of sensation, for the ideal, if you will, went out to the moon.

'Thy starry sway
Has been an under-passion to this hour,'

he cries, in 'Endymion'; and it is to the moon, always, that he looks for the closest symbols of poetry.

Keats has a firm common sense of the imagination, seeming to be at home in it, as if it were literally this world, and not the dream of another. Thus, in his most serious moments, he can jest with it, as men do with those they live with and love most. 'The beauty of the morning operating on a sense of idleness' is enough to set him on a distant journey, in a moment of time; and he can reason about the matter so subtly and in such eloquent prose as this: —

'Now it appears to me that almost any man may, like the spider, spin from his own inwards, his own airy citadel. The points of leaves and twigs on which the spider begins her work are few, and she fills the air with a beautiful circuiting. Man should be content with as few points to tip with the fine web of his soul, and weave a tapestry empyræan — full of symbols for his spiritual eye, of softness for his spiritual touch, of space for his wanderings, of distinctness for his luxury. But the minds of mortals are so different, and bent on such diverse journeys, that it may at first appear impossible for any common taste and fellowship to exist between two or three under these suppositions. It is, however, quite the contrary. Minds would leave each other in contrary directions, traverse each other in numberless points, and at last greet each other at the journey's end. An old man and a child would talk together, and the old man be led on his path and the child left thinking.'

'Man should not dispute or assert, but whisper results to his neighbour,' he affirms; 'let us open our leaves like a flower, and be passive and receptive, budding patiently under the eye of Apollo, and taking hints from every noble insect that favours us with a visit.' That passive and receptive mood was always his own attitude towards the visitings of the imagination; he was always 'looking on the sun, the moon, the stars, the earth and its contents, as materials to form greater things'; always waiting, now 'all of a tremble from not having written anything of late,' now vainly longing to 'compose without fever,' now reminding a friend: 'If you should have any reason to regret this state of excitement in me, I will turn the tide of your feelings in the right channel by mentioning that it is the only state for the best kind of poetry — that

JOHN KEATS

is all I care for, all I live for.' Perhaps it is this waiting mood, a kind of electrically charged expectancy which draws its own desire to itself out of the universe, that Mr. Bridges means when he speaks of Keats' 'unbroken and unflagging earnestness, which is so utterly unconscious and unobservant of itself as to be almost unmatched.' In its dependence on a kind of direct inspiration, the fidelity to first thoughts, it accounts, perhaps, for much of what is technically deficient in his poetry. When Keats gave his famous counsel to Shelley, urging him to 'load every rift with ore,' he expressed a significant criticism, both of his own and of Shelley's work. With Shelley, even though he may at times seem to become vague in thought, there is always an intellectual structure; Keats, definite in every word, in every image, lacks intellectual structure. He saw words as things, and he saw them one at a time. 'I look upon fine phrases like a lover,' he confessed, but with him the fine phrase was but the translation of a thing actually seen by the imagination. He was conscious of the need there is for the poet to be something more than a creature of sensations, but even his consciousness of this necessity is that of one to whom knowledge is merely an aid to flight. 'The difference,' he says, in a splendid sentence, 'of high sensations, with and without knowledge, appears to me this: in the latter case we are continually falling ten thousand fathoms deep, and being blown up again, without wings, and with all the horror of a bare-shouldered creature; in the former case our shoulders are fledged, and we go through the same air and space without fear.' When Keats wrote poetry he knew that he was writing poetry; naturally as it came to him, he never fancied that he was but expressing himself, or putting down something which his own mind had realised for its own sake. 'The imagination,' he tells us, in a phrase which has become famous, 'may be compared to Adam's dream — he awoke and found it truth.' Only Keats, unlike most other poets, never slept, or, it may be, never awoke. Poetry was literally almost everything to him; and he could deal with it so objectively, as with a thing outside himself, precisely because it was an almost bodily part of him, like the hand he wrote with. 'If poetry,' he said, in an axiom sent to his publisher, 'comes not as naturally as the leaves to a tree, it had better not come at all.' And so, continually, eagerly, instinctively, yet in a way unconsciously, he was lying in wait for that winged, shy guest, the 'magic casements' always open on the 'perilous seas.' 'The only thing,' he said, 'that can ever affect me personally for more than one short passing day is any doubt about my powers for poetry: I seldom have any; and I look with hope to the nighing time when I shall have none.' His belief that he should 'be among the English poets after his death' meant more to him, undoubtedly, than such a conviction usually means, even to those most careful of fame. It was his ideal world, the only aspect of spiritual things which he ever saw or cared to see; and the thought of poetry, apprehended for its own sake as the only entirely satisfying thing in the world, imprisoned him as within a fairy ring, alone with his little circle of green grass and blue sky.

'To load every rift with ore': that, to Keats, was the essential thing; and it meant to pack the verse with poetry, with the stuff of the imagination, so that every line should be heavy with it. For the rest, the poem is to come as best it may; only once, in 'Lamia,' with any real skill in narrative, or any care for that skill. There, doubtless, it was the passing influence of Dryden which set him upon a kind of experiment, which he may have done largely for the experiment's sake; doing it, of course, consummately. 'Hyperion' was another kind of experiment; and this time, for all its splendour, less personal to his own style, or way of feeling. 'I have given up "Hyperion,"' he writes; 'there were too many Miltonic inversions in it — Miltonic verse cannot be written but in an artful, or, rather, artist's humour. I wish to give myself up to other sensations.' He asks Reynolds to pick out some lines from 'Hyperion,' and put a mark, x, to the false beauty, proceeding from art, and 1, 2, to the true voice of feeling. It is just then that he discovers Chatterton to be 'the purest writer in the English language.' A little later he decides that 'the marvellous is the most enticing, and the surest guarantee of harmonious numbers,' and so decides, somewhat against his inclination, he professes, to 'untether Fancy, and to let her manage for herself.' 'I and myself cannot agree about this at all,' is his conclusion; but 'La Belle Dame sans Merci' follows, and that opening of 'The Eve of St. Mark,' which seems to contain the germ of both Rossetti and Morris, going, as it does, so far along the road that Chatterton had opened up and then wilfully closed. It was just because Keats was so much, so exclusively possessed by his own imagination, so exclusively concerned with the shaping of it into poetry, that all his poems seem to have been written for the sake of something else than their story, or thought, or indeed emotion. Even the odes are mental picture added to mental picture, separate stanza added to separate stanza, rather than the development of a thought which must express itself, creating its own form. Meditation brings to him no inner vision, no rapture of the soul; but seems to germinate upon the page in actual flowers and corn and fruit.

Keats' sense of form, if by form is meant perfection rather of outline than of detail, was by no means certain. Most poets work only in outline: Keats worked on every inch of his surface. Perhaps no poet has ever packed so much poetic detail into so small a space, or been so satisfied with having done so. Metrically, he is often slipshod; with all his genius for words, he often uses them incorrectly, or with but a vague sense of their meaning; even in the 'Ode to a Nightingale' he will leave lines in which the inspiration seems suddenly to flag; such lines as

'Though the dull brain perplexes and retards,'

which is nerveless; or

> 'In ancient days by emperor and clown,'

where the antithesis, logically justifiable, has the sound of an antithesis brought in for the sake of rhyme. In the 'Ode on a Grecian Urn,' two lines near the end seem to halt by the way, are not firm and direct in movement: —

> 'Thou shalt remain, in midst of other woe
> Than ours, a friend to man, to whom thou say'st.'

That is slipshod writing, both as intellectual and as metrical structure; and it occurs in a poem which is one of the greatest lyrical poems in the language. We have only to look closely enough to see numberless faults of this kind in Keats; and yet, if we do not look very closely, we shall not see them; and, however closely we may look, and however many faults we may find, we shall end, as we began, by realising that they do not essentially matter. Why is this?

Wordsworth, who at his best may seem to be the supreme master of poetical style, is often out of key; Shelley, who at his best may seem to be almost the supreme singer, is often prosaic: Keats is never prosaic and never out of key. To read Wordsworth or Shelley, you must get in touch with their ideas, at least apprehend them; to read Keats you have only to surrender your senses to their natural happiness. You have to get at Shelley's or Wordsworth's point of view; but Keats has only the point of view of the sunlight. He cannot write without making pictures with his words, and every picture has its own atmosphere. Tennyson, who learnt so much from Keats, learnt from him something of his skill in making pictures; but Tennyson's pictures are chill, conscious of themselves, almost colourless. The pictures of Keats are all aglow with colour, not always very accurate painter's colour, but colour which captivates or overwhelms the senses. 'The Eve of St. Agnes' is hardly more than a description of luxurious things: 'lucent syrops, tinct with cinnamon,' a bed, with 'blanched linen, smooth and lavender'd,' moonlight through painted windows, 'warmed jewels'; yet every word throbs with emotion, as the poet 'grows faint' with the lover. Tennyson's 'Palace of Art' is full of pictures, each in its frame, or of statues, each in its niche; but the pictures and statues are no more than decorations in a house of thought, somewhat too methodically arranged there. To Keats, the thing itself and the emotion were indistinguishable; he never saw without feeling, and he never felt without passion. That is why he can call up atmosphere by the mere bewitchment of a verse which seems to make a casual statement; because nothing, with him, can be a casual statement, nothing can be prosaic, or conceived of coldly, apart from that 'principle of beauty in all things' which he tells us that he had always loved, and which to him was the principle of life itself.

GEORGE DARLEY (1795–1846) [1]

DARLEY has said more explicit things about himself, in a single letter to Miss Mitford, than any one else has ever said about him. 'My whole life has been an abstraction — such must be my works': that is his final summing up; yet, as he thinks of the fierce critical work to which so much of his time was abandoned, he defines himself as 'like one of Dante's sinners, floating and bickering about in the shape of a fiery tongue, on the Slough of Despond.' 'A heat of brain mentally Bacchic,' he finds in himself, and he admits: 'I have seldom the power to direct my mind, and must only follow it'; and the mind itself he calls 'occasional, intermittent, collapsive.'

Every phrase is a self-revelation, and there is little more to be said. Imagination, of a kind, he had, as the incoherent

---

[1] (1) *The Errors of Ecstasie*, 1822. (2) *The Labours of Idleness*, prose and verse, 1826. (3) *Sylvia*, 1827. (4) *Nepenthe*, privately printed, 1835. (5) *Thomas à Becket*, 1840. (6) *Ethelstan*, 1841. (7) *Poetical Works*, 1908.

rhapsody of 'Nepenthe,' only later printed in full, is enough to show us. But Miss Mitford, when she roused the author to his grateful confessions, had not read it to the end, as she confessed to the world afterwards. Nor is any one else likely to fix his mind sufficiently on these bright motes in the air. Even 'Sylvia,' which has a kind of pretence at story-telling, baffles the attention. Only the few loveliest of the songs can be lingered over.

For Darley was, as he said of himself, 'a day-dreamer of no ordinary extravagance, and was perpetually creating such labyrinths of thought around him that no wonder if he was sometimes lost in them.' 'Some of his compositions,' he says also, 'were less irregular, and, indeed, as works of fancy their novelty of conception and imagery may perhaps recommend them with those who have just as severe a contempt for meteors, and just as profound an admiration for paving-stones, as I wish them.' Yet it will surprise no one who reads 'Sylvia' that George Darley has been forgotten so soon, and that he made so little fame in his time. It is full of fancy, gaiety, and blithe singing; there are lyrics that echo Elizabethan airs with an almost deceptive music; the blank verse is continually dropping jewelled words by the way, and there is a strained antic quality in the motley prose, like a jangling of fools' bells. But there is no clear path through this fairy maze, this no man's land in which there are no laws, even of an inverted logic; nothing that happens matters, and we are hardly aware of what is happening. 'The benefit of a perfectly unrestricted design,' though it seemed to Darley to 'afford him the best chance of succeeding,' may be said rather to have left him with no chance whatever of success. Before abandoning the reins to one's caprice, it is well to know what instinct or sense of direction there is in the fantastic animal. Caprice is apt to turn in a ring, and come back to the starting-place in the end, which is much the case with 'Sylvia.' Before it is over, before it has even got to its best moment, in the delirious procession of the fairies, we are a little tired of the journey. The whole extravagance once over, we look back as on a confused dream, out of which we still remember some delicate, thin, festal music of flutes.

I am not sure that Darley was not right, and most others wrong, in thinking that he had put his best, most living work into the two unactable plays of 'Thomas à Becket' and 'Ethelstan.' Incoherent, desultory, there are in them fine madnesses, dramatic moments, a flitting and aspiring energy, a coming and going of a strange, personal poetry. The queen's dwarf Dwerga, in 'Becket,' is, as he realised, 'the highest creation in the work.' 'I wrote it,' he says, 'with delight, ardour, and ease,' and there is a fine Middletonian grotesque in the infamous creature dieted on —

> 'rich snails that slip
> My throttle down ere I well savour them;
> Most luscious mummy; bat's milk cheese; at times
> The sweetbreads of fallen moon-calves, or the jellies
> Scummed after shipwreck floating to the shore.'

The blank verse has rich Elizabethan echoes in it, and can speak with this dignity, in the mouth of Becket: —

> ''T is reasonable,
> I do confess, to think that this fine essence,
> Grandeur of soul, should breathe itself throughout
> The mien and movements: every word should speak it,
> Howe'er so calm — like the pleased lion's murmur!
> Each tone, glance, posture, should be great with it.
> All levity of air, too buoyant cheer,
> The o'er familiar smile, salute, and chat
> Which sinks us to the low and common level,
> Should be dismissed, and giant-minded things
> Disclaim the pigmy natural to most men.'

Yet the plays are the experiments of a lyrical poet, and must be read chiefly for the bravery of the writing.

As a lyrical poet, Darley is most himself and at his best in 'Sylvia.' In most of his other songs (which have now and then a plaintive Irish colour cadence, like that used by him in more than one poem, in which he anticipates a masterpiece of a later writer) there is often an attempt to spin his web out of too thin a substance, which breaks in his hand. Everywhere there are little snatches, little flutterings of song, which are felt for a minute and then are gone. 'The Maiden's Grave' and 'Love's Devotion' are dainty elegies; 'Heroa' would have pleased Landor, and 'Robin's Cross' must please all. But the best lines are in lyrics made consciously after Elizabethan models, and they are rarely so good as these two almost supremely good ones: —

> 'He who the Siren's hair would win
> Is mostly strangled in the tide.'

Darley's good things are for the most part either scattered or broken. They could never be mended or brought together, and he is not likely to be remembered for more than these bright fragments.

JEREMIAH JOSEPH CALLANAN (1795–1829) [1]

CALLANAN said of himself, in one of his most personal poems:

> 'I only awoke your wild harp from its slumber,
> And mingled once more with the voice of those fountains
> The songs even Echo forgot on her mountains.'

'It is Callanan's distinction — a great one, though ignored till now,' says Dr. Sigerson, who speaks with authority — 'that he was the first to give adequate versions of Irish Gaelic poems.' As we commonly find in modern Irish poets, even in the most remarkable of them, James Clarence Mangan, Callanan's original poems are not to be compared with those which he re-created from the Irish. Some of these have, with all the Irish agility of lilt and sombre passion in the substance, a certain rarity in the style, close to the feeling which it renders. The last stanza of 'The Outlaw of Loch Lene,' with its lovely

[1] (1) *The Recluse of Inchidony*, 1830. (2) *Poems*, 1861.

Irish rhythm, has a combination of naïveté with imagination that is rarely to be found beyond the Celtic borders. Listen to this tune: —

> ' 'T is down by the lake where the wild wind fringes its sides,
> The maid of my heart, the fair one of heaven resides;
> I think as at eve she wanders its mazes along
> The birds go to sleep by the sweet wild twist of her song.'

It is that word 'twist' which drops the pinch of salt into the bowl.

SIR THOMAS NOON TALFOURD (1795–1854) [1]

'Ion' is the work of a man who might well have been the friend of Lamb. It is, as he himself calls it, 'the phantom of a tragedy,' but it is a kindly and gentle shade, and it still makes pleasant reading, though it can never have lived on the stage with more than what came to it from Macready's 'extraordinary power of vivifying the frigid and familiarising the remote.' Frigid, though his own word, is not quite the word which describes that almost idyllic quality which, attractive in itself, is rather apart from the purpose of drama. Everywhere there is a sort of faint irrelevant eloquence, and what might well be a simple statement, that the headsman and his sword are ready, is thus rendered: —

> 'Even now the solemn soldiers line the ground,
> The steel gleams on the altar, and the slave
> Disrobes himself for duty.'

Talfourd came to the drama oddly, from Hannah More's 'Sacred Dramas,' through Addison's 'Cato.' What began so far away from us comes in the end to have a certain kinship with Browning's early drama, in a frank and manly pathos and sense of friendship. The poetry never gets quite beyond the state of poetical feeling. Talfourd seems unable to get

[1] (1) *Ion*, 1836. (2) *The Athenian Captive*, 1838. (3) *Glencoe*. (4) *The Castilian*, 1853.

over his surprise, that anything so 'feeble in its development' should have succeeded for its moment even on the stage, and reminds us that it was never really intended to be acted.

JOHN HAMILTON REYNOLDS (1796–1852) [1]

It is as a friend, companion, and fellow worker of Keats that Reynolds is best remembered, though in his day he made a little place of his own as a satirist, in the unsigned 'antenatal Peter,' as Shelley called the brilliant parody of Wordsworth. It was reviewed by Keats in 'The Examiner,' and the review led to Shelley's 'Peter Bell the Third.' Its author said afterwards: 'Ah, which is the serious poem?' in order to answer: 'The Burlesque, by its having a meaning.' 'Peter Bell' was the radiant, gentlemanly mockery of a poet by a poet, itself a kind of homage and criticism in one.

'I am the mighty mental medlar,
I am the lonely lyric pedlar,
I am the goul of Alice Fell';

says the 'real Simon Pure.'

Reynolds had a good technique in comic verse, and a poetical feeling which expresses without quite achieving itself in some of his sonnets and songs. But, as he said of himself, he 'had not the heart to rush at Fame'; or, as it has been said of him since, 'he was too light a weight for a grave age.' His early work was imitative, but with a boyish freedom. 'Safie,' dedicated to Byron, was full of Byronisms such as —

'Despair is poison of the heart,
It rankles in a feeling part.'

'The Eden of Imagination' is a pleasant dream of a paradise after Leigh Hunt.

[1] (1) *Safie, an Eastern Tale*, 1814. (2) *The Eden of Imagination*, 1814. (3) *The Naiad*, 1816. (4) *Peter Bell*, 1819. (5) *The Fancy*, 1820. (6) *Odes and Addresses to Celebrated Persons* (five by Reynolds and the rest by Hood), 1825. (7) *The Garden of Florence*, 1831.

'The graceful willow, weaving to the breeze,
A green Narcissus of surrounding trees.'

He longs for 'such a scene of lusciousness and rest' (Keats-like), and in a naïve footnote declares: 'I know no one so fit to inhabit this Eden of Imagination as Mr. Wordsworth.' Finally there comes 'The Naiad,' a bright pastoral, with some songs of a quaint youthfulness, recording the time when 'his breast was young Maria's shrine.' Later on, the influence of Keats absorbed all others, and some of Reynolds' own impulses seem to have communicated themselves back to Keats. It was in answer to two pleasant, Hunt-like sonnets on Robin Hood that Keats wrote his ballad-song of 'Robin Hood.' It was with Reynolds that he was to have collaborated in a book of rhymed tales after Boccaccio; 'Isabella' was probably written to go with 'The Garden of Florence' and 'The Ladye of Provence' in the book published by Reynolds in 1821. The best of Keats' epistles was one written to Reynolds, and we see its wild fantasies, about the 'Lapland Witch turned maudlin Nun,' and the rest, reflecting, as in a mirror, something of the irresponsible insobriety of the writer of 'Peter Bell' and 'The Fancy.'

It was in 'The Fancy' that Reynolds was perhaps most himself; for that book, 'strictly familiar but by no means vulgar,' full of gusto, the record of a single gay corner of a period, suggests the man 'good with both hands,' with his 'gamecock-looking head,' as Hood described him. The prose, perhaps better than the verse, of it, but both rattling well together, combine in a nonsense book as taking and irrelevant an impromptu as his life.

DAVID HARTLEY COLERIDGE (1796–1849)[1]

HARTLEY COLERIDGE impressed the people who met him hardly less than his father; he seemed to them a person of

[1] (1) *Poems*, 1833. (2) *Poems*, edited by his brother, 2 vols., 1851.

equally essential genius. But behind his wonderful talk, in the depths of his sensitive and perturbed nature, there was a vast inertia; and the one, like the other, was an inheritance. Wrecked nerves, hauntings in sleep, absent-mindedness amounting almost to hallucination, an 'impotence of will,' together with 'melancholy recklessness,' a sense of what he called '*triste augurium,* uneasy melancholy,' 'the feeling or fantasy of an adverse destiny,' buried somewhere in his mind: how could he, with all these legacies, do much to turn to effect that other fainter legacy, an instinct almost of genius? He spoke of himself as 'one of the small poets,' and he was right; his verse is just such poetry as can be improvised by genuinely poetical natures in which the soil is thin. His was always 'a young lamb's heart among the full-grown flocks,' as it was said by Wordsworth, to whom he owed so much as a poet and as a man. And, as he said of himself, in one of his best sonnets: —

> 'I lived like one not born to die,
> A thriftless prodigal of smiles and tears.'

'For I have lost the race I never ran,' he tells us, and he seems really never to have started on that race as more than a comforting diversion. There are splendid single lines and passages in his sonnets, sometimes as tenderly fanciful as this: —

> 'But when I see thee by thy father's side,
> Old times unqueen thee and old loves endear thee';

sometimes as full of significant and pungent imagery as here: —

> 'Or being bad, yet murmurs at the curse
> And incapacity of being worse,
> That makes my hungry passion still keep Lent
> In keen expectance of a Carnival.'

The first two lines might occur in 'The Unknown Eros,' the two latter in 'Modern Love.' The sonnets are full of poetical thought, and are as pleasant for their substance as for their easy, gracious form. Besides the sonnets, which are of many kinds, there are a few lyrics, some, like the lullaby, 'When on my Mother's Arm I lay,' Elizabethan in colour, as are some of the sonnet endings, not without charm of cadence. We feel everywhere, even in the blank verse, really good of its kind, an accomplished master of language and versification. An attractive temperament is seen through them all. What is it, then, that is not in a work which remains ineffectual in the end? Is salt the ingredient that is lacking?

WILLIAM MOTHERWELL (1797–1835) [1]

WILLIAM MOTHERWELL was the son of an ironmonger; he was born at Glasgow, October 13, 1797, and died there of softening of the brain, November 1, 1835. He was a lawyer's clerk and a journalist, and he published in 1827 an important collection of Scottish ballads, under the title of 'Minstrelsy, Ancient and Modern.' In 1832 he collected the original poems which he had printed at intervals in the newspapers, and was engaged on a life of Tannahill, and with Hogg, on an edition of Burns, at the time of his death. A collected edition of his poems, with unpublished or uncollected pieces, was brought out in 1846.

Motherwell was an adventurer or a trespasser on many provinces, and one has to turn continually to his exact date to find out whether he is anticipating or echoing something with which we are already familiar. He imitates old English poetry more in the spelling than in the spirit; his Scottish writing is naturally more like the real thing, as in the famous 'Jeanie Morrison,' and in the better 'Willie' song, which, if they do not 'strike a few bold knocks at the door of the heart,' as John Wilson said of his ballads, have at least a suggestion of sincerity in their speech. His Norse war-songs and sword-

[1] (1) *Renfrewshire Characters and Scenery*, 1824. (2) *Poems, Narrative and Lyrical*, 1832. (3) *Poetical Works*, 1846.

songs, his Turkish battle-songs and all the other exotic compositions into which and into the 'Cavalier' songs he put most of his force, have the fine ringing clink of what is not after all sure steel. Starting from Gray he points the way to the versifying Macaulay. Some of his light jingles he apparently caught from Moore, while in others, more languid in flow, he seems to anticipate some of Tennyson's early cadences. But there is, among his various attempts at ghastliness (one of which, 'The Madman's Love,' would be striking if it had less rhetoric and came to an end sooner), a poem called 'The Demon Lady,' which is either a clever but extravagant imitation of Poe, or else, as it more likely was (for Poe knew his work and quotes a poem of his), one of the obscure and almost accidental origins of Poe's elaborate method of repeated effects. Motherwell wrote with vigour, but his work is a series of experiments, all detached, and akin only in their general aim at giving striking expression to striking subjects. He was an artificer rather than an artist.

SAMUEL LOVER (1797–1868) [1]

SAMUEL LOVER is best known to English readers as the writer of a wild drollery called 'Handy Andy,' which they are too easily inclined to take as a pattern of Irish life. He wrote better things in prose, and the poetical feeling which disguises itself in them is to be felt, speaking through athletic rhythms, in such uproarious ballads as 'Widow Machree' and such dainty ballads as 'The Whistling Thief,' which is as good as many similar things of Heine, and in some ways better. They are not quite like anything else, even in Irish work done before and after them, like 'The Groves of Blarney' of Richard Alfred Milliken, who wrote that irresistible solemn nonsense ode,

[1] (1) *Songs and Ballads*, 1839. (2) *Irish Lyrics*, 1858. (3) *Rival Rhymes*, 1859. (4) *Volunteer Songs*, 1859.

which Peacock would have envied. There is little of Lover's verse to be interested in, but the best things give one a queer kind of pleasure.

ROBERT POLLOK (1798–1827) [1]

The final criticism of Pollok's 'Course of Time' was written by Frere on the fly-leaf of that strictly prose production.

> 'Robert Pollok, A. M.! this work of yours
> Is meant, I do not doubt, extremely well,
> And the design I deem most laudable;
> But since I find the book laid on my table,
> I shall presume (with the fair owner's leave)
> To note a single slight deficiency:
> I mean, in short (since it is called a poem),
> That in the course of ten successive books
> If something in the shape of poetry
> Were to be met with, we should like it better;
> But nothing of the kind is to be found,
> Nothing, alas! but words of the olden time,
> Quaint and uncouth, contorted phrase and queer,
> With the familiar language that befits
> Tea-drinking parties most unmeetly matched.'

DAVID MACBETH MOIR (1798–1851) [2]

For a short time Moir obtained a sympathetic public in response to a series of 'Domestic Verses' inscribed to the memory of three small children. They express a natural grief with sincerity, but it is the utterance of a man who mistakes feeling for poetry. The many people who once wept over 'Casa Wappy' were so sorry for the father that they hesitated to put his verse to any test but the easy one of pathos. When he writes a festival ode to Burns there is the same genuine

---

[1] *The Course of Time*, 2 vols., 1827.
[2] (1) *The Legend of Guenevere*, 1824. (2) *Domestic Verses*, 1843. (3) *Poetical Works*, 2 vols., 1852.

feeling and the same incapacity to render it into poetry. Nowhere in all this fluent and specious versification is there more than such improvisations as the 'hurried life' of a professional man is likely to leave time for.

WILLIAM THOM (1798–1848) [1]

THE life of William Thom was full of misery and distraction. He endured all the agonies of poverty and privation, with intervals during which he was feasted in London as a celebrity, and received large sums in charity from admirers in America and in India. He once said to his hosts at a dinner: 'I retire to my loom, gentlemen, and those who would best serve me, buy my webs.' He appears to have been a good weaver, but not a thrifty one. At nearly the age of fifty he speaks of himself, quite justly, as 'not yet come to years of discretion'; he lived not without a certain disorder, having his own way in his habits and morals. But there is no doubt that this random, reckless, defiant creature was a man of unusual force and charm, and a man who can characterise his feelings as he goes away from his wife's burial as 'a trifle of sad thinking,' is not without that sense of style which comes from some fineness of mind. Personally, we are told, he was small, thickset, and somewhat lame, with 'a face which was creased and wrinkled all over, wherever a wrinkle could be, and had an expression at once shrewd, humorous, insinuating, and woebegone.' The description suggests the actual qualities of his work, in which many strange contradictions are not less strangely harmonised.

Thom was an instinctive artist, and though he imagined that he had learned largely from his 'ill-fated fellow-craftsman,' Tannahill, and though he certainly and naturally learned from Burns, he discovered for himself a kind of finish, a technique

[1] *Rhymes and Recollections*, 1844.

that seems really elaborate, and is far beyond that of any other Scots-writing lyric poet of the time. His sense of rhythm and of epithet is equally certain and unusual. Something which we rarely find in Scottish verse (or only in Burns, who had everything) gives a curious quality to Thom's work: a tender irony, which mixes with deep human feeling and with an almost playful sense of the beauty of things and sounds. This irony sometimes turns fierce, and can be as grim as in the biting ballad of the nettle and the 'stricken branch.' It gives salt to sympathy, and adds finish, a kind of mental distinction, to poems that tend to go the Scots way down to sentimentality.

Like most Scottish poets, Thom sought for much of his inspiration, or for adequate forms for it, in the national airs, to which his musical sense guided him. There is one instance, which he has set down in one of those notes which supplement the masterly prose 'Recollections,' in which even he could not better what he called 'a most romping stamping tune, with neither time nor measure' (though it had both), and which I must record here for the joy of it: —

> 'Did ye meet my wife, Jenny Nettle, Jenny Nettle?
> Did ye meet my wife, coming frae the market?
> A bag o' meal upon her back,
> A bag o' meal upon her back,
> A bag o' meal upon her back,
> And a bairnie in a basket.'

But look at almost every poem of Thom and you will find a rhythm in which the cadences are elaborated and variously balanced, and in which lilt and alliteration combine to produce a rare singing music, not usually of pure beauty, but with something strange, strong, often grotesque in it. There are artful breaks, like the repetition, outside the normal measure, in

> 'That waur green, green when he was near me.'

Sometimes the turns and pauses are mere effects of harmony, oftener they are all for meaning, but a meaning which seems to evoke sound in its own image. A satirical poem called 'Chants for Churls,' written at the time of the birth of the Free Church, would be a pure delight, read properly, to one who did not even grasp the sense of the not too difficult words. Has Mr. Kipling ever done so much with the hammer and anvil as this : —

> 'We've kirks in ilka corner,
> An' wow but we can preach!
> Timmer tap, little sap,
> Onything for bread.
> Their sermons in the draw-well,
> Drink till ye stretch.
> We're clean sairt sookin' at it,
> The deil's dazed lookin' at it,
> Daud him on the head!'

There is hardly a poem which has not its own lilt, and an epithet or two which come as if by surprise. The feeling often passes beyond mere personal record, and becomes almost dramatic. 'In my very very heart I found it,' he could say of any of his poems, in the true sense, and he asks indignantly: 'Who are they that beat about in the substanceless regions of fancy for material to move a tear ? ' He was 'a man who had something to say,' it was rightly said of him by one of his first and best critics. Yet what is after all chiefly remarkable in him is the rare, almost unerring, art of his verse, which, as the work of a lame, drunken, flute-playing weaver, is not less than astonishing.

THOMAS HOOD (1799–1845) [1]

HOOD is one of the great artists in English verse, especially

[1] (1) *Odes and Addresses to Great People,* with J. H. Reynolds (who wrote five), 1825. (2) *Whims and Oddities, in Prose and Verse,* 2 vols., 1826–27. (3) *The Plea of the Midsummer Fairies,* 1827. (4) *Epping Hunt,* 1829. (5) *The Dream of Eugene Aram,* 1831. (6) *Hood's Own,* 1839. (7) *Whimsicalities,* 1844. (8) *Memorials, edited by his Daughter,* 1860. (9) *Miss Kilmansegg,* 1870. (10) *Complete Works,* 11 vols., 1882–84. (11) *The Haunted House,* 1886. (12) *Complete Poetical Works,* edited by Walter Jerrold, 1906.

in his serious play with double and treble endings. No one else could have written such a stanza as this: —

> 'Still, for all slips of hers,
> One of Eve's family —
> Wipe those poor lips of hers
> Oozing so clammily.'

The rhymes would be laughable if Hood's sensitive finger had not trembled on them and touched them into pathos. His verse has a strong beat, as in 'The Song of the Shirt,' in which a certain poise and weight are given to a lilt, something as Campbell did, but with an artifice more obvious, in 'The Battle of the Baltic.' He uses repetitions and refrains with less artifice than Poe, who must have learnt the exact shape of certain metres from him; and he has a musical art, unique in him, of getting crescendos, sometimes by an unexpected new line added with sudden effect to a refrain, like that which ends and intensifies 'The Song of the Shirt.' At moments he leaves all that is peculiar, and what is most personal in his verse, to fall into older-fashioned cadences as satisfying as these, both funereal: —

> 'Saving those two that turn aside and pass,
> In velvet blossom, where all flesh is grass';

and, more mental in its picture: —

> 'When grass waves
> Over the past-away, there may be then
> No resurrection in the minds of men.'

And he has a quality, so simple and straightforward that it is hardly distinguishable from prose, which allows him to say at times final and perfect things like the famous: —

> 'We thought her dying when she slept
> And sleeping when she died.'

It becomes didactic, but does not lose its sharpness and neatness, in: —

> 'But evil is wrought by want of thought
> As well as want of heart.'

An art of saying almost unforgettable things is part of his various skill, and belongs to the antithetical mind, which turns easily from a pun to a moral contrast.

Hood learnt, in form, matter, and subject, from several of his contemporaries; metrically, no doubt, from Coleridge, who, he tells us with pride, was 'friendly to my rhyme'; and, in epithets and natural colour from Keats, whose 'La Belle Dame sans Merci' he echoes closely in the ballad of 'The Water Lady,' while the closing imagery of the 'Ode on Melancholy' is almost transferred to his own 'Ode to Autumn.' Lamb, whom he honoured nobly, he comes sometimes to resemble, but, in verse, for the better; so that the little cameo-like poem of 'Ruth,' so tender, finished, and restrained, is really what Lamb would like to have done, but was never quite to accomplish. At his best, Hood has a style which seems to come to him naturally, and to suit his needs; but he invented another style by the way, of which the main ingredients were Elizabethan.

It is difficult sometimes to know how far Shakespeare, or one of the melodious minor people of his time, is being consciously followed in the cadences of some of the longer poems. 'The Plea of the Midsummer Fairies' is full of sweet fancy, woven with a pleasant ingenuity, after one of the manners of the narrative poets of our Renaissance. 'Hero and Leander' is done after a slightly different manner, and its sophisticated feeling would have been understood by the people who came after Marlowe, and began to embroider upon a plain outline. 'Lycus the Centaur,' with its swaying metre, is a kind of classical extravaganza, and here the curious sympathy for what is unhuman in things, for the unearthliness of fairies, sea-nymphs, and Circe's beasts, perhaps culminates. Tragic mischief, which in the others was of a graver kind, becomes here almost a horrible thing, into which he puts beauty.

Yet in all this, with its charm, strangeness, and a kind of

novelty in its combinations, we have not yet come to the essential Hood. In 'The Haunted House' it is often thought that we find him. Scarcely, though the quality by which he resembles Hawthorne, the sense of a mystery enveloping real and mouldering things, is there, and traverses a poem too long and too detailed to maintain its suspense throughout. Not even Poe has experimented so carefully and deliberately in this particular kind of evil glamour. In 'The Elm-Tree' we have the Hawthorne feeling again, and again the idea is hardly serious enough to justify so many stanzas. In 'The Dream of Eugene Aram' Hood achieves. Here what has been fanciful in the rendering of sensation becomes a dreadful and penetrating humanity, and we realise that Hood is, above all, an artist of the human heart.

Hood's verse is the broken-hearted jesting of a sick buffoon, to whom suffering has brought pity and taught the cruel humour of things. It is natural to him to be sentimental and fantastic at once, a tender-hearted Fantasio who has 'passed the equinoctial of Queubus with the Vapians,' 'a fag for all the town,' as he calls himself: —

> 'I am a shuttle-cock myself,
> The world knocks to and fro.'

Once or twice he arraigns the justice of things on his own behalf, as when he says, in a rare self-confession: —

> 'But oh! as many and such tears are ours
> As only should be shed for guilt and shame.'

With him there is —

> 'Death, death, and nothing but death,
> In every sight and sound,'

till his aspect becomes at moments almost that of a death's head grinning in a mirror. He mocks, as he laments, without bitterness; and can write a gay elegy: —

> 'What can the old man do but die?'

but there is always a consciousness of how near death is.

The thought of it is never out of his head; and while in 'Hero and Leander' he sets it to a pageant of watery beauty, and in 'The Bridge of Sighs' makes a great tune out of it, and sets his verse shivering with the horror of it in 'Eugene Aram,' he also plays with it, and will have his fooling. It is dreadful to recollect how much of what is mere trivial fun in his copious and miscellaneous work (making a collected edition a kind of posthumous cruelty) was written by a man joking for money, lest he should 'die beyond his means.' That recollection takes out some of the pleasure with which we can still read the best of the comic poems. 'That half Hogarth,' Lamb called him, praising 'a prime genius and hearty fellow'; but does the epithet quite characterise him? The best pieces are not always the most famous, as for instance the mainly meaningless 'Miss Kilmansegg,' which has hardly more than a juggler's agility in its tap-tap of a ceaseless ball rising and falling like a shuttle-cock. A little space fitted best for the due exercise of that riotous fun which would come whenever Hood called it, but not always go when the somersaults were over; a fun never other than sharp, salt, alert, but most significant, not in any meaning at the back of it, but in the sting of its rhymes and the crackle of its puns, perhaps the most accurate in the language.

'Eugene Aram' is a masterpiece of horror, and in it Hood perfects that style which has an emphasis far beyond epigram, because it comes straight from the heart and carries with it an awful inwardness of thought. When, here, he says:—

>'A dozen times I groaned; the dead
>Had never groaned but twice,'

there is the same quality and calibre as in the moral reflection in 'The Song of the Shirt':—

>'O God, that bread should be so dear
>And flesh and blood so cheap!'

Since the 'Ancient Mariner' there has been no such spiritual fear in our poetry, and the nightmare comes to us as if out of our own bed, the sensations translate themselves into our own nerves. The words reach us like a whisper, from which it is impossible to escape. That imagination, which had hardly shown itself among the thick flocks of fancy in all the other poems, is here, naked, deadly, and beautiful.

In 'The Song of the Shirt' this drama passes into an indignant song, not less human, and coming with its splendid lyric quality to prove that a conviction, a moral lesson if you will, can turn red-hot and be forged into a poem. Here, too, is 'modernity,' but of a kind that can be contemporary with every age. Only one more human thing exists in the work of Hood, and that is one of the greatest English poems of its kind, 'The Bridge of Sighs.' It has lost nothing by becoming the property of all the world, like the last lines of the Emperor Hadrian, in which there is not more final a moral, or some of those outcries and lamentations in the Old Testament, to which it seems almost to go back and snatch a form. The fragility of the metre, its swiftness, as of running water, the piercing daintiness of the words, which state and denounce in a song, go to make a poem which is like music and like a cry, and means something terribly close and accusing. A stone is flung angrily and straight into the air, and may strike the canopy before it falls back on the earth. That saying of —

'Anywhere, anywhere
Out of the world!'

has passed through interpreters, and helped to make a rare corner of modern literature; and the pity of the whole thing is like that of a great line of Dante, not less universal.

THE MINORS

'He and his muse might be *minors*.' — Johnson's Dictionary.

IN order that I may omit no one coming within the limits of my list who has written anything in verse that is, or was

334 ROMANTIC MOVEMENT IN ENGLISH POETRY

once thought, tolerable, I have strung together, a little indiscriminately, the names which follow. I hope that the word or two in which I have tried to characterise them may be enough to at least suggest the view I take of their claim to be mentioned. They are given in chronological order.

The earliest I find is ELIZABETH CARTER (1717–1806), who, besides writing very indifferent verses, was a good scholar in many languages, and translated Epictetus. Next comes the REV. JOHN SKINNER (1721–1807), who wrote the rollicking song of 'Tullochgorum,' which Byron admired for the swing of it. CHARLES ANSTEY (1724–1805), a good Latin scholar, who wrote a clever poem on a decayed Macaroni, and the more famous 'New Bath Guide' (with its 'watered tabbies, flowered brocades'); he wrote with facility, which is perhaps what his son meant by 'a sudden and peculiar operation of the mind (not easily described) resolving itself, as it were, incontinently into verse.' EDWARD JERNINGHAM (1727–1812), who Miss Burney tells us was 'all daintification in manner, speech, and dress,' wrote worthless verses during the whole of a long life. JANE ELLIOTT (1727–1805) made a lasting fame by writing one ballad, 'The Flowers of the Forest.' JOHN HOOLE (1727–1803) was a translator, in the manner of Pope, of Tasso, Metastasio, and Ariosto. THOMAS PERCY (1729–1811), famous for his 'Reliques,' may be forgiven for intruding some of his own unimportant verse among so many authentic treasures. RICHARD CUMBERLAND (1732–1811), an indifferent dramatist, the writer of a rather ghastly epic on 'Calvary,' in one of his odes, dedicated to Romney, anticipates the later worship of 'Grasmere's calm retreat,' 'stately Windermere,' and 'Keswick's sweet fantastic vale.' ROBERT JEPHSON (1736–1803), a writer of tragic and comic plays, was praised by Walpole, whose 'Castle of Otranto' he adapted for the stage. MRS. PIOZZI (1741–1821), Johnson's friend, wrote verse in one century and lived nearly twenty years into the next. HANNAH COWLEY (1743–1809) was the Anna

Matilda of the two cooing partners in the Della Cruscan couple (the other was Robert Merry, an even worse versifier); but in spite of her abandonment to the sickening and platonic love-duet between two poetasters, she has left some comedies, among them 'The Belle's Stratagem,' which are still sometimes seen on the stage. CHARLES MORRIS (1745-1838), 'the inimitable Captain Morris,' was punch-maker and bard of the Beefsteak Society, and he wrote songs savoured to its table. HENRY JAMES PYE (1745-1813), the 'Poetical Pye,' meatless and savourless, was poet laureate from 1790 to 1833. ANNA SEWARD (1747-1809), the Swan of Lichfield, who while living had 'thrown an unfettered hand,' she tells us, 'over the lyre of Horace' (unfettered, that is, by too close an acquaintance with the text in Latin), left a cruel legacy to Sir Walter Scott, — her poems to publish. CHARLOTTE SMITH (1749-1806), who translated 'Manon Lescaut,' and was a guest of Hayley at Eartham, wrote better verse than her host's, genuine in its observation of nature, and not without a small personal skill and taste. NEIL DOUGLAS (1750-1823), 'minister of the Word of God,' wrote a pious play, in tedious ten-syllable couplets, 'the Royal Penitent, or True Repentance Exemplified by David, King of Israel,' in which he is concerned partly in giving 'Serious Hints at this Awful Crisis' of 'David's unhappy affair with Bathsheba.' LADY ANNE BERNARD (1750-1825) wrote, at the age of twenty-one, the popular and still remembered 'Auld Robin Gray.' RICHARD BRINSLEY SHERIDAN (1751-1816) jingled once or twice in rhyme to put a moment's pause to his prose liveliness. WILLIAM ROSCOE (1753-1831), the first English student of the Renaissance, wrote indifferent verses about slavery when he was young, and for children when he was old. GEORGE ELLIS (1753-1815), the writer of 'Poetical Tales by Sir Gregory Gander,' light and lively society verses, was one of the collaborators of Canning and Frere in the 'Anti-Jacobin.' THOMAS JAMES MATHIAS (1754-1835), a somewhat clumsy and spiteful satirist in English, was a fine scholar in Italian, and, besides writing 'Poesie Liriche' of his own, made numerous translations of English poets. GEORGE DYER (1755–1841) wrote verse and prose of no importance, but Lamb has immortalised his name. WILLIAM SOTHEBY (1757–1833) attempted many forms of literature, and wrote copious and tedious rhyme, worthless tragedies in blank verse, and scarcely more tolerable translations of Wieland, Virgil, and Homer. WILLIAM THOMAS FITZGERALD (1759–1829), whose 'creaking couplets' Byron denounced and Horace Smith parodied, is only to be remembered by the 'Loyal Effusion' of the 'Rejected Addresses.' DR. SAYERS (1763–1817) was a pedantic writer of unrhymed verse, of whom sufficient notice will be found in what I have written about Southey, his pupil in metre. JAMES GRAHAME (1765–1811) was a descriptive and didactic writer, whose blank verse has a certain natural simplicity. CATHERINE MARIA FANSHAWE (1765–1834) leaves a rhyming riddle, which is remembered only because it was attributed to Byron. RICHARD ALFRED MILLIKIN (1767–1815) wrote a radiant parody of a street-ballad (itself afterwards parodied by Father Prout), the unforgettable 'Groves of Blarney.' LADY DACRE (1768–1854), a woman of many accomplishments, did some translations from Petrarch for Ugo Foscolo. Among the fashionable rhymers in verse was WILLIAM ROBERT SPENCER (1769–1834), who suffered justly in the 'Beautiful Incendiary' of the 'Rejected Addresses,' and who was 'one of the living ornaments, if I am not misinformed, of this present poetical age, A. D. 1811,' as Lamb says meaningly. ROBERT ANDERSON (1770–1833), a writer of songs and ballads in the Cumberland dialect, had little quality beyond a crude uncomely humour which seems to have been characteristic of the dancing, ale-drinking, 'night-courting' Cumberland peasantry of that time. SIR ALEXANDER BOSWELL (1775–1822), the son of Johnson's Boswell, in the intervals of printing at his private press wrote poems after many masters, and

THE MINORS

a few good hearty ballads (like 'Jenny dang the Weaver') of his own. MATTHEW GREGORY LEWIS (1775–1818), of 'The Monk,' wrote some verses called 'Alonzo the Brave,' in which he prepared a rhythm for serious use by Mr. Swinburne. WILLIAM STEWART ROSE (1775–1845) outdid the humble Hoole in translation, in the original metre, of Ariosto's 'Orlando Furioso.' ALARIC ALEXANDER WATTS (1775–1802), who had, we are told by his son, 'a nicely delicate discrimination in the perception of tender shades of feeling,' succeeded in drawing tempered eulogies from Lamb, Coleridge, and Wordsworth, which are read to-day with amazement. JOHN HERMAN MERIVALE (1779–1844) wrote an 'Orlando' of his own in the Italian manner, and better work as a translator from the Greek anthology. GEORGE CROLY (1780–1860), a prose writer, attempted in verse the usual Byron and Moore, bloodthirsty and Eastern, far-fetched and rhetorical, without even success in imitation. THOMAS PRINGLE (1780–1834) is remembered by his poem, 'Afar in the Desert': the verse has a vigorous stride, but Coleridge is certainly wrong in classing it 'among the two or three most perfect lyric poems in our language.' LUCY AIKIN (1781–1864), who wrote in verse 'Epistles on Women,' was better in her memoir-writing in prose and her private letters. JOHN MITFORD (1781–1859) was a learned editor of Pickering's Aldines, but an indifferent writer of verse. JOHN FINLAY (1782–1810) wrote some pleasant youthful verses, in some of which, as he says, 'nature's varieties wildly combine,' but in no unseemly manner. CHARLES ROBERT MATURIN (1782–1824), the author of 'Melmoth the Wanderer,' which is still, since Balzac, taken seriously in France and remembered, but hardly more than by name, in England, wrote three plays in verse, of which the first, 'Bertram,' had an immense popular success; a just, but under the circumstances ungenerous, review will be found, quite out of its place, in the middle of Coleridge's 'Biographia Litteraria.' THOMAS MITCHELL (1783–1845) was the best translator of Aristophanes before Frere, who reviewed him in the 'Quarterly,' kindly and discriminatingly, in an article which has never been excelled as a study and example of translation. The REV. JOHN EAGLES (1783–1855) wrote in 'Felix Farley' some dog-Latin and English doggerel of his own, and here and there a passable lyric; but he was happiest in his renderings of some of Vincent Bourne's Latin poems; the owl one and the solemn Billingsgate: 'Londini ad pontem, Billingi nomine, porta est.' JOHN KENYON (1784–1856) was a noble friend of poets, but his own verse was of little value. ROBERT BUCHANAN (1785–1873), professor of logic, wrote a play called 'Wallace,' which was performed twice for a charitable object at Glasgow. HEWSON CLARKE (1787–1832) was a satirist, who is only remembered because Byron replied to him, rather rudely, in one of his own satires. EDWARD QUILLINAN (1791–1851), who married Dora Wordsworth, wrote some pleasant light verses for albums, and showed a gentle and amiable nature in the sonnets on his dead wife and child. SIR JOHN BOWRING (1792–1872) did some service to English readers by his translations from poets of many countries, Russian, Batavian, Spanish, Servian, Polish, Hungarian, Bohemian, but they were done into very indifferent verse. JOHN ANSTER (1793–1867), besides writing some valueless verse of his own, did a translation of Goethe's 'Faust,' which remains one of the best for lightness of touch on rhymes and rhythms. ROBERT STORY (1795–1860) was a Northumberland poet, of whom Carlyle said that he had 'a certain rustic vigour of life,' but his work was mostly over-ambitious and of little value. THOMAS HAYNES BAYLEY (1797–1830) was once famous as the writer of cheap and common verses for music, some of which have survived with the cottage harmonium; in his day he was a sort of bad second to Moore. HERBERT KNOWLES (1798–1827) wrote a poem at the age of eighteen which Southey and Dr. Garnett admired to excess; it has a few good phrases, tolerable ideas, and an intolerable metre. JOHN

BANIM (1798–1842), the Irish novelist, wrote 'Soggarth Aroon' and one or two other sombre and passionate songs. JOHN MOULTRIE (1799–1874), who was praised by Wordsworth and Gifford, wrote a 'Protestant Hymn to the Virgin, and some vigorous sonnets, one of them setting' an anonymous editor of Coleridge's letters and conversation 'conspicuous on the Dunce's loftiest stool.' MRS. CATHERINE GRACE GODWIN (1798–1845) was praised by Wordsworth; Wordsworth was not a critic. MARY HOWITT (1799–1888), a copious writer, who was born a Quaker and died a Catholic, and who lived almost through an entire century, has left some fanciful verse, written, under the influence of Coleridge, in the new unearthly manner. And lastly there was ALFRED BUNN, known as the 'Poet Bunn,' who was born at the end of the eighteenth century and died in 1860, endeared to posterity by his nickname.

The reader may be referred to selections from four poets: Byron (Blackie, 1904); Coleridge (Methuen, 1905); Keats (Jack, 1907), and Clare (Clarendon Press, 1908), which contain introductions partly taken from this book.

INDEX

INDEX

Aikin, Lucy, 337.
Anderson, Robert, 336.
Anster, John, 338.
Anstey, Charles, 334.

Baillie, Joanna, 63.
Banim, John, 339.
Barbauld, Anna Lætitia, 30.
Barham, Richard Harris, 263.
Barton, Bernard, 217.
Bayley, Thomas Haynes, 338.
Beattie, George, 234.
Beattie, James, 26.
Bernard, Lady Anne, 335.
Blake, William, 37.
Bloomfield, Robert, 74.
Boswell, Alexander, 336.
Bowles, William Lisle, 65.
Bowring, John, 338.
Boyd, Henry, 107.
Brydges, Samuel Egerton, 65.
Buchanan, Robert, 338.
Bunn, Alfred, 339.
Byron, George Gordon, Lord, 239.

Callanan, Jeremiah Joseph, 318.
Campbell, Thomas, 191.
Canning, George, 106.
Carlyle, Thomas, 297.
Carter, Elizabeth, 334.
Cary, Henry Francis, 122.
Clare, John, 288.
Clarke, Hewson, 338.
Coleridge, David Hartley, 321.
Coleridge, Samuel Taylor, 123.
Colman, George, the Younger, 67.
Combe, William, 28.
Cornwall, Barry. See Procter, B. W.
Cowley, Hannah, 334.
Crabbe, George, 52.

Croly, George, 337.
Cumberland, Richard, 334.
Cunningham, Allan, 227.
Curran, John Philpot, 36.

Dacre, Lady, 336.
Darley, George, 315.
Darwin, Erasmus, 23.
De Vere, Aubrey, 232.
Dermody, Thomas, 170.
Dibdin, Charles, 34.
Douglas, Neil, 335.
Dyer, George, 336.

Eagles, John, 338.
Elliott, Ebenezer, 209.
Elliott, Jane, 334.
Ellis, George, 335.

Fanshawe, Catherine Maria, 336.
Finlay, John, 337.
Fitzgerald, William Thomas, 336.
Frere, John Hookham, 75.

Gifford, William, 37.
Godwin, Mrs. Catherine Grace, 339.
Grahame, James, 336.

Hayley, William, 32.
Heber, Reginald, 215.
Hemans, Felicia Dorothea, 293.
Hogg, James, 97.
Home, John, 23.
Hood, Thomas, 328.
Hoole, John, 334.
Howitt, Mary, 339.
Hunt, James Henry Leigh, 218.

Jephson, Robert, 334.
Jerningham, Edward, 334.

Keats, John, 298.
Keble, John, 286.
Kenyon, John, 338.
Knowles, Herbert, 338.
Knowles, James Sheridan, 216.

Lamb, Charles, 161.
Landor, Robert Eyres, 207.
Landor, Walter Savage, 172.
Lewis, Matthew Gregory, 337.
Leyden, Dr. John, 171.
Lloyd, Charles, 167.
Lockhart, John Gibson, 295.
Lover, Samuel, 324.
Luttrell, Henry, 73.

Maginn, William, 286.
Mathias, Thomas James, 335.
Maturin, Charles Robert, 337.
Merivale, John Herman, 337.
Millikin, Richard Alfred, 336.
Milman, Henry Hart, 265.
Mitchell, Thomas, 337.
Mitford, John, 337.
Mitford, Mary Russell, 234.
Moir, David Macbeth, 325.
Montgomery, James, 119.
Moore, Thomas, 200.
More, Hannah, 30.
Morris, Charles, 335.
Motherwell, William, 323.
Moultrie, John, 339.

Nairne, Carolina, Lady, 73.
Nicholson, William, 213.

O'Keeffe, John, 34.

Peacock, Thomas Love, 230.
Percy, Thomas, 334.
Piozzi, Mrs., 334.
Pollok, Robert, 325.
Pringle, Thomas, 337.

Procter, Bryan Waller, 236.
Pye, Henry James, 335.

Quillinan, Edward, 338.

Reynolds, John Hamilton, 320.
Robinson, Mrs. Mary, 61.
Rogers, Samuel, 68.
Roscoe, William, 335.
Rose, William Stewart, 337.

Sayers, Dr., 336.
Scott, Walter, 108.
Seward, Anna, 335.
Shelley, Percy Bysshe, 268.
Sheridan, Richard Brinsley, 335.
Skinner, John, 334.
Smith, Charlotte, 335.
Smith, Horatio, 189.
Smith, James, 189.
Sotheby, William, 336.
Southey, Caroline Anne Bowles, 233.
Southey, Robert, 148.
Spencer, William Robert, 336.
Story, Robert, 338.
Strong, Charles, 228.

Talfourd, Thomas Noon, 319.
Tannahill, Robert, 161.
Taylor, Ann, 213.
Taylor, Jane, 213.
Tennant, William, 217.
Thom, William, 326.
Thurlow, Edward, Baron, 209.
Tighe, Mrs., 121.

Watts, Alaric Alexander, 337.
White, Henry Kirke, 228.
White, Joseph Blanco, 169.
Wilson, John, 231.
Wolcot, John, 27.
Wolfe, Charles, 266.
Wordsworth, William, 78.